A STUDY OF
ELIZABETHAN AND JACOBEAN TRAGEDY

A STUDY OF ELIZABETHAN AND JACOBEAN TRAGEDY

BY

T. B. TOMLINSON

CAMBRIDGE
AT THE UNIVERSITY PRESS

MELBOURNE UNIVERSITY PRESS
1964

PUBLISHED BY
THE SYNDICS OF THE CAMBRIDGE UNIVERSITY PRESS
Bentley House, 200 Euston Road, London N.W.1
American Branch: 32 East 57th Street, New York 22, N.Y.
West African Office: P.O. Box 33, Ibadan, Nigeria
AND
MELBOURNE UNIVERSITY PRESS
Parkville N.2, Victoria, Australia

©

CAMBRIDGE UNIVERSITY PRESS
1964

Printed in Great Britain by
THE STELLAR PRESS LTD.
UNION STREET, BARNET, HERTS.

CONTENTS

v

EDITIONS OF PLAYS

For the quotations used I have consulted the following editions:

Beaumont and Fletcher (Select Plays), Mermaid, 2 vols. (London, 1887)

The Tragedies of George Chapman, ed. Parrott (London, 1910)

Five Plays of John Ford, Mermaid Dramabooks (N.Y., 1957)

The Plays of John Marston, ed. H. H. Wood, 3 vols. (Edinburgh, 1934)

The Plays of Christopher Marlowe, World's Classics (London, 1939)

Thomas Middleton (Ten Plays), Mermaid, 2 vols. (London, 1887-90)

The Changeling, ed. N. W. Bawcutt, Revels Plays (London, 1958)

The Works of Cyril Tourneur, ed. Allardyce Nicoll (London, 1930)

Webster and Tourneur (Chief Tragedies), ed. J. A. Symonds, Mermaid (London, 1948)

Works of John Webster, ed. F. L. Lucas, 4 vols. (London, 1927)

The Minor Elizabethan Drama, Everyman (London, 1910)

Elizabethan Plays, ed. Hazelton Spencer (London, 1934)

PREFACE

The study of Elizabethan and Jacobean tragedy has suffered from the twin evils of excessive concentration on scholarly 'background' (textual variants, biographical material, mediaeval and Tudor history and philosophy, etc.) and, more recently, a tendency to abstract themes and ideas from the plays in which they are embodied (or alternatively to illustrate Elizabethan 'themes' from isolated examples taken at random from various plays and with no reference to the quality of the work considered). In this study I have attempted to combine a consideration of general issues which affect English tragedy with particular comment on the plays. The amount of detailed comment needed on a given play will clearly vary, but I felt it was of first importance to deal with plays as wholes, or at least with significant sections of plays, rather than illustrating 'themes' and problems from isolated scenes and passages. The meaning of a play, and consequently its place in English literary history, is dependent on the quality of the dramatist's insight. We cannot take any play as significant of a trend or development unless at the same time we are considering how good (or bad) it is.

The first two chapters raise questions about the special contribution drama has to make to English literature (What is the nature and validity of the truths about experience the *dramatist* is led to see? How does 'dramatic' truth differ from other kinds of truth?) and about the key position Shakespeare occupies in relation to other dramatists. These are followed by detailed studies of key plays of the period. Here it seems to me essential to stress qualitative differences between well-known plays and to see three playwrights – Shakespeare, Middleton, Tourneur – as dominating the period and offering, when taken together, a controlling insight into what we now find of value in Elizabethan and Jacobean drama. The way to place accurately the other dramatists (including, I feel, the less impressive Webster) is first to see the sort of tensions and oppositions that arise between the work of these three.

The book concludes with a comment on elements in seventeenth-century society which, for various reasons, helped defeat the drama, to the consequent impoverishment of English literature and English life. Where any society loses its grip on the substance of dramatic truth and dramatic experience an attenuation or etiolation follows which – at least in the case of English literature – the cultivation of poetry alone as a dominant form cannot overcome. With English literature, and English life, we have to wait for the rise to maturity of the novel – comparatively late in the nineteenth century – for the body and substance of literature, lost with the eclipse of tragedy in the seventeenth century, to be replaced.

I have not considered textual problems except in the few cases where they are directly relevant to the overriding concern of what is, and what is not, of value in Elizabethan drama to us now. Most of the textual arguments at present being conducted – as particularly in the case of the Middleton-Tourneur controversy – seem to have got to the point of attrition. Short of any major discoveries being made in this field, our information is so uncertain that it is better to decide from internal evidence alone what are the major interests and achievements of a given writer.

Some of the chapters in this book are in part based on articles I have written for *Essays in Criticism* ('Tourneur's Critics'), *The Journal of English and Germanic Philology* ('*The Changeling*'), and *The Melbourne Critical Review* ('Shakespearean Criticism').

MELBOURNE   T. B. T.
January, 1963

PART 1
ELIZABETHAN
TRAGEDY

CHAPTER I

THE ELIZABETHAN TRAGIC WORLD

In the most general terms, great tragedy presents us with the problem: why is it that we are most acutely aware of the good and the valuable when they are attended by evil, chaos, loss, destruction? in what sense does order depend on the presence of disorder? Thinking specifically of English literature, these questions are brought up with such extraordinary vividness and richness by the Elizabethan playwrights that a further generalization may be possible: the central paradox of Elizabethan tragedy in particular seems to be that it sees the good and the valuable as – at least in part – actually nourished and supported by chaos and evil. This is not a matter either of the 'pity and terror' we may feel at tragic loss, or of the regenerative force of love and goodness seen the more keenly because it is in opposition to evil and tragic destruction. It is a more complex question than these, and one indeed which cannot satisfactorily be grasped in philosophical, ethical, or religious terms. Terms like 'good' and 'evil', in particular, must be taken only as approximations in any argument about Elizabethan tragedy, and their significance will change from play to play. Nevertheless there is a sense in which, for the Elizabethans generally, to experience the tragic and the chaotic is at the same time to experience the energy and richness of life itself. Thus Shakespeare is at his greatest, not in the last plays, but in the tragedies. In part this means that in tragedy he has seen and felt more keenly than elsewhere the central mystery of death and the loss of human potentiality. More than this, however, it means that in the tragedies there is a richer sense of the manifold possibilities of living than any Shakespeare achieved in the earlier or later plays.

And this is so, I think, not because tragedy illuminates by contrast the nature of goodness, but because what Shakespeare has seen in the chaos and destruction of tragedy – even, possibly, in evil itself – is a source of energy and vitality greater than any he found elsewhere. Less richly, and with greatly varying emphases, the writing of the other Elizabethan dramatists bears out the truth of this central paradox: the deepest response to evil and good, or to the valuable and the chaotic, sees them as, in some sense, dependent on each other for their form, substance, and very existence.

My main aim in this introductory chapter is to develop further such general questions about the nature of the Elizabethan tragic world and the continuing relevance it may have for us today. Clearly these are questions which in the end can only be answered in terms of a full critical examination of the value (or otherwise) of particular plays. Themes of 'appearance and reality', 'accident and design', 'the condition of nature' have long been a popular refuge for criticism, but they are meaningless except in so far as they can be seen embodied in the quality of the dramatic writing given us over the whole extent of a given play. And where this can be done, what emerges will only with difficulty, or for purposes perhaps of quick summary, be called a 'theme' at all. For drama – great drama, at least – is never merely a matter of 'dramatized philosophy', or 'illustrated Christianity', or even 'eternal truths rendered in human and dramatic terms'. Each major play we consider is a fresh experience, a fresh insight; not something already implicit in, and hence merely dramatized from, a Thomist philosophy, or a concept of Tragedy derived from earlier writers, or an attitude to the breakdown of feudal society obtainable from material outside the limits of the play. The critic who can claim that the problem of justice is the same for Shakespeare as it was for Socrates, and further that the solution Shakespeare offers 'is that of St Augustine and St Thomas, translated . . . into a pagan analogue'[1]

[1] M. D. H. Parker, *The Slave of Life* (London, 1955), p. 130.

has missed both what Shakespeare has to say and the sense in which he *has* it to say. Further, he has not realized what drama is, what the nature of *dramatic* truth must inevitably be.

On the other hand, general questions about a given period must arise, and one of the first we have to ask – developing its implications wherever possible in terms of specific plays – is: What is the particular contribution that the plays, and the plays alone, have to make to our sense of the valuable in the Elizabethan experience? What is it that the tragic drama has to say which, even in an age as prolific as the Elizabethan, is not to be found expressed in any other form? What is the *nature* of tragedy? Again, it is easier to say what the answers to these questions are not, than to glimpse what they might be. Obviously, drama does not merely illustrate in other, more 'human', terms what Donne, for instance, said in his. When the phrase 'the play as a dramatic poem' is taken to mean simply that plays and poems are the same thing and offer identical insights, one has some sympathy with readers who want to return the critical emphasis to concepts of character and action.[1] But equally obviously, any explanation which stops at saying that the Elizabethans were intensely interested in the theatre, or in people ('drama is a social art'), is merely skating the surface of the problem. These remarks may be true as generalizations, but the trouble with them is that they could too easily apply to other ages – even other national dramas – as well. The Elizabethan insights are – at their best – always intensely particular.

Clearly, then, if we are looking for the nature of the Elizabethan dramatic insight – or more specifically of its tragic insight – we must find some approach which cuts through matters of form and technique and reveals what tragedy has to say about the human condition. There is, I think, one very particular sense in which

[1] Cf. William Rosen, *Shakespeare and the Craft of Tragedy* (Harvard, 1960). Mr Rosen's thesis, however, leads him to see Shakespeare as placing man's 'nobility of spirit' against 'the fearful elements of the world'; Mr Rosen is thus adopting what seems to me a quite unacceptable position (see the discussion of Clifford Leech's thesis below, and note 1, p. 6).

Shakespeare, at least, can be said to have founded his plays on a peculiarly *Elizabethan* view of the relations between man and the tragic universe around him, and this is the sense brought out most clearly by L. C. Knights in his examination of Nature in *Lear* and *Macbeth*. Professor Knights does not claim that his approach to tragedy is exhaustive, or the only one possible, but it is, I think, a better starting point for general formulations than any other suggested so far. However, before looking at this in some detail, it is important to distinguish other approaches which at first sight look complementary or even similar to his, but which in fact are radically different. Many, if not all, recent approaches seem to me insubstantial in that they have missed the essential points made by Professor Knights and also those made by Dr Leavis in his shorter studies of Shakespeare.

For instance, it is clear that almost all recent critics, English and American, are concerned to stress, in different ways and with different qualifications, what is nevertheless basically the same point: the isolation of the tragic hero from the universe, or the people, around him. The trouble with this kind of approach is that it almost always ends by attempting to make what is undoubtedly one element in some plays, the key element in all. One of the clearest and most uncompromising formulations is Clifford Leech's in his book *Shakespeare's Tragedies*. Despite Dr Leavis's earlier remarks in *Education and the University* on the nature and function of Shakespeare's verse in *Macbeth*, Professor Leech feels free to claim that 'When we think of Shakespeare's tragedies . . . what we recall is made up of an indifferent universe and certain characters who seem to demand our admiration'.[1] The centre of the tragic vision, for Professor Leech, is in the hero who shares with all of us a

---

[1] C. Leech, *Shakespeare's Tragedies* (London, 1950). And compare theses like that of D. G. James, *The Dream of Learning* (Oxford, 1951) which stresses Shakespeare's imaginative ability to 'see things as they really are', but develops this in terms of Shakespeare's 'forcing apart . . . of virtue from life itself'. For Mr James, *Lear* is a play 'designed to exhibit suffering and helpless virtue' (p. 111). Compare also Geoffrey Bush, *Shakespeare and the*

human weakness but who is greater than we are because he shows
'an increasing readiness to endure, an ever greater awareness';
and what this 'awareness' consists in is simply a clearer and steadier
vision of man's plight in the face of an alien universe, and in the
face of a 'justice' which is 'indifferent' and 'cares no whit for the
individual'.[1] This, like Bradley's earlier but basically similar approach, would if it were true certainly give a clear account of
man's place in the universe and would consequently offer a
rationale for the view that drama has indeed a unique function in
the Elizabethan age: the 'character' element in drama brings home
man's plight, and man's nobility, in more specific terms than
poetry could. But the trouble is, as we shall see more fully later on,
little or nothing in Shakespeare's universe, or even Webster's,
corresponds to Professor Leech's idea of it. Terms like 'an indifferent universe'– or its complement 'dramatic irony'– are completely inadequate in the face of the health and vitality given us, as
Dr Leavis points out,[2] in Banquo's 'This guest of summer . . .' or
even in Lady Macbeth's 'All our service,/ In every point twice
done . . .'. Approaches like that of Professor Leech can serve to
stress, as it should be stressed, the human *suffering* in these plays –
especially in *Lear* with its agonized questioning so reminiscent of
Sophocles: 'Who is it that can tell me who I am?' – but they are
quite misleading on the relationships this suffering bears to the
world of nature given us in *Macbeth*, or the different universe
given us in *Lear*, or the investigation of the flux of nature, different
again, in *Antony and Cleopatra*.

Professor Leech's over-simplification of the tragic world of
Shakespeare is mirrored in another, much more commonly held,
approach. Recent publications reveal a growing body of criticism

---

Natural Condition (Harvard, 1956). For similar approaches to later, Jacobean tragedy see
C. Leech, *John Webster: A Critical Study* (London, 1951); and Robert Ornstein, *The Moral
Vision of Jacobean Tragedy* (University of Wisconsin, 1960).

[1] Leech, *Shakespeare's Tragedies*, p. 14.
[2] F. R. Leavis, *Education and the University* (London, 1943).

which centres on *Lear* and talks in terms of Lear's 'spiritual journey' of self-discovery on the Heath; of the redemptive aspects of the play and Lear's discovery, through suffering, of his one-ness with humanity; and of the great positive value of love, conceived variously in Christian and Humanist terms. Formulations of this kind – and there are many more than I have suggested here – look at first sight as if they offer a more positive approach than those of the 'irrational universe' type, but on inspection they turn out almost invariably to be merely variations of it. Undeniably, Shakespeare in *King Lear* (and elsewhere) *is* preoccupied with what several critics call the 'mystery of human suffering', and it is equally clear that this is one reason why he felt compelled to write plays as well as poems. But critics, and audiences, neglect at their peril the dominating qualities of Shakespeare's dramatic verse as it changes from play to play. It is the fabric of the verse, varying from play to play and from situation to situation, which offers, not a 'background' of order or chaos, but the very substance of the play; and this is a substance which, as we shall see, changes radically with each fresh insight, each new tragedy written. With *Lear*, even though this play appears to fit 'redemptive' theories better than most (the struggle is waning to find nobility in Macbeth's character sufficient to fit any such theories), nevertheless neglect of the true importance of the verse fabric ends either in isolating Lear and Cordelia from the natural world around them, or, as in the 'pathetic fallacy' theories, using the natural world merely as background. The characters appear, once again, as in total opposition to or in isolation from a chaotic universe (the storm), or a chaotic and evil society (Edmund and the bad daughters), and the play's complex and particular insights are lost. The way is then opened to over-generalized pronouncements about human love as a value in itself, and once generalizations about Shakespeare's world are permitted, sentimentality beckons at every turn of the argument. The following are typical of many recent formulations of the problem of suffering in *Lear* and its relation to the other plays:

> Descent may be, and perhaps must be, a preliminary to ascent; and from Shakespeare's hell there is an open but not easy path to heaven. Essentially it is love's path. Truth to one's Self, fidelity to Love, and creative mercy are inseparable ... Shakespeare traces the soul's journey from the pit of chaos, to a point where it seems about to unfold celestial wings ...[1]

> As Lear is revealed to us in the last scene of the play ... he represents for us the final affliction of suffering humanity; but he represents, too, the tenderness, the love of suffering humanity, and the dignity, the almost mystical dignity, with which that love is invested. It is a moment too solemn for tears. In his figure, as his great heart falters and dies, we recognise a supreme value that the ancients never knew, a value which surpasses – for us, at least – even the Sophoclean value of justice: the value of human love.[2]

In both these examples, the very softness of the critical prose itself betrays sentimentality and an inadequate response to Shakespeare's much tougher, and more particular, view.

Of course one must admit that there are tougher minded critics in plenty. For instance Professor John Lawlor, in his book *The Tragic Sense in Shakespeare*,[3] writes critical prose which could not be accused of the softness and sentimentality of most of the redemptivists. But even Professor Lawlor's view seems to me to be

---

[1] John Vyvyan, *The Shakespearean Ethic* (London, 1959), pp. 204-5.

[2] Harold S. Wilson, *On the Design of Shakespearian Tragedy* (Toronto, 1957), pp. 208-9. In the many other articles and books offering similar 'redemptivist' interpretations of *Lear* and the other plays there are minor differences of emphasis. Some see Lear as foolish but redeemed; others as the good man struggling on behalf of humanity against Edmund and the bad daughters. Some see a background of 'order' in the poetry; others merely 'dramatic irony'. In all these cases the hero's personality is given as the main issue, the order (or lack of it) merely background; or alternatively Shakespearean order is something we might find as readily in St Thomas Aquinas (cf. Parker, *op. cit.*).

[3] J. Lawlor, *The Tragic Sense in Shakespeare* (London, 1960). For a similar approach to *Macbeth*, see C. C. Clarke, 'Darkened Reason in *Macbeth*', *The Durham University Journal*, N.S. XXII, 1960, 11-18.

one which fatally isolates the protagonists from the world in which Shakespeare presents them as living and acting. Much of the book is devoted to a discussion of the freedom of choice a tragic hero is given, and though the discussion is much fuller, and the argument much keener, than that of the many earlier critics who chose the same ground, it still seems to me to be looking in the wrong directions. Concentration on the tragic choice leads often to what looks in fact like sophistical argument:

> To the question what is Fate? we can make no adequate answer. But our question is simpler. How can the dramatist represent Fate without impairing his character's power of choice?; and to this we may now attempt a reply. Fate must be shown as a limitation of the character's field of choice – not, be it emphasized, his power of choosing, but the things there are to choose from. His whole universe must be narrowed to a single 'either-or'; *and the 'or' must represent what he cannot do without ceasing to be the character introduced or established for us.*
>
> (p. 121, my italics)

Even apart from the shaky logic of the argument here, the reduction of choice to these rigid alternatives is false to our sense of the *manifold* possibilities of life in Shakespeare's play (here *Macbeth*). Concentration to this degree on the tragic choice offered the protagonist tends to reduce everything else the verse of the play has to offer to mere background, and so it is not surprising that when Professor Lawlor comes to make claims for the imagery and 'word-play' in *Macbeth* he tends to see it merely as 'reinforcing' thematic structures on the one hand, and, on the other, lending 'deepest irony' to Banquo's speech about Macbeth's castle. The poetry is thus denied its most positive impact on us, and the uniqueness of Elizabethan dramatic insight is fatally obscured.

More particularly – and here Professor Lawlor's account is characteristic of a growing body of opinion about Shakespeare – the dominating themes of the tragedies tend by this method to be stated exclusively in terms of the natural bond between man and man. 'Here again,' says Professor Lawlor of the gathering of the forces of right at the end of the tragedies, 'we meet the unwearied Shakespearian sense of the endlessly fruitful possibilities of the natural tie . . .'[1] Taken by itself this could be a true enough statement, but it is disturbing when we realize that Professor Lawlor is here thinking of the specifically human relationships or alignments *and of these alone*. Responding to the whole range of the drama and poetry in a Shakespearean tragedy, we realize that this concept of 'the natural' is a crippling limitation of Shakespeare's deeper insights.

And it is indeed a deeper insight into Shakespeare's view of 'the natural', and of our possible relations to it (and hence of order, value and, ultimately, tragedy), which is absolutely essential if we are to see either the true nature of his plays or the particular contribution the drama as a whole has to make in the Elizabethan age. The greatness and individuality of drama certainly depends on its ability to deal with people and their problems more fully and deeply than short poems, at any rate, can readily do. On the other hand, a poetic drama is not a tale illustrated in verse. Clearly we respond to the poetry in fuller and more demonstrably specific ways than this. It is on questions of this kind that Professor Knights's concept of the relations between man and the natural world given us in Shakespeare's plays is so immensely valuable. Like Dr Leavis, Professor Knights rejects any concept of Shakespearean tragedy which would see it in terms of a simple opposition between man and an irrational universe, or in terms of the natural bond between man and man, or even between man and an essentially benevolent natural 'order'. The point, rather, is that in the fabric of Shakespeare's verse the world of nature is given us as having an existence which, paradoxically, is at once independent of, and intimately related to, man's status and worth. Any full

---

[1] Lawlor, *op. cit.*, p. 125. For a similar interpretation of the 'Nature' theme in *Lear*, see John F. Danby, *Shakespeare's Doctrine of Nature* (London, 1949), p. 131.

realization of nature, Shakespeare is saying, must ultimately be in terms of man's consciousness; but the Shakespearean tragic paradox includes also a demonstration that nature, so far from being mere background or illustration of a morality or goodness truly grounded in man alone, is in *itself* an indispensable source of nourishment, the given body of experience and substance sustaining and supporting human life. The tragic hero often fails to see this, or sees it only imperfectly. But the *plays* see it, and consequently see human life as 'closely related to the wider setting of organic growth, as indeed, in a quite concrete and practical way, directly based on man's dealings with the earth that nourishes him'.[1] Moreover, it is the Shakespearean verse which gives us the highly particularized substance of the natural world. Talking of the Lear-Cordelia relationship towards the end of the play, Professor Knights says: 'Lear's "ungovern'd rage" is compared, as before, to elemental fury ("as mad as the vex'd sea"), and his mock crown is fittingly made up of "idle weeds", astonishingly present in the clogged movement of the lines that list them. Yet co-present with these – and given emphasis by the lift and smooth sweep of the verse – is "our sustaining corn" '.[2] Now if we can assume for the moment that Shakespearean – and possibly other – dramatic verse has indeed this kind of status and importance, we can summarize the argument so far in the form of two propositions, both to be further developed later on: First, Professor Knights's view of the man-nature relationship in Shakespeare offers the truest insight into what part men – 'characters' – may play in the total complexity of drama. Second, these truths about man and the natural world are particular insights to be grasped only by responding to the quality of the verse and structure of a given play. *Dramatic* truth always has a meaning and significance different from any other. For all the attention given in recent years

[1] L. C. Knights, *Some Shakespearean Themes* (London, 1959), pp. 125-6.
[2] *Ibid.*, p. 130.

to the 'irony' and 'imagery' of Shakespeare's verse, few I think
have seen clearly the implications of this sort of argument.[1]

I want to leave for a separate chapter any fuller consideration of
what – given these terms of argument and criticism – Shakespeare's
varying positions and achievements are over the range of three or
four of his tragedies. At the moment I want to ask a different
question: What happens when we attempt to extend Professor
Knights's formulation of the complex man-nature relationship in
Shakespeare to some of the other Elizabethans and Jacobeans?
Shakespeare is the centre of attention, undoubtedly, in these
matters. But what specific relations – if any – do the others bear to
him? How does he figure in the conflicting patterns of development in Elizabethan and Jacobean drama which we will be looking
at more fully in succeeding chapters?

Here the clearest and in many ways one of the most interesting
comparisons is with the verse – and all that this implies in terms of
the play's dramatic thought and structure – of Marlowe's
Tamburlaine. The whole problem can best be seen initially in terms
of a contrast between energy as defined in *Tamburlaine* and energy
or vitality as variously interpreted by Shakespeare and some of the
other leading dramatists. Basically, we are still concerned with the
question of what the natural world around us has to do with tragic
or dramatic writing. In Marlowe's *Tamburlaine* there are repeated
assertions of the energy of nature (either within Tamburlaine's
control or beyond it), clustered around repeated idea-images:
Fortune's wheel; God; Jove; Black Jove; Zenocrate 'the loveliest
maid alive'; 'Nature that framed us'; etc., etc. But in almost every
case of this kind that one can think of, the assertion is of a vitality
which is self-contained, dependent so to speak on a concept of
energy or beauty no further developed than this, and having,
almost, no more substance than is implied in the barest statement

[1] See, however, Derek Traversi, *An Approach to Shakespeare*, 2nd ed. (London, 1957):
and the Pelican Guide No.2, *The Age of Shakespeare* (London, 1955).

or definition of itself. With *Tamburlaine* the deepest issues seem to
be limited to this attempt of the denotative verse, with its firm but
unexpansive imagery, to control and limit a simply conceived
force; and therefore whenever such generalized energy or vitality
is brought to focus in imagery, it tends to be imagery of definition
and limitation rather than of growth and possibility:

> The god of war resigns his room to me,
> Meaning to make me general of the world.
> Jove, viewing me in arms, looks pale and wan,
> Fearing my power should pull him from his throne.
> Where'er I come the Fatal Sisters sweat,
> And grisly Death, by running to and fro,
> To do their ceaseless homage to my sword;
> And here in Afric, where it seldom rains,
> Since I arriv'd with my triumphant host,
> Have swelling clouds, drawn from wide-gasping wounds,
> Been oft resolv'd in bloody purple showers,
> A meteor that might terrify the earth
> And make it quake at every drop it drinks.
> Millions of souls sit on the banks of Styx,
> Waiting the back return of Charon's boat . . .

In this passage the imaginative possibilities we glimpse in the concept of brute force releasing fertility and abundance are sternly
repressed by the verse. In the lines 'And here in Afric, where it
seldom rains . . . Have swelling clouds . . .' Marlowe seems
momentarily prepared to contemplate a more complex relation
between destruction and fertility, but even this image ends in the
rhythmic stiffness of '. . . Been oft resolv'd in bloody purple
showers'.

With others of the Elizabethans however, and particularly
Shakespeare, the whole enterprise is different. To all of the Elizabethans some concept of a vitally alive and energetic universe is
important, but the ways in which most choose to express it imply
a force more obviously life-giving and fertile than anything in

Marlowe, or at any rate in *Tamburlaine*. Furthermore, in most cases, the concept is one which more readily yields suggestions that a given play is incorporating wide experience within itself, is attached to or rooted in life in ways which differ widely from play to play, but which are generally more satisfying than are Marlowe's in *Tamburlaine*. Thus, for instance, and most obviously, Shakespeare again and again demonstrates a complex alliance with the natural world. For him it is a matter, not of a simple, generalized concept of an 'energy' to be 'restrained' by clear diction and firm rhythm, but of a response to the natural world of growth and decay, of wholeness and disorder mixed. 'Energy' and 'vitality' in Shakespeare are therefore never felt simply as energy or vitality, but as particular manifestations of growth and possibility called up by a given situation. And just as the Shakespearean sense of energy is essentially one of diversity and particularity of substance, so 'control' is present in the total complexity of his verse, rather than in any simplified firmness of mind expressing itself in denotative imagery. Thus when Antony claims Cleopatra's kisses – 'the nobleness of life is to do thus . . .'– we know that this romantic concept of life is being qualified by verse which at the very same time asserts the solidity and energy of ordinary experience; and this assertion is made, furthermore, in and by the very terms that Antony himself chooses in his attempt to *reject* the pressing claims of everyday existence: 'Our dungy earth alike feeds beast as man . . .' Here a romantic impatience with life, and an assertion in specific terms (our 'dungy earth' feeding beast and man) of the sustaining strength of life, are combined in complex dramatic poetry. But the real contrast with Marlowe is in the effortless proliferation of such images in Shakespeare, implying, or rather enacting, the presence of endlessly diversified growth, bound up with and indeed emerging from tragedy itself. The images need not, of course, paint the natural world pictorially. It is enough that they assert the strength of life in particular relationships (often relationships to death itself, or tragedy) rather than in generalized concepts:

> Now all labour
> Mars what it does; yea, very force entangles
> Itself with strength; seal then, and all is done.

There is nothing pictorial or imagistic about this verse, but it is nevertheless impossible to read it as a generalized statement, or as an assertion of one thing (e.g. force) checked by another (acceptance of failure). The sense of 'labour' or 'force' in the verse is one with the sense of 'marring' and 'entanglement'; and entanglement is inseparable from the idea of strength.

As well as *Antony and Cleopatra*, *Macbeth* and even *Lear* are, as we shall see, packed with life and energy of this, notably un-Marlovian, kind. In all these plays it is a case of mankind seen as necessary to the realization of the possibilities in nature; but also of nature seen as having a sustaining energy of its own, in a sense independent of the lives of men and proliferating in boundless possibilities of growth. Thus nature is inexhaustible because never channelled into simple concepts of energy, force, or vitality, and in exhibiting growth and life of this kind it transcends the force of assertion inherent in mere energy, and presents man, whose consciousness is necessary to the whole process, as nevertheless dependent on a whole world of life and growth beyond the bounds of his own personality.

Critical distinctions of this kind must be the basis for our attempt to place other Elizabethan plays in relation to Shakespeare's. What is implied is that we must be prepared to recognize the existence of certain general problems, but treat these wherever possible as at once typically 'Elizabethan', and at the same time problems which change their nature with the changing fabric and quality of each new play considered. Certainly some general formulations can be made confidently about the Elizabethan age. Concepts of energy and the control of energy; chaos and a sense of order or degree related to the chaotic; the moral and the good receiving substance and energy from the evil they fight – these may fairly be said to be the dominant critical problems that arise as we look over the range of Elizabethan and Jacobean tragic drama. As in the case of the Marlowe and Shakespeare comparison, however, and even within the range of a single playwright, the very nature and status of a problem will always be found to be dependent on the nature and quality of the dramatic verse and structure of a given play.

Most important of all in this respect, if we add some consideration of the leading Jacobeans to the comparison of Shakespeare's verse with that of *Tamburlaine*, it becomes clear that *all* these writers are doing something which is different from Shakespeare in kind as well as degree. Shakespeare is thus far more than merely a more intelligent and experienced Marlowe. The leading Jacobeans are something other than merely lesser versions of the supreme artist Shakespeare. Tourneur's verse and dialogue in *The Revenger's Tragedy*, for instance, embrace varied traditions of moral thinking and feeling often far removed from Shakespeare's. There is always a sense, in Tourneur's verse at its best, of a firmly grasped and basically very simple moral position. For all the complexity of some of the issues at stake, sin is sin for Tourneur – at least in a sense that it is not for Shakespeare, and certainly not for Fletcher and Ford. Tourneur's ideas are often complex ones, but where the later writers prevaricate, he can see and grasp with great firmness the dangerous attraction of the sins and vices his characters contemplate, and even of the still more dangerous double sin, to 'rub hell o'er with honey' (the 'sin robed in holiness'), which represents the ultimate in vice for people in the Tourneur world. For Tourneur's sense of sin, focused by and in his wit and the crisp rhythmic movement of his verse, is more than a simple rejection of sin and it can therefore contemplate steadily the vice and luxury indulged by the characters in the play:

O, that marrowless age
Should stuff the hollow bones with damned desires!
And, 'stead of heat, kindle infernal fires
Within the spendthrift veins of a dry duke,
A parched and juiceless luxur. O God! one,
That has scarce blood enough to live upon . . .

There is even, as we shall see later, a sense in this verse that the very images of the luxury condemned contain also a kind of energy which – under the control of Tourneur's verse structure – may be a source of power for the wider moral vision of the play as a whole.

Tourneur's is immensely valuable dramatic poetry and it has a clear moral strength in the midst of – perhaps closely linked to – the vividly realized sin and evil. Certainly no simple concept of 'decadence' (e.g. a decadence from Shakespeare's high standards of dramatic art) will explain the positive contributions Tourneur makes to the drama of his age. Yet in this verse there is no more than the merest hint ('A parched and juiceless luxur . . .') of anything which would remind us of Shakespeare's reliance on the capacity of the natural world to sustain and nourish the good and the wholesome in man. Tourneur's play shares with – let us say – *Macbeth* a clear realization of evil, and also a sense of the potential vitality in the thing condemned. It is also related to Shakespeare in that it entertains the possibility of a play ot wit being at once a controlling and a liberating activity over the whole range of a play's developing structure. We could say therefore that *Macbeth* and *The Revenger's Tragedy* are both 'Elizabethan' in that they draw on a common fund of energy which is greater and more freely ranging than that available to any later society. We could particularize further and say that, within the larger terms of this 'Elizabethan' comparison, the two plays are related in more specific ways – for instance in their intelligent use of a sense of 'wit' – which clearly set them apart from the more simply energetic *Tamburlaine*.

But the total or final vision of the two is different, in kind as well as in degree. Not only does Tourneur reject – or ignore – Shakespeare's sense of nature and the natural; his sort of wit is also very different from anything in Shakespeare, and this largely because it is clearly orientated towards what Miss Bradbrook calls the 'jingling sententious couplet' and all that this implies in the sense of a need to mingle complex verse with a simpler, less ambiguous moral vision. The very 'control' or 'order' which in a generalized way is common to both playwrights is nevertheless also a very different matter when we consider it for what, in the last analysis, it is – part of the given substance of the plays. Thus we feel Shakespeare's sense of order is far the more rewarding of the two simply *because* it is less a mere sense of order and control; it is more continually related to manifold and constantly changing possibilities in life. And, on the other hand, though Tourneur's grasp on energy and vitality yields possibilities and insights that even Shakespeare's doesn't, it is also clearly narrower, driven more consistently to seek vitality in evil and the negative passions like Vendice's anger and scorn. Hence it is not surprising that his verse, though firm and crisp, is correspondingly less flexible than Shakespeare's, more unequivocally devoted to a simple need to order and control.

I started by claiming at the beginning of this discussion that the most valuable insights into the true nature of the dramatic experience which Shakespearean drama provides could best be seen in terms of the plays' ability to affirm complex relations – and oppositions – between man and the universe that sustains him. Shakespeare's art is great not least in that, offering a highly individual demonstration of the dramatic, it at the same time offers a *normative* vision of life and drama. The other key writer in our period – apart from Tourneur – is Middleton. With Middleton the nature of tragedy as we see it in Shakespeare's 'normative' plays develops and changes – if anything more radically still.

Thinking of Tourneur one could say that he relies in part on older concepts of sin and morality (which, however, are by no means entirely Shakespeare's) and that he also uses and develops a Revenge convention common to other writers of the time. But none of these things can be said of Middleton's great plays. He is in no clearly marked 'tradition' or 'convention'. Certainly there is an 'Elizabethan' vitality informing, and helping to mould, the verse and structure of *The Changeling*, but equally clearly the emphasis has now swung more towards the need for a new kind of clarity and control. The clear texture of the writing has, even in *The Changeling*, little of the excitement of Tourneur or the richness of Shakespeare. New areas of experience – for instance, in *The Changeling* a world of clear-sightedness and judgment radically disturbed by an underworld of passion; in *Women Beware Women* the world of bourgeois buying and selling – these are now brought under control. And since the areas of experience are different, the kind of control exercised will be different too. Oversimplifying for the sake of brevity, we could say that in Tourneur Shakespeare's preoccupations with the *whole* range of the natural world have narrowed to an intense preoccupation with the nature of sin and guilt, vividly and specifically realized. In Middleton, however, the drama is moving in another direction still. Here it embraces man's attempt to relate the deeply personal in himself to a society which is infinitely less capable than is Shakespeare's natural order – radically disturbing though this can be – of responding *to* the personal.

All these distinctions must be critical and qualitative ones. We are not 'tracing patterns of development', so much as seeing what – if anything – is given us in the quality of the dramatic writing before us. Thus to develop distinctions already suggested between *Tamburlaine* and other tragedies: compared with Tamburlaine, the verse in *The Revenger's Tragedy* has a life and energy which is more flexible, more valuably self-aware than Marlowe's. And

Middleton, though using a spare and quite obviously un-Shakespearean dialogue, can nevertheless rely on detailed contact with a new world of middle-class experience which, though barren in comparison with Shakespeare's universe, has its own relevance to us now, and certainly has richer possibilities than ever simple force or energy by itself could have. However strong it is – and it has strength and energy – Marlowe's world in *Tamburlaine* is, compared with either Middleton's or Tourneur's, too self-supporting, too far out of touch with the sustaining details of life itself. If we compare, for instance, the clarity and control which are admittedly a very marked feature of Marlowe at his best –

> I hold the Fates bound fast in iron chains,
> And with my hand turn Fortune's wheel about;
> And sooner shall the sun fall from his sphere
> Than Tamburlaine be slain or overcome.

– if we compare this with a representative quotation from a Middleton play, we shall see immediately that Middleton's sense of control and clarity has a substance Marlowe's lacks. Or rather, where the given 'substance' of Marlowe's verse tends to be merely a controlled but generalized (and hence comparatively *in*-substantial) force or energy, Middleton's very sense of control is far the more impressive of the two *because* it incorporates within itself the particular and moulds itself to this. And what the particular gives us – though not here in Shakespearean terms – is always a sustainingly solid reality:

> Get out again, for shame! the man loves best
> When his care's most, that shows his zeal to love:
> Fondness is but the idiot to affection,
> That plays at hot-cockles with rich merchants' wives,
> Good to make sport withal when the chest's full,
> And the long warehouse cracks. 'Tis time of day
> For us to be more wise; 'tis early with us . . .

In this speech, from Act I of *Women Beware Women*, the substance and fabric of the given society – the rich merchants' wives, the full chest, the long warehouse 'cracking' – is present, as something far more than mere illustration or background, in the clear texture of the verse. It is more, too, than something simply rejected. Middleton is strongly critical of this factorship-in-love, but his verse is subtle and clear enough to draw sustenance from the object criticized. In that steady, just barely excited rhythm, the images establish the presence of a sustaining solidity in the very merchandizing of love towards which our active criticism is nevertheless always directed.

Clearly there is no possibility of imposing on the Elizabethan-Jacobean age a pattern of development in which one attitude or achievement inevitably leads on to, and is superseded by, the next. The very word 'pattern' implies something too neatly organized to fit our sense of the varied activity that the age – even in tragedy alone – commands. In particular, just as surveys of Shakespeare which see all in terms of a simple development from the histories through the tragedies to the last plays inevitably miss what is given as fresh material in each play, so a critical attack which sees playwrights as 'building on the shoulders' of their predecessors misrepresents both individual plays and the true relations between one writer and another. In all period studies, simple teleological patterns and hindsight are an ever-present danger. There is a widely held view which presents *Twelfth Night,* for instance, as the apotheosis of Shakespearean (and Elizabethan) comic drama.[1] Falstaff's crudity – necessary as it was earlier on – is held to be refined and purified in the later play, the cloak-bag of guts scaled down to Sir Toby's size and importance. Similarly, there are plenty of attempts to show how tragedy 'grew out of' the history plays. Now, the concealed danger here lies not so much in the judgments

[1] Cf. H. B. Charlton, *Shakespearean Comedy* (London, 1958).

J. F. Danby appears to adopt the teleological principle of interpretation with approval (see his chapter 'Killing the King', in *Shakespeare's Doctrine of Nature*).

given on individual plays, as in the critical method adopted. The attitude of mind that assumes that Shakespeare's achievements must be judged in terms of a continuous straight-line progress which simply makes clearer and clearer his final vision of comedy or tragedy begs every critical question. The grossness of *Henry IV* and the dramatic structure adopted in that play, so far from being unfortunate necessities to Shakespeare at that stage of his writing, are essential values he establishes there and nowhere else. They cannot adequately be described in terms of what later became tragedy or what later became comedy. *Henry IV* is a greater play than *Twelfth Night*; it can also be seen, when the blinkers are off, as a play quite as great as some at least of the tragedies. The sense of 'progression' from play to play does indeed demand that we look at the histories in the light of what Shakespeare later had to say, but this only because and in so far as we are different people after having read, say, *Lear* – and proved it to be a great play – than we were before. Whether any given new experience raises or lowers our estimate of the earlier play cannot be assumed merely in terms of the 'workshop' theory of Shakespearean – or Elizabethan – development. In the particular case of *Henry IV*, it is I think true that this comparatively early play offers something more richly intelligent than anything in the later comedies. One of the many reasons why we value Elizabethan literature so highly now is that it demonstrates in what ways sheer coarseness and vulgarity can be valued as part of the substance of life itself, and this even while these same qualities are being criticized for their comparative inefficiency and lack of direction. And this is what is being demonstrated, more clearly perhaps than anywhere else, in the Falstaffian element of *Henry IV*. The Falstaffian world in the play must – in terms of sheer political and moral necessity – give way to Hal's. But this means, not that Falstaff is seen as something to be rejected as worthless, but that the sheer necessity of Hal's rise to power and control involves a gain which is also a related and very particular kind of loss. And this in turn means that the whole play of *Henry IV* – sustaining Falstaff's grossness even while it criticizes it – can never be truly represented as merely a cruder version of *Twelfth Night*. The later play may have its own particular insights, but they are not such as can outweigh the richer world of *Henry IV*, including as this does the 'roasted Manningtree ox', the 'stuffed cloak-bag of guts'.

And so with the whole range of Elizabethan-Jacobean tragic drama. The nature of the 'dramatic' means that truth and value as given in plays are only to be defined in terms of the structure and fabric of the writing in each play considered. Drama cannot be seen merely as working towards a lively illustration, in 'human terms', of a truth about man or the universe held, in other terms, outside the given play or in other plays available. Tourneur's and Middleton's attitudes and achievements are different in kind as well as in quality from Shakespeare's, or Marlowe's, 'and the rest'. Nor does any of these writers merely illustrate or enliven philosophical truths available to the persistent reader of Aquinas or Machiavelli or Bacon or Plutarch. When literary critics reduce plays like *Antony and Cleopatra* to Plutarch's level one can merely gesture despairingly at what is obviously the failure of modern criticism to educate teachers of literature today:

> But these two lovers . . . are greater than their failings; their love is equal to the last sacrifice, more than equal to it. They triumph in their love; and in so far as we may be capable of sharing in their experience vicariously, we triumph with them. For their story is a true one; it is all in Plutarch, though only Shakespeare could show us that it is there.[1]

On the other hand, there *are* relations to be grasped between plays and between the work of different writers. Few critics nowadays would wish to retreat into an escapist neo-classical world of criticism where plays are seen in terms of 'what they set

[1] H. S. Wilson, *op. cit.*, p. 211.

out to do', or the 'kind' to which they belong. For one thing, some Elizabethan plays are poor or, what is worse, positively unhealthy. And conversely, some plays can and must be seen – by virtue of their sheer quality – as dominating and controlling the insight we now have into what a given period could and could not do. Basically it is a question of using the quality of insight in the best plays in order to see what nowadays remains as of value in Elizabethan drama, and what does not. Among the dramatists, Shakespeare, Middleton and Tourneur seem to me to occupy this controlling position. The tensions and oppositions between the respective achievements of these three dramatists are the key at once to the position and worth of the lesser figures and to an understanding of the true nature of tragic drama.

And Shakespeare himself, though he does not exhaust the possibilities of tragedy, has a prior claim on our attention, not only because his is the widest and deepest enquiry, but also because his position, as we consider it from play to play, shifts more radically than does that of any other single writer.

CHAPTER II

SHAKESPEAREAN TRAGEDY

I cannot, of course, pretend to deal with Shakespeare's plays in one chapter. What I want to do is look at his position as it seems to me modern criticism is now tending to explain it, and in particular to consider more fully some of the problems raised in the previous chapter. Focusing the argument on a closer examination of key Shakespeare plays, our main concern will be to develop more fully questions about the nature of drama. If it is misleading to think of plays as merely 'dramatizing' fundamental truths having an independent existence in philosophy or theology, what then – taking Shakespeare as the leading case in point – is *dramatic* truth?

Looking at Shakespearean criticism of the last 30 years or so, two facts or generalizations stand out from many others as both pre-eminently important and, by now, established. The first is the apparently largely negative one that Shakespearean tragedy – whatever this may mean – offers us a radically different experience from one play to the next. Even leaving *Antony and Cleopatra* out (as quite obviously a puzzling play), we are now inclined to ask, more urgently than before, what precisely *is* the link between the equivocations of *Macbeth* and the radical questionings of *Lear*? And what has *Othello*, for instance, to do with the others, taken as a group? In a vague sense, these were always obvious questions to ask, but it's only fairly recently that the true importance of such distinctions has been recognized.[1] Nowadays it is seen not as a matter of Shakespeare putting the same point differently, but of his dealing with different areas of experience in different plays. All

---

[1] *The Age of Shakespeare*, Pelican Guide No.2; L. C. Knights, *Some Shakespearean Themes* (London, 1959); D. A. Traversi, *An Approach to Shakespeare* (London, 1957).

the plays in question may usefully, though loosely, be termed 'tragedies', but the differences between them are more than matters of 'form' or 'expression'. Shakespeare's basic attitudes and outlook in *Lear* are radically different from, for instance, his attitudes in *Macbeth*.

The second general point, related to the first, is one which took shape first in Dr Leavis's extraordinarily penetrating remarks on *Macbeth* in *Education and the University*. In this book Dr Leavis dealt briefly, though probably more authoritatively than anyone before or since, with the 'character' question in Shakespeare's plays. More importantly, in the course of so doing he raised an issue about Shakespearean tragedy generally which is of far greater – because far wider – importance than the Bradleyan 'character' issue from which it arose. Talking of the inadequacy of a strictly Bradleyan interpretation of the plays, Dr Leavis argued that Shakespeare attacks us not through character alone but, as it were, simultaneously through his evocation of character, his imagery, the juxtaposition of opposing scenes and opposing values, etc., etc. 'For Shakespeare's blank verse is a convention (so subtle that we forget it to be one) that enables him to play upon us, not merely through our sense of the character speaking, but also, and at the same time, directly; and the question, how much of the one and how much of the other it may be in any particular case, does not arise.' From this position, there quite naturally arose an interpretation which treated Shakespearean tragedy, or at any rate certain tragedies, as an establishing of values as well as a recognition of tragic waste, tragic inevitability. Talking of the 'temple-haunting martlet' scene, Dr Leavis concluded: 'But more; its "pendent bed", secure above the dizzy drop, is its "procreant cradle"; and "procreant" is enforced by "breeds": all these suggestions, uniting again with those of "temple" and "heaven", evoke the contrast to "foul murder" – life springing swift, keen and vulnerable from the hallowed source.'[1] This, I think, was the really valuable contribution *Education and the University* had to make to Shakespeare studies. Many critics, neo-classical and modern alike, had wanted to see something like this positive quality in Shakespeare. Bradley himself, after writing impressive criticism on the pessimism of *Lear*, attempted to answer his own question (Is man here represented as the 'plaything of a blind or capricious power?') by an evocation of the spiritual rebirth of the protagonist. He even suggested an amended title for the play: *The Redemption of King Lear*. The trouble with this approach was, first that it wouldn't fit all the plays; and more important, even if it could have been made to fit *Lear*, it assumed a play less impressive than everybody, including Bradley, felt *Lear* to be. Lear's personal regeneration alone (if this were Shakespeare's main point) would be not merely ludicrously inadequate in the face of, notably, Cordelia's death and Lear's own concluding speeches, but also too vague and amorphous a value to put up against the (on the Bradleyan hypothesis) cruelly alien universe against which Lear had been 'fighting'. And as we saw in Chapter I, in any view of Shakespearean tragedy in which the heroes are representing mankind in a struggle against an irrational and possibly vicious universe, the audience-hero identification which results is apt to end in a sentimental indulgence quite alien to the tough sensibility we feel to be there, behind and in the text as a whole. Such a view will inspire, for instance, something like the vague emotionalism Maxwell Anderson apparently wants to evoke by Esdras's speech at the end of *Winterset*:

> On this star,
> in this hard star-adventure, knowing not
> what the fires mean to right and left, nor whether
> a meaning was intended or presumed,

[1] F. R. Leavis, *Education and the University*, p. 124; see also pp. 115-16. The best single essay available on poetic tragedy is Dr Leavis's 'Tragedy and the Medium', in *The Common Pursuit* (London, 1952).

man can stand up, and look out blind, and say:
in all these turning lights I find no clue,
only a masterless night, and in my blood
no certain answer, yet is my mind my own,
yet is my heart a cry toward something dim
in distance, which is higher than I am
and makes me emperor of the endless dark
even in seeking!

But Shakespeare's writing is demonstrably sharper and tougher than this. At the same time, his 'universe' is, at least in *Macbeth* and *Antony and Cleopatra* – very possibly also in *Lear* – less unequivocally alien. We cannot assume from his plays a simple evaluation of the 'Heroic Man *versus* the Universe' kind.

It was, I think, Dr Leavis's attack on the problem which permitted a solution to worries of this kind and opened the way for a more interesting and valuable enquiry. He, with L. C. Knights, broke through the dichotomy between character and action inherent in earlier interpretations and enabled us to see, emerging from the plays, values very different from Bradley's; different, too, from those of almost any other critic before or since.[1] Their work was – and is – far more important than anything implied by the apparently merely negative result of proving Bradley wrong about the relative importance of character in drama. Freed from worrying too much about any personal triumph of Lear, or Othello, or Macbeth, criticism could begin to discover, and discriminate between, the true values that emerge from each of Shakespeare's plays. The clearest case is *Macbeth* itself where, for all the dramatic irony hinging on it, the 'temple-haunting martlet' speech, and other passages like it, assert life arising out of

---

[1] Like Professor Knights, I should like to record my admiration for the work of G. Wilson Knight. Personally I cannot accept his readings of some of the plays, but his comments are often invaluable, and obviously distinguished.

In addition all modern critics must owe a considerable debt to Bradley, some of whose insights can in fact be valuably disentangled from his limiting 'character' approach (cf. section 5 of 'The Substance of Tragedy', *Shakespearean Tragedy* (London, 1949 edn.), pp. 31-39).

death and negation. And it doesn't matter in this connection whether these suggestions come – as is the case partly with the 'naked new-born babe' speech, the 'broad and casing air' and others – from the doomed hero or not. Our vision is not entirely his.

These, then, are I think the two most important, interrelated (and largely neglected) insights that modern criticism at its best has arrived at. Firstly, Shakespeare's achievement is a positive one in a sense far beyond Bradley's understanding; secondly, his tragedies give us experiences which, from play to play, differ in kind as well as in quality or emphasis. The two insights are interrelated because, starting from the supposition that Shakespeare presents specific values of the kind Leavis, for instance, finds in *Macbeth*, we then have to assume that a play as different from this as *Lear* will embody a different evaluation of experience, will in fact be a different play in far more than the purely technical sense. Certainly there is something about all or most of these plays which does seem to imply a generic concept of Tragedy. If we think of the puzzling but highly important and valuable case of *Antony and Cleopatra*, where a broadness of comic vision includes scenes like the Thyreus one, or the Charmian gossip scene immediately after the great love scene in Act I, or Cleopatra mocking Antony as he tries to tell her he's going back to Rome –

> *Antony* You'll heat my blood; no more.
> *Cleopatra* You can do better yet, but this is meetly.
> *Antony* Now, by my sword,–
> *Cleopatra*   And target. Still he mends . . .
>   I, iii, 79 ff.

– all this would seem to set the play off against the other tragedies and consequently give them a kind of grouping together, for all their differences. *Antony and Cleopatra* is obviously a great and – in the wider sense – serious play, but also it has a broader, wittier vision of life than *Macbeth*, *Hamlet*, *Othello* and, most notably,

Lear. On the other hand, this distinction, true as it is, should never be used in such a way as to obscure the inadequacy of *any* completely generalized formulation about the nature of 'Shakespearean Tragedy'.

In spite of this, however, and even among those who see much of what was implied in Dr Leavis's attack on problems of Shakespeare criticism, attempts are still being made to group Shakespeare's plays together in such a way as to make them yield a single dominating or central concern. The temptation to do this for Shakespeare will always exist, because the deeply serious nature of the plays seems to imply a developing and consistently held purpose. Even Professor Knights's book *Some Shakespearean Themes* stresses – far more markedly than did most of his earlier essays on which the book is largely based – a consistent development which he claims to find in Shakespeare's thought and writing. For instance Professor Knights quotes and discusses lines from Sonnet CXXIV: 'And finally, allied with a capacity for self-searching and moral discrimination, there is a groping for some certitude to set over against the perpetual flux of things, an intimation that love alone "stands hugely politic, That it nor grows with heat nor drowns with showers". . . . And when that patient passionate exploration has reached its centre there will be a marvellous celebration of values that are not only in wish but in fact "builded far from accident" . . .'[1] There is, surely, something drastically wrong with a statement that Shakespeare was 'groping for some certitude to *set over against* the perpetual flux of things'? It is of course likely that Shakespeare wanted to create by his art a life that was indeed 'builded far from accident', and this, if he had ever achieved it, would have involved a gathering together and

---

[1] L. C. Knights, *op. cit.*, pp. 50-1. I am not, of course, suggesting that Professor Knights rests his case on this sonnet. On the other hand, compared with his work as it appeared in earlier essays (cf. 'Shakespeare's Use of Nature', *Sewanee Review*, Vol. 64, 1956), *Some Shakespearean Themes* as a whole relies heavily – I think myself too heavily – on presenting a distinct line of development in Shakespearean thought and writing.

hardening of a set of values and attitudes gradually developed from the earliest plays. But fortunately he nowhere succumbed to this temptation. Had he done so, his dramatic art would have withered immediately. He cannot be seen as writing plays which reject or rise above the life which gave them birth. It is often assumed that Shakespeare's drama is a testing process, or one which asks questions about fundamental human or divine values (as Justice, Love, Mercy, Grace). And indeed – particularly if we are thinking of a play like *Lear* – this is in part true. But the total or final vision of both *Lear* and the other tragedies is always something other than an assertion that Love, or Mercy, or Grace is now seen the more clearly because it has been subjected to a testing process, or because it has been finally, by the purging fire of tragedy, distilled from what previously obscured our vision. Indeed what seems to me to blur even Professor Knights's invaluable insight into the nature of tragedy in *Lear* is his summing up of that play in terms of 'an affirmation *in spite of*'.[1] Putting the emphasis like this, though it fits *Lear* better than most of the tragedies, is dangerously close to over-simplifying the relations Shakespeare establishes between the valuable in nature and the tragically chaotic; and it is untrue, I think, to Professor Knights's own more revealing insights.

The truer position I think is that Shakespeare, even while he is firmly rejecting, let us say, Edmund's concept of nature and the natural, is at the same time incorporating some of Edmund's vitality into the play's total vision or dramatic truth. Without Edmund, the play would be slightly less terrifying; but its final achievement – the 'truth' it yields – would also be less substantial. A clearer case would be the insistence we shall find Shakespeare making, in *Antony and Cleopatra*, on the sheer *value* of Nilus' mud and slime, or the flies that are imaged as blowing Cleopatra's body

---

[1] *Ibid.*, pp. 116-119. And compare his statement, rather puzzling in the light of the analysis he gives the whole play, that in *Lear* 'The positives that emerge from the play are indeed fundamentally Christian values, but they are reached by an act of profound individual exploration . . .' (p. 91).

'into abhorring'. Here Shakespeare is in fact saying as clearly as he can that value and the good can never exist 'far from accident'. Shakespeare is no idealist: life for him is neither a testing of pre-existent values, nor a confusion of flux and 'accident' obscuring an ideal state (e.g. Platonic, or Humanist, or Christian). Rather, it is itself an indispensable source of value, an enriching of the artist's total vision: the particular kind of vitality *Antony and Cleopatra* displays would be impossible without the flies and mud, because they are part of it.

If there is any point at all in taking Sonnet CXXIV, for instance, as a microcosm of Shakespeare's larger purposes, it is in the sense that his *art* is, at its greatest, 'builded far from accident'; but such a statement is only true in so far as it admits that his art at once sustains and receives nourishment from 'accident' and the flux of life.[1] This is in fact one of the principal ways in which the great plays give us a demonstration of the true nature of 'dramatic' (as opposed, for instance, to philosophic) truth – truth, that is, the fabric of which takes shape and nourishment from the flux of life it criticizes. There are no absolute values in Shakespeare; and there is certainly no Scale-of-Being philosophy which assumes an absolute above and beyond mankind. His art is always nourished from below, and he defines or demonstrates the true and the good by assembling life, in each new play, in forms and shapes it had not taken, even in his own plays, before. And this, again, must mean that each of his tragedies states a complex truth which is different, in form and substance, from 'truth' in any other play. Therefore when we are looking at the relations between Shakespeare's plays we will be seeing, not a consistent purpose illustrated, but a set of relations which can only be grasped by actually putting one whole play, in all its complexity, up against others. We can accept readily

[1] For a full discussion of *Antony and Cleopatra* in this light see S. L. Goldberg, '*Antony and Cleopatra*: The Tragedy of the Imagination', *The Melbourne Critical Review*, 1961, pp. 41-64.

enough a further contention of Professor Knights, that *King Lear* is the 'great central masterpiece, the great exploratory allegory to which so many of the earlier plays lead and on which the later plays depend'.[1] But even this is acceptable only in so far as *Lear* can be demonstrated to be a greater play than the others and consequently provides some explanation for the firmness and achievement which we quite independently recognize to be there in most of the later writing. Even *Lear* cannot be used as a background of information necessary in order to explain what is happening in *Macbeth, Antony and Cleopatra*, and the last plays. It is for this reason that a later formulation by Professor Knights of the position of *Lear* in the Shakespeare canon is worrying: 'The resulting freedom from inner tensions is seen alike in the assured judgment and the magnificent vitality of *Macbeth, Antony and Cleopatra*, and *Coriolanus* . . .'[2] There may possibly be a sense in which the writing of *Lear* resulted in a 'freedom from inner tensions' in the later tragedies – though personally I doubt this – but if this *is* so, surely the 'freedom' is loss as well as gain? The radically disturbing quality of *Lear* is one of its distinctive and most valuable qualities.

These broad generalizations are important as a starting-point for an evaluation of Shakespeare. Without attempting to go through the plays in detail, I want now to see how such generalizations work out in some of the plays and what relations, if any, there are between the tragedies. In a brief survey of this kind, *Hamlet* and *Othello* are special cases for very many reasons, and I would prefer therefore, for the sake of clarity, to draw examples and suggest patterns of achievement from the other plays, leaving aside the particular difficulties of these two.[3]

[1] L. C. Knights, *op. cit.*, p. 158.

[2] *Ibid.*, p. 159.

[3] See E. Jones, *Hamlet and Oedipus* (London, 1949); and F. R. Leavis, 'Diabolic Intellect and the Noble Hero', *The Common Pursuit.*

King Lear, first, presents us with a tragic view in which the distinctive quality is one of radical questioning. Whatever our total impressions of this play, we are never allowed to forget the pressing, impertinent questions about Nature and Justice which come to a head in the storm scenes where Lear enthrones the Fool and the 'madman' Edgar as justices. Despite the Fool's placing comments ('Cry you mercy, I took you for a joint-stool') this is a very different and I think a more radically disturbing enquiry than is Macbeth's juggling with good and evil. The focal point of it is Lear himself, but the enquiry comes from all aspects and sections of the play, spreading out far beyond the central character. Nature itself, from Edmund's 'Now, gods, stand up for bastards!' onwards to the storm scene, poses the question in one form, and the play mingles this with Lear's own enquiry:

> *Kent* I know you. Where's the king?
> *Gentleman* Contending with the fretful elements;
> Bids the wind blow the earth into the sea,
> Or swell the curled waters 'bove the main,
> That things might change or cease; tears his white hair,
> Which the impetuous blasts, with eyeless rage,
> Catch in their fury, and make nothing of . . .
>
> III, i, 3 ff.

This is a nature which includes and embraces both the 'eyeless rage' of mere destruction and also a fury which is vital even when threatening destruction ('Or swell the curled waters 'bove the main . . .'). Lear's own protest against a seemingly hostile universe is in fact being put against, and modified by, this view of a natural order which is at once destructive and powerfully energetic.

There are countless other passages in the play where the verse asserts a similar view of the universe and the relationship of man and man's values to it. To take just two short but very important ones as examples:

You sulphurous and thought-executing fires,
Vaunt-couriers to oak-cleaving thunderbolts,
Singe my white head! And thou, all-shaking thunder,
Strike flat the thick rotundity o' the world!

III, ii, 4-7

Filial ingratitude!
Is it not as this mouth should tear this hand
For lifting food to't? But I will punish home . . .

III, iv, 14-16

In the first of these the character's passionate need to 'strike flat' the offending world is valid, but is opposed by the 'thick rotundity', the essential, solid reality of the world itself. In the second, the character's indignant protest against what is in a sense undeniably a cruel world, at the same time is seen as containing the possibility of 'hand' feeding 'mouth' in a more stable and substantial order of things. In both extracts the very thickness of texture of the verse and its rhythmic firmness and vitality are part of the assertive quality within the question being asked.

The briefness of each of these quotations might be taken as misleading. Actually, the play is continually throwing up suggestions of this kind and this is again and again seen to be the way in which Shakespeare's dramatic verse works. Especially in *Lear*, and even in *Macbeth*, it is a matter not so much of long speeches or arguments, but of the speed, compression and subtlety of Shakespeare's investigating, probing mind. Reading (or listening to) the verse with attention, we are conscious of suggestions of vitality springing from the very terms of tragic protest and tragic destruction. If we think of the comparatively sterile world evoked, often, in Ibsen, or even Middleton, the nature of Shakespeare's grasp should be immediately apparent.

To return more specifically to *Lear*. This is a play, then, where the natural world presents itself as an equivocal issue to mankind, but also as a presence on which mankind must always depend. It can be wolfish and cruel; or it can suggest growth, vitality and possibility; or it can present itself as both destructive and vital at the same time. It is, however, never, or seldom, sterile and arid in the Ibsen sense.

But, we must go further still than this in our attempt to sum up the play's final statement. *Lear* is further removed from *Macbeth*, and certainly from *Antony and Cleopatra*, than criticism of this kind would in itself suggest. Most notably, the juggling fiends and the equivocation which begin *Macbeth* are replaced in *Lear* by a sense of driving action more like that of ancient tragedy. This is best seen and felt in the combination of our considerable sympathy for Lear himself with the cumulative, crushing questions which he, and the play generally, ask again and again about the nature of justice, and the nature of man in the face of an apparent utter lack of justice. The questions put in and by the storm scenes are repeated yet again in Act IV when Lear, dressed fantastically in wildflowers, brings finally into the open the undercurrent of sex which he, Edgar, Edmund and others have been suggesting all along:

> Thou shalt not die: die for adultery! No:
> The wren goes to 't, and the small gilded fly
> Does lecher in my sight.
> Let copulation thrive . . .
> To 't luxury, pell-mell! for I lack soldiers.
> Behold yond simpering dame,
> Whose face between her forks presageth snow;
> That minces virtue, and does shake the head
> To hear of pleasure's name;
> The fitchew nor the soiled horse goes to 't
> With a more riotous appetite.
> Down from the waist they are Centaurs,
> Though women all above:
> But to the girdle do the gods inherit,
> Beneath is all the fiends':
> There's hell, there's darkness, there is the sulphurous pit,
> Burning, scalding, stench, consumption; fie, fie, fie! pah, pah!
>
> IV, vi, 114-133

Here Shakespeare has brought the slightly more generalized questions and comments of Acts II and III down to a psychological comment based on very specific observation. Before the speech finally dissolves into the threatening anarchy of Lear's complete breakdown in the final lines ('Burning, scalding, stench . . .'), the 'matter and impertinency mixed' focuses the earlier questions about nature and justice onto what Lear has been led by events to see as possibly the only significant basis for human behaviour. He *sees* the gilded fly ('Does lecher in my sight . . .') and he sees therefore one obvious connection between this and behaviour generally. What, then, of Justice: 'None does offend, none, I say none.' The directness and force of this questioning process, easily stripping every shred of pretence and evasion from mankind, is unique in Shakespearean drama. It is certainly very different from anything in *Macbeth*, and the toughness of despair in and behind the writing is jolted into the foreground yet again with the death of Cordelia later on and the presentation of the last joke played by the universe against Lear: the fact that he dies on the point of seeing a last hope where none is possible.

For all its difficulty, we have in *Lear* a play which is in a sense simpler than *Macbeth*. It probes issues, if not more subtly, then at any rate more radically and directly. Like *Macbeth* it includes the concept of a nature which is full of growth and possibility, but man's part in this seems to be not to hold difficult issues in balance, but to state as disturbingly and radically as possible what can, under certain circumstances, be the terrifying injustice of tragedy. Rightly, then, *Lear* is the Shakespeare play which most clearly depends on a comparatively straightforward action, though by this I mean not simply the story, but story as organized to drive home again and again the tough questioning of Nature and Justice in which lies the play's most obvious and most disturbing impact.

The final impression of this play is one which can for our purposes be summed up in terms of the impact of the last scenes.

There is toughness and directness still in the verse:

> Why should a dog, a horse, a rat, have life,
> And thou no breath at all? Thou'lt come no more,
> Never, never, never, never, never!

There is also, however, in the sudden flexibility of lines like those
that follow immediately, great and positive sympathy for mankind
faced with the inevitability of tragic fact:

> Pray you, undo this button: thank you, sir.
> Do you see this? Look on her, look, her lips,
> Look there, look there! (Dies)

It has been a play where a comparatively simple action has put
the toughest and most disturbing questions in all drama, but also
one which could contain an equally straightforward energy, and
sympathy.

Macbeth presents a radically different picture. As a number of
critics have pointed out, much of its initial impact is bound up with
a juggling of values like that of the witches early on: things are and
are not, at the same time:

> My thought, whose murder yet is but fantastical,
> Shakes so my single state of man that function
> Is smother'd in surmise, and nothing is
> But what is not.   I, iii, 139-42

From this less direct, but nevertheless moving and subtle enquiry,
spring constant suggestions, affirmations of growth and possibility
in the face of – perhaps *from* the very fact of – instability and sin.
Shakespeare is not here concerned with the magnificent violence
of *Lear* or with the radical questions this in itself suggests. Nature
and the universe in *Macbeth* are, again, equivocally presented, but
the equivocations are different ones and, surprisingly, the natural
world appears in the end as far less potentially destructive. Dr
Leavis's comments on the 'temple-haunting martlet' speech are a
case in point, and in fact the play is, for all its equivocations, packed

with suggestions of firmness and growth. Macbeth and Lady Macbeth, in the certainty of crime and destruction, are themselves continually the occasion for the author's assertion of values. The verse they speak presents us with their crime and their thoughts, but at the same time and in the very act of doing so establishes firmly the actual presence of the 'sure and firm-set earth', the real possibility of being '. . . As broad and general as the casing air'. In particular, the development of attitudes in 'If it were done when 'tis done', from the equivocal, almost hysterical beginning, to the strongly metaphorical, almost Blakean insight at the end, is highly significant in this connection (though it is too difficult a speech for detailed comment here).[1] The point relevant to our enquiry at the moment is simply the presence of values and metaphorical, dramatic statement emergent from the more personal opening lines. The last section of the speech is a statement of values (though of a highly complex and metaphorical kind) rather than anything that could be summed up in terms of Macbeth's personality, or even of his personal problems of the moment.

There is one further point about *Macbeth* and the dramatic verse in it I should like to make here. In the following speech on the occasion of Duncan's death there is, despite the dramatic irony, arising out of it in fact, the familiar assertion of values:

> Here lay Duncan,
> His silver skin lac'd with his golden blood;
> And his gash'd stabs look'd like a breach in nature
> For ruin's wasteful entrance; there, the murderers,
> Steep'd in the colours of their trade, their daggers
> Unmannerly breech'd with gore: who could refrain,
> That had a heart to love, and in that heart
> Courage to make's love known?   II, iii, 118-25

[1] See *Education and the University*, pp. 78-83. However, Dr Leavis's line of approach to dramatic poetry is often misunderstood and taken as consisting merely, or largely, in detailed examination of the text (cf. Graham Martin, '*Macbeth*, I, vii, 1-28', *Interpretations*, ed. John Wain (London, 1955), pp. 17-30, where the 'examination' is in fact a fragmentation of the text).

Duncan's 'silver skin' laced, significantly, with his *golden* blood, presents, as do his 'gash'd stabs' and the 'breach in nature/For ruin's wasteful entrance', at once the fact of destruction and the presence of wholeness, perfection. The further point made by this speech looks forward to *Antony and Cleopatra*. In *Macbeth*, and particularly in *Antony and Cleopatra*, Shakespeare sees not only the clear presence of vitality and value in tragedy, but also a kind of solidity, a kind of rough activity of a deliberately more 'ordinary' kind ('Steep'd in the colours of their *trade* . . .'). Before closing this particular speech he moves on to the lines which, by their sheer impudence and wit, have embarrassed editors since the First Folio:

> . . . their daggers
> Unmannerly breech'd with gore:

There is nothing here that one could state even summarily as a 'value' or an 'attitude'. It is an odd image, because the 'breeching' is clearly a pun: one of its implications is certainly literally that of being 'unmannerly breech'd' (i.e. in the sense of improperly trousered! – though there is also a further sense that, for daggers, this is a very 'mannerly' breeching indeed). This note in Shakespeare increases, of course, in *Antony and Cleopatra*, and I take it to represent the ability constantly to evoke and rely on a sort of witty reality, actuality. There is a tough comedy or wit here which, as well as being highly metaphorical, asserts the solid actuality and liveliness of experience itself. It is not easily described as a value, but it works as such. Even in the subtleties and oddness of the metaphor here, there is a realization of the actual, the tangible – even, in a sense, the ordinary.

This, finally, is one of the dominant notes in *Antony and Cleopatra*. This play is as subtle as *Macbeth*, but the area of experience touched on is wider and hence the cast of the play entirely different. Much of it depends on juxtapositions of the kind evident in the movement from the utter conviction of the play s opening comment, to the slightly hollow but nevertheless impressive lyricism of the lovers' talk, and then (with an obvious comment) to the bawdy, lively gossip on love and marriage between Charmian and the maids which follows. This kind of movement of scene and image establishes the sort of flux, the sort of ambivalence of death and vitality which Shakespeare sees at this stage of his writing.

Stiffening this further is the sense throughout the play of an exploration of the complexity and toughness of actual experience itself, an exploration suggested in parts of *Macbeth* and, later, in the knotted complexity of *Cymbeline* and *The Winter's Tale*. Constantly in *Antony and Cleopatra* we have a sense of the dramatic dialogue, the verse, being foreshortened, forced into ellipses. It halts, and skips over expected connections, rehearsing by this movement and this tone the difficulty, the knottedness of actual life and actual experience. (One is forced to add here, 'experience as Shakespeare sees it at this moment', but this is a necessary begging of the question, because the verse does actually prove its point, 'for the moment', about what experience is like.) There are many examples from many sections of the play, but the following are typical:

> It hath been taught us from the primal state,
> That he which is was wish'd until he were;
> And the ebb'd man, ne'er lov'd till ne'er worth love,
> Comes dear'd by being lack'd.   I, iv, 41-44

> Yon ribaudred nag of Egypt –
> Whom leprosy o'ertake! – i' the midst o' the fight,
> When vantage like a pair of twins appear'd,
> Both as the same, or rather ours the elder,–
> The breese upon her, like a cow in June! –
> Hoists sails and flies.   III, x. 10-15

> . . . now all labour
> Mars what it does; yea, very force entangles
> Itself with strength . . .   IV, xiv, 47-49

Mixed with the 'difficulty' of the imagery (cf. the sudden oddity
of the 'cow in June'), and with the movement of the action of the
play, this kind of abruptness of thought and rhythm constitutes
what is for Shakespeare almost a new order of thought – a reliance now on the lively, solid *vulgarity* given in the images of the
'ribaudred nag', 'the breese upon her', and in the character of
Cleopatra herself 'hopping forty paces through the public street'.

It is difficult, finally, to stress too much the precise kind of importance that the fact of such widely differing imagery, verse, and
action has in these three plays. In *Antony and Cleopatra*, much of the
uniqueness of the play depends on new images, new *facts* almost,
that Shakespeare uses. There was equivocation in plenty in
Macbeth, but in *Antony and Cleopatra* the paradoxical, ambivalent
verse is put in terms of life emerging from Nilus' slime, of Cleopatra (to take the opposite paradox) blown 'into abhorring', of the
flag rotting itself with motion, and so on. These images add up not
simply to a statement that all things are paradoxical, but to a statement that in these circumstances – the circumstances specifically of
apparent futility, 'riggishness', mud and slime – there is life and
growth.

Given this outline of Shakespeare's basic positions, and of some
of the possibilities that emerge, we can now turn to other writers.
The connection between Shakespeare and the rest of the Jacobeans
I should like to leave tentatively suggested, rather than worked out
in the kind of detail which could be suffocating. The best way of
placing him, in fact, is I think simply to state his position in the
context of others.

Briefly, however, the sort of superiority he has, particularly over
Webster, can be put in terms of clarity of texture. This means, of

course, clarity of and about particular issues, but it is useful at this
stage to see the importance the clarity itself has. It is, basically, a
clarity of control, of moral certainty. Where Webster only just
rescues his plays from notebook brilliance, Shakespeare can launch
into issues of infinite, even bewildering complexity without losing
his clarity of meaning and emphasis. With Webster, the notebook
technique was an easy way of holding off for the moment the
confusion which broke out finally in, for instance, the central
scenes of *The Duchess*. Shakespeare, on the other hand, never
hesitates, even in the later tragedies, in the face of complexity or
difficulty. His confidence is justified when we recognize that,
though the plays are far too complex to sum up or gather together
easily, we still have no doubt about the emphasis of (and in) important passages. Nobody could mistake, for instance, the clarity
in the interrelation of levels of comment in Philo's opening speech
in *Antony and Cleopatra*:

> Nay, but this dotage of our general's
> O'erflows the measure; those his goodly eyes,
> That o'er the files and musters of the war
> Have glow'd like plated Mars, now bend, now turn
> The office and devotion of their view
> Upon a tawny front; his captain's heart,
> Which in the scuffles of great fights hath burst
> The buckles on his breast, reneges all temper,
> And is become the bellows and the fan
> To cool a gipsy's lust. Look! where they come.

On one level (to use a possibly misleading phrase since there is no
break between 'levels'), this is the statement of an observer, or
'character', to the effect that Antony has declined. As such, it has
its truth. On the other hand, the verse is so powerful that many
other meanings, which have nothing to do with Philo, emerge
from the dialogue. The actual vitality centring in Antony (and it
doesn't particularly matter when, at what stage of his career we
like to see this as active) is there:

those his goodly eyes,
That o'er the files and musters of the war
Have glow'd like plated Mars, now bend, now turn . . .

Also, the life and movement at the heart of the play's central paradox are called up immediately in that oddity of movement in
which Antony is pictured as turning his gaze from war to Cleopatra. It is a studied image, reaching far beyond mere character, and
a difficult one, because the vitality is in the very movement *from*
war, in the tawny front itself, and even in the 'gipsy's lust'. Even
the certainties of 'office and devotion' shift between war and
Cleopatra, and without being destroyed by this. The verse merges
gain with loss, futility with activity, in Shakespeare's firmest
manner. But – and this is the real point – as we read the passage we
are in no doubt, for all the complexity, as to Shakespeare's precise
meaning.

It is this clarity of definition and achievement in Shakespeare
that enables him also, in the tragedies and in plays like *Much Ado*
and the last plays, to make much more than did any other writer
of the increasing and widely representative Jacobean preoccupation with unchastity. The comedies and the last plays are here the
clearest case. Like Webster and Tourneur, and to a certain extent
Middleton, Shakespeare is concerned in these plays with the possibility of the instability of Jacobean values extending as far as the
obvious, traditional image of purity, woman. In plays of this kind,
it is not so much a matter of whether the women are or are not in
fact unfaithful, but whether the violence and suspicion of the
world around them has any comment to make on the kind of
purity they represent. It is the suspicion of unchastity which is the
great fact. If suspicion can fall, and stick, as easily as it does in
Much Ado and *Cymbeline* and *The Winter's Tale*, what hope has the
purity that Hermione and Hero and Imogen represent got of
meaning *anything* in such a world? As it turns out in Shakespeare,
this purity has in fact a meaning, but neither Webster nor

Tourneur is so certain. In any case, the important point here is the moral control, in situations as extreme as the ones these plays represent, that Shakespeare has. Again, it can be seen best in terms of the clarity and precision of his writing. By comparison, even Tourneur balances dizzily on the edge of the abyss.

But the most interesting case, in many ways, is Middleton. Obviously his range, compared with Shakespeare's, is cripplingly small. On the other hand, his achievement is a positive one in a sense denied to Webster or even Tourneur. His limited naturalism is, first of all, beautifully clear and firm. Though he goes much further than any of the others in expressing a certainty of sin and unchastity, even in his main characters, he is never in danger, as Webster certainly is, of being swamped by this. There is a sense throughout his plays that he has passed beyond the kind of worries that tormented both Webster and Tourneur. He is firmly in contact with a refreshingly new area of experience and therefore of a new kind of drama. His certainty of this, in the text of his best plays, gives him a control and firmness different from Shakespeare's but, in the Elizabethan-Jacobean context, almost as important. Of course his plays are quite obviously sparer than Shakespeare's, far less richly conceived – almost, in the case of some, to the edge of aridity. But the important point is that, after Shakespeare, nobody in the drama could have had any real expectation of commanding, for any length of time, experience of the Shakespearean kind. With Webster, for instance, for all the evocative splendour of patches of his verse, grasp and control are so lacking as seriously to endanger the very substance of his plays. What Middleton, unlike the rest, did was simply to respond to the urgency of fresh demands, even at the risk of losing much of what Shakespeare had achieved. His triumph is one which recognizes and even hastens the end of the Shakespearean age (as it had been variously interpreted by Webster, Tourneur and the rest) and at the same time suggests new possibilities. His greatness comes not from equalling or rivalling Shakespeare, but from the certainty with which he gave shape to the need for – and to some extent the inevitability of – change.[1]

We shall find, therefore, that both Middleton and Tourneur take up positions radically different from Shakespeare's. By the same token, however, their art will be a further demonstration of the more general proposition than an essentially dramatic insight is always unique, and never a mere illustration of truths conceived outside the given play we are studying. There are ways in which we can relate plays to each other, or to the common fund of energy available in a given period; but these will only be valid in so far as we also allow the verse and structure of a great drama its fully particularized, and unique, insights.

But before looking in more detail at the tragic world of the Jacobeans, there are some particular problems which must be raised in terms of the minor Elizabethans, notably Marlowe and Kyd.

---

[1] It is impossible to forget that Middleton, in turn, was followed by the sentimental Heroic Drama which ignored – or could not cope with – his insight and his lead. But though this may cast some doubt on the 'inevitability' of the 'change' Middleton initiated (it was not a change which had an immediate and pervasive influence) the quality of his drama stands. And his insights into middle-class living were in fact picked up and developed, though not fully until the advent of the nineteenth-century novel and George Eliot (see *Conclusion*, below).

CHAPTER III

ENERGY *VERSUS* CONTROL: MARLOWE

Tamburlaine (*c.* 1587) and *Faustus* (*c.* 1588) are the only two plays in which Marlowe reveals the sort of staying-power and consistency of purpose we would expect of a major dramatist. The rest, obviously, are brilliant fragments only. Furthermore, even in the two major plays, the 'consistency of purpose' is of a very special, and in the case of *Tamburlaine* at least, a drastically limited kind. Marlowe's reputation as a major dramatist can rest safely enough on *Faustus*; though in recognizing even this achievement, we will again, as in the case of *Tamburlaine*, be recognizing Marlowe's comparative isolation. He cannot be seen unequivocally as the 'founder of Elizabethan drama'.

This is not to say that he is totally unrelated to the Elizabethan age of drama. We pick up, for instance, Bale's *King John* from the years before *Tamburlaine*, see that any sort of nonsense passes for dramatic dialogue, and recognize immediately what a fund of freshness and energy even *Tamburlaine* displays compared to this:

> By the popys auctoryte I charge them yow to fight
> As with a tyrant agenst Holy Chyrchys ryght;
> And by the popes auctoryte I geve them absolucyon
> *A pena et culpa*, and also clene remyssyon.

> Sedycyon *extra locum*.

> Alarum! Alarum! tro ro ro ro ro, tro ro ro ro ro, tro ro ro ro!
> Thomp, thomp, thomp, downe, downe, downe, to go, to go, to go!

Gorboduc might be considered by some a fairer comparison, but even though it is not as silly a play as Bale's, the verse and the

whole cast of mind in those long speeches are stiff and dull beyond
relief. Marlowe is the first, in tragedy at least, who shows himself
to be in any way in touch with the common fund of sheer vitality
we recognize to be characteristically Elizabethan:

> Forsake thy king, and do but join with me,
> And we will triumph over all the world:
> I hold the Fates bound fast in iron chains,
> And with my hand turn Fortune's wheel about;
> And sooner shall the sun fall from his sphere
> Than Tamburlaine be slain or overcome.
> Draw forth thy sword thou mighty man-at-arms,
> Intending but to raze my charmed skin,
> And Jove himself will stretch his hand from heaven
> To ward the blow, and shield me safe from harm.
>   I, ii, 171-80

The trouble with this sort of dramatic dialogue, over the whole
range of the play, is not that it lacks energy, but that it does not
know what to do with it. When we add to our description of this
verse as 'energetic' the fact that it is also surprisingly controlled
and firm – 'surprisingly', that is, for a play so obviously dominated by the excitement of sheer discovery and freshness of insight – we are also virtually signing the death-warrant of *Tamburlaine* as a surviving major drama. Certainly, in the 'Fortune's
wheel' passage and others like it, Marlowe's control is considerable. Reading it closely, we realize immediately that Marlowe is
not identifying himself with Tamburlaine. The claims Tamburlaine makes *for himself* are indeed comically inflated (it is even
dramatically appropriate that they should be so), but the connotations of the verse generally – the imagery of the iron chains
and the sun falling from his sphere and, even, Jove's hand from
heaven – are so clearly limited by the specific diction and the
firm rhythm that the total impression is one which firmly opposes
the hero's claims. Of course Tamburlaine doesn't hold the Fates
bound fast in iron chains, or move Fortune's wheel as he pleases;

nor are we meant to think he does, literally. With most of Marlowe's verse in *Tamburlaine*, the tendency is in fact towards the vernacular rather than towards the heavy latinisms and rhetorical complications of, for instance, a play like *Sejanus*, or *Caesar and Pompey*. In Marlowe's play energy and the control of energy are such that they successfully resist that heaviness of texture which, in many Jacobean plays, underlines extravagant claims to a pitch altogether beyond serious attention. We know exactly what Tamburlaine means and how far he is to be allowed to go in his persuasive assault on our emotions and sympathies. The precision of the verse both limits the largeness of the claim he is making and at the same time gives it some sharpness of definition and credibility.

But when we consider this sort of verse over the whole range even of Part I of the play, the effect is very different. Even in 'Fortune's wheel', the degree of control clearly involves a marked stiffness in the verse, and with other passages this is even more obvious. Tamburlaine's wooing of Zenocrate is pretty representative:

> Zenocrate, lovelier than the love of Jove,
> Brighter than is the silver Rhodope,
> Fairer than whitest snow on Scythian hills . . .
> With milk-white harts upon an ivory sled
> Thou shalt be drawn amidst the frozen pools,
> And scale the icy mountains' lofty tops,
> Which with thy beauty will be soon resolv'd.
>
> I, ii, 87-101

There is no give-and-take in Marlowe's sense of control here. His contempt of the average, the limited, leads him (and Tamburlaine) to the hundred Tartars, the martial prizes and five hundred men, the flights of imagination over the mountains 'which with thy beauty will be soon resolv'd'. But to this he opposes a control which is negative because it nowhere responds to or incorporates

the natural world as Shakespeare's, for instance, does. Zenocrate
and the icy pools are not in imaginative and fruitful relation to
each other, but merely carefully delineated images of the same
thing. In this play control is too simply a matter of the deliberate-
ness with which one image is separated from another, a cold
clarity which achieves firmness and order at the tremendous cost
of refusing to allow images – or people – to interact at all. It is
indeed a matter, not of energy and control interpenetrating, but
of energy *versus* control. No matter what the dramatic situation
being presented, the sense of order in the verse is always the same,
and so both it and the energy presented lack substance and true
focus.[1]

The issue is one of what use Marlowe makes of the resources of
his native language. The play's use of language is sterile. There is
no sense in it of the possibility of imaginative development either
for Marlowe or his successors. To this we must now add that
Tamburlaine suffers, not merely in comparison with the later
Elizabethans, but also in comparison with the best of early English
drama. In particular there are illuminating comparisons we can
make, not now in terms of the pathetic *King John*, but in terms of a
very different kind of 'early' writing, the presence of which must
surely have lingered in Marlowe's time, though steadily repressed
as Popish stuff by the late Tudor monarchy:[2]

> Lord, what these weders ar cold, and I am ylle happyd;
> I am nere-hand dold, so long have I nappyd;
> My legys thay fold, my fingers ar chappyd,
> It is not as I wold, for I am all lappyd
> In sorow.

---

[1] Similar points are often made in terms of Marlowe's theme or plot in *Tamburlaine*, cf.
U.M. Ellis-Fermor, *Christopher Marlowe* (London, 1927). However, Professor Ellis-Fermor
tends to see it merely as a matter of Marlowe having 'committed himself to a theme that
was in its essence undramatic' (pp. 44–5); the implication being that Marlowe on this
occasion simply chose the wrong sort of theme for a play. The more significant issue seems
to me to be Marlowe's undramatic *imagination*, and the quality of his verse.

[2] A. P. Rossiter, *English Drama from Early Times to the Elizabethans* (London, 1950).

In stormes and tempest,
Now in the eest, now in the west,
Wo is hym has never rest
    Myd-day nor morow.
But we sely shepardes, that walkys on the moore,
In fayth we are nere-handys outt of the doore . . .
We ar so hamyd,
For-taxed and ramyd,
We ar mayde hand-tamyd,
Withe thyse gentlery men.

This is not 'good in its way' but good. Here in the shepherds' complaint – and elsewhere in abundance in the cycle – is a quickly
pointed play of mind, and a sharpness of syncopation in the play of
image and rhythm that it would be impudent to patronize by any
of the usual labels ('Exciting, and potentially good; but we must
wait for Marlowe to develop drama as we know it'). In fact, the
liveliness of the *Secunda Pastorum* underlines better than anything
else outside Shakespeare himself the essential sterility of *Tamburlaine*. In *Tamburlaine* Marlowe had a point to make – if we are
prepared to see him as more than a crude preparation for Shakespeare – but the play as a whole suffers because, in the very act of
attempting a genuine revolution, it turns its back on much of the
existing life in English poetry and drama. Consciously or unconsciously, Marlowe in this play side-stepped the kind of writing
that the Mysteries at their best provide, just as earlier everybody
except Wyatt had avoided the syncopated rhythms, closely allied
to the verse of the Wakefield cycle, of early English poetry. They
were held to be 'crude'; and so Tottel's editorship, so far from
being an advance, becomes a convenient representation of the
turning away of English poetry from liveliness of this particular
kind.[1] Marlowe represents a clear advance on most of the poetry

[1] See D. W. Harding, 'The Rhythmical Intention in Wyatt's Poetry', *Scrutiny*, vol. XIV,
1946, pp. 90-102; and 'The Poetry of Wyatt', in Pelican Guide No. 1, *The Age of Chaucer*
(London, 1954), pp. 197-212. Professor Harding notes some exceptions to his generalizations about the regularizing of English poetic rhythms in the fifteenth century and later.

espoused (and often rewritten) in Tottel; but in no sense does *Tamburlaine* represent the English language used more intelligently or more fruitfully than it is in the Wakefield plays.

The comparatively limited point that Marlowe does effect in *Tamburlaine* is one which can be seen clearly enough, but which is often obscured by attempts to set the play in a line of development leading directly to Shakespeare. For it is a point that Marlowe was led to make not despite his limitations but because of them, and it consists in a clear though still stiffly uncompromising recognition of the essential sterility at the heart of his hero's ambitions. This is a different issue from the more negative one of an over-simple control in the verse, though it is certainly related. Briefly, the point is that there is a tendency in the play initially to see energy as vitality, a life-giving activity constantly supporting the hero; but, almost contemporaneously, there is an opposing tendency to see it in life-denying terms, as something brutal, limited, ultimately sterile. After the Fortune's wheel speech early on, these tendencies gradually become more at odds until, with the Damascus scenes, Marlowe's early calm has deserted him and the question he put so clearly and confidently early on – 'What of the hero who is not prepared to submit to what is nevertheless and all the time the logic of necessity?' – has become more urgently personal. The surviving interest that we have in the play today centres on this movement from a slightly too rigid control at the beginning to turbulence and alarm near the end.

(Wyatt himself, of course, is the most outstanding exception.) In early Tudor stage verse there are also (as Harding again notes) passages which show a liveliness and substantiality probably related to traditional poetic rhythms. Compare, for instance, the Pardoner's tale from *The Play Called the Four PP.* (published 1544) by John Heywood:

> This devil and I walked arm in arm,
> So far till he had brought me thither
> Where all the devils of hell togither
> Stood in array in such apparel . . .
> Their horns well gilt, their claws full clean,
> Their tails well kempt, and, as I ween,
> With sothery butter their bodies anointed –
> I never saw devils so well appointed . . . (ll. 872 ff.)

The ways in which the play develops this point can be summarized in terms of the opposition between Tamburlaine and Zenocrate. Tamburlaine's personality focuses the driving energy of the play, its lyrical exuberance, and the sense of the conqueror's progress actually becoming more and more effortless as the obstacles to overcome get bigger and bigger. Thus we note that Tamburlaine has barely digested Mycetes before swallowing his ally, Cosroe, as well; and he has laid the foundations of his future career long before the conquest of Bajazeth is completed.

But this urge for life and freedom and almost unrestricted energy is opposed in the play by a realization of the grim brutality – the sterility, ultimately – of it all. One of Tamburlaine's earliest 'conquests' is Zenocrate, the symbol of a beauty he constantly tries to relate to his ideal of military power. In fact, however, as the action develops, the presence of Zenocrate constantly underlines the grim logic of necessity which assumes a larger and larger part in the play as Tamburlaine's career develops. At intervals in his military progress, Tamburlaine returns to Zenocrate:

> Zenocrate, the loveliest maid alive,
> Fairer than rocks of pearl and precious stone . . .
>
> III, iii, 117 ff.

But the intervals are selected ones. Here, of course, it is the occasion of Tamburlaine's particularly vicious subjugation of Bajazeth. The controlled and sympathetic lyricism of this passage brushes up against the harsher realities of the quest for power and the savagely uncompromising verse this, in turn, entails. Having conquered Bajazeth, Tamburlaine uses him as his footstool:

> Now clear the triple region of the air,
> And let the Majesty of Heaven behold
> Their scourge and terror tread on emperors.
>
> IV, ii, 30-32

Marlowe is being forced to temper what at first seemed the glorious freedom of Tamburlaine's military career with the realization that the logic of events has captured his hero. Even the famous 'What is beauty' speech is, significantly, sandwiched between the killing of the Virgins – the hoisting of their 'slaughtered carcasses' on the city's walls – and the final command for the slaughter of Damascus:

> But go, my lords, put the rest to the sword.
> (*Exeunt* all except Tamburlaine)
> Ah, fair Zenocrate! divine Zenocrate!
> Fair is too foul an epithet for thee . . . v, i, 134 ff.

The compulsiveness of Tamburlaine's career, unsettling the triumphant ease of his victories, and always at odds with the beauty of Zenocrate and all this represents for Tamburlaine, is seen working most clearly and impressively in the Damascus scenes with their imagery of the white, red and coal-black tents:

> *Messenger* Pleaseth your mightiness to understand,
> His resolution far exceedeth all.
> The first day when he pitcheth down his tents,
> White is their hue, and on his silver crest,
> A snowy feather spangled-white he bears,
> To signify the mildness of his mind,
> That, satiate with spoil, refuseth blood . . . iv, i, 48 ff.

The pageantry of this is just sufficiently restrained to allow the grimness of it to emerge and stand as a fact. As the passage goes on, the ornament and decoration of the opening lines, with their even cadences and their imagery of the snowy feather and the silver crest, gives way to plainer statement –

> Then must his kindled wrath be quenched with blood

– and, finally, to the rhythmic insistence of

> Black are his colours, black pavilion,
> His spear, his shield, his horse, his armour, plumes,
> And jetty feathers, menace death and hell;
> Without respect of sex, degree, or age,
> He razeth all his foes with fire and sword.

These images thread through the ensuing dialogue:

> And when they see me march in black array,
> With mournful streamers hanging down their heads . . .
>> IV, ii, 119 ff.

> As now when fury and incensed hate
> Flings slaughtering terror from my coal-black tents,
> And tells for truth submissions comes too late.
>> V, i, 71-3

Each of them recalls the beautiful but clear and uncompromising change of colour in the Messenger's speech when the pastoral opening, by a simple change of colour and rhythm, merged into the more threatening pageantry of blood and then into the still ceremonial but utterly uncompromising black. The sequence of colours means that none is complete without the other two. This verse is not concerned with whether towns will surrender or not, but with the completeness of the picture of Tamburlaine's behaviour as it now stands. There will in fact be no surrender, because red must follow white, black red. Neither Damascus nor Tamburlaine can escape this fact. The swift nuptial announcements that follow these battles are a personal triumph for Tamburlaine, but they can hardly gloss over the difficulties raised by Marlowe in the larger context of the play as a whole. Tamburlaine and Zenocrate have long been at odds, and it must be an uneasy truce indeed between the attitudes they represent:[1]

> *Zenocrate* Yet would you have some pity for my sake,
> Because it is my country's and my father's.
> *Tamburlaine* Not for the world, Zenocrate, if I have sworn.
> Come; bring in the Turk.
>> IV, ii, 123-6

[1] Putting this issue as a matter of the values focused by the opposition of these two characters is I think more rewarding than concentrating, as many do, on the conflict in Tamburlaine's mind (a conflict which in fact is rudimentary and feebly conveyed in the verse). On Tamburlaine's mental struggles see, for instance, G. I. Duthie, 'The Dramatic Structure of Marlowe's *Tamburlaine the Great*, Part I', repr. in *Shakespeare's Contemporaries*, eds. Max Bluestone and Norman Rabkin, Prentice-Hall, 1961.

Part II of the play continues to develop the same sort of point, though now it is increasingly put in terms of Tamburlaine's war – enunciated in Part I – against the gods:

> Come, let us march against the powers of heaven,
> And set black streamers in the firmament,
> To signify the slaughter of the gods.
>
> Part II, v, iii, 48-50

This is set against Theridamas's more grimly controlled speech, also, like Tamburlaine's own, cast in terms of the Damascus tent imagery:

> For Hell and Darkness pitch their pitchy tents,
> And Death, with armies of Cimmerian spirits,
> Gives battle 'gainst the heart of Tamburlaine.
>
> Part II, v, iii, 7-9

Tamburlaine is at last openly at war against a fate which is pictured in imagery remarkably reminiscent of the inflexible necessitarianism of his own early progress. Despite the operatic nature of much of Part II, this is a just and necessary conclusion to the series, and in the closing scene Tamburlaine crawls vainly over his map of the yet unconquered sections of the world. We know the sons will never be able to take his place, for the attempt to 'set black streamers in the firmament' has been made and has failed.

Points like these are made in *Tamburlaine* and they are not of a kind we shall get from any other Elizabethan or Jacobean play, certainly not from Marlowe's unfortunate admirer, Chapman. But on the other hand the serious limitations we first ascribed to this play have not been removed, because essentially the quality of the verse is still the same. The lines move with a firm deliberation which Marlowe applies equally to *any* situation, any imagery. The fabric of the verse – the denotative imagery, the rigid control – is the same in those speeches on Damascus as it was when Tamburlaine saw only the lyrical beauty of Zenocrate, as yet unthreatened by war and fatalism. Or if it is not precisely the same, it is too nearly so to establish anything in the play that could be called expansively imaginative – anything, that is, that could make a sense of control and order something other than merely restrictive and defensive. Virtually, Marlowe's claim to greatness of achievement – as opposed to the sense of exciting potential we always glimpse through his plays – rests on *Doctor Faustus*.[1]

The terms used to describe the very limited achievement of Tamburlaine – 'energy *versus* control' – do not fit the new attitudes developed in *Faustus*, though some modification of them may in the end be found to do so. But initially the gap, in both intention and achievement, between the two great Marlovian plays can hardly be stressed enough. There is an obvious temptation to compare the physical aspirations evident in *Tamburlaine* with what at first appear to be the scholarly, intellectual aspirations in *Faustus*. But whatever Marlowe may have thought privately about the 'School of Night' philosophies and about atheism, Faustus is a play preoccupied at least as much with the damnation of a Christian soul as with the aspiring, scholarly mind.[2] The outstanding impression from Acts I and II, in fact, is the intelligence and scrupulous fairness of Mephistophilis, and by contrast, therefore, the weakness and limitations imposed by Marlowe on Faustus in this situation.

---

[1] Even *Edward II* seems to me to lack substance. Some of the verse in it has its interest if one is thinking of the puzzling emergence in Marlowe of poetry in the 'Hero and Leander' vein. But as a whole the play wavers uncertainly. In particular the writing for Mortimer, Lancaster, etc, is lacking in character, lifeless; the problem of rebellion should, surely, have been the centre of this play, but it is never in Marlowe the live and substantial issue it so quickly becomes in Shakespeare. We are therefore left with tantalizingly brilliant fragments of poetry only:

> But what are kings, when regiment is gone,
> But perfect shadows in a sunshine day?   v, i, 26-27.

[2] Cf. M. M. Mahood, *Poetry and Humanism* (New Haven, 1950), pp. 67-74. Many critics recognize, as Miss Mahood does, the importance of the undermining irony in *Faustus*, and also of traditional Christian concepts in the play. On the other hand the more difficult question that follows from this – what status and significance has Marlowe given his free-thinking hero – has not had the attention it should. (For some suggestive comments see Arthur Mizener, 'The Tragedy of Marlowe's *Doctor Faustus*', *College English*, Vol. 5, 1943, pp. 70-75.)

Mephistophilis's points about his own and Lucifer's fall from heaven could not be more clearly or more significantly put, and yet it is the supposedly intelligent scholar who cannot or will not see the point. As Faustus himself later on admits, something has happened to turn his freedom of spirit towards stubborn hardness of heart, and part of Marlowe's point in the play is that in this particular situation intelligence, so far from liberating Faustus, is above all the constricting factor, the very thing which prevents him from seeing the obvious.

To a large extent the basic terms of the problem in this play are still – as in *Tamburlaine* – comparatively simple and even static ones. The opposition between a free intelligence – given at least a qualified endorsement in the lyricism of sections of the verse – and the threat, or rather certainty, of a specifically Christian damnation is clearly, and comparatively simply, maintained almost to the very end of the play. For all the new flexibility in Marlowe's verse, there is little in *Faustus* which reminds us of the manifold possibilities of life in Shakespeare's mature tragedies, or even of attitudes held in the less complex Jacobeans. For instance as we shall see there is an element of almost deliberate simplicity in Tourneur's handling of sin and damnation, but this is always set against the near-metaphysical complexity which dominates *The Revenger's Tragedy*, and it therefore tends to have the quality of a quick summing-up of experience rather than a basic attitude to it. But in *Faustus* Marlowe constantly uses familiar liturgical phrases with a sureness and lightness of touch which establishes their validity in the play at least as firmly as it does the hero's evasion of them:

> O God,
> If thou wilt not have mercy on my soul,
> Yet for Christ's sake, whose blood hath ransom'd me,
> Impose some end to my incessant pain . . .
>   ll. 1482 ff.

The verse in this and similar speeches is so powerful that for the moment, at least, God's existence is proved:

> Oh, I'll leap up to my God! Who pulls me down?
> See, see, where Christ's blood streams in the firmament!
> One drop would save my soul, half a drop: ah, my Christ!
>
> ll. 1461-3

The speech, and its ironic picking up of earlier dialogue, are too well known to need lengthy quotation here. The important point is that the play includes, as part of its total vision, a more specifically devotional attitude than any other outside mediaeval drama.

And yet its attitudes are not those of mediaeval drama. Obviously *Faustus*, though in some ways shutting the door – or attempting to – on future developments, is still a play that offers a much more exploratory interpretation of the Elizabethan world than ever the mediaeval plays could of theirs. The keenest questionings of natural justice in the Mysteries and Moralities come from passages like the shepherds' complaint at the beginning of the Wakefield *Secunda Pastorum*. But even these are never of the kind that consider the possibility of an order different from their own. The sense of enquiry or protest they show, valuable though it is, is never one which suspects the possibility of any answer other than the obvious one given usually at the end of the plays. Marlowe, on the other hand, whatever his final conclusions, gives real status to the problem of humanist attitudes in a Christian world. He knows that a fresh order of experience is at hand and is concerned to say something about it. For the other main term in his enquiry – sustained in much the same clear, simple way as the Christian attitudes – is the energetic potential focused on the freethinking Faustus himself. The Christian position given in the play is firmly and surely held, but it is always presented as an *achieved* attitude or value. Constantly it is given us either in the liturgical phrases, pointing to unshakably established values of the past rather than to an exciting future; or through the persistent, drily conservative irony of Mephistophilis himself. The energy is with the hero. In the section near the end of the play from which comes Faustus' final realization of what 'Christ's blood' means, Marlowe opposes to these traditional values both the hero's own anarchic vitality and his lyrical praise of Helen. And the speech to Helen, in particular, has much the same note as his early hymn of praise to magic. Whatever *Faustus* is, it is not simply the tragedy of a man who sees he has lost irrevocably the hope of salvation.

The real critical problem with *Faustus*, then, is what emerges when the two terms of the enquiry – briefly, Christianity and freethinking Humanism – are put up against one another in the play? It is no longer simply a matter of controlling or containing Faustus's energy and vitality. A new term, which has a value and a solidity much greater than that of a mere control of verse structure, has been added. Much of what I have said so far oversimplifies the play's position, but I made the points initially in this way because I wanted to avoid any suggestion that subtlety of a Shakespearean kind is given us in this play – Marlowe is depending on simpler and more specifically Christian-Humanist terms than any later writer did – and yet at the same time I wanted to stress that it is not merely a matter of 'irony' undercutting the hero's position. The Christianity incorporated in the play is of a more positive kind than any formulation in terms of irony alone would suggest.

For a truer view of the play I want now to look at the ways in which the two terms of Marlowe's drama, though never changing character radically as they would in later plays, tend to merge and interact. In this connection the quality of the opening soliloquy is of first importance.

With the opening lines we are launched into the play, casually in sympathy with Faustus's off-hand treatment of the conventional virtues: 'Why, Faustus, hast thou not attained that end...? Affords this art no greater miracle...?' The list goes on. And at the end of the soliloquy, eleven lines of powerful verse in praise of magic seem to assure us that Marlowe is well and truly behind his hero:

> Oh, what a world of profit and delight,
> Of power, of honour, of omnipotence
> Is promis'd to the studious artisan!
> All things that move between the quiet poles
> Shall be at my command: emperors and kings
> Are but obey'd in their several provinces,
> Nor can they raise the wind, or rend the clouds;
> But his dominion that exceeds in this,
> Stretcheth as far as doth the mind of man . . .
>
> ll. 81 ff.

And so, at this particular point, he obviously is. The authentic note of Marlowe the free-thinker, throwing off the shackles of mere temporary power

> But his dominion that exceeds in this,
> Stretcheth as far as doth the mind of man . . .

is clinched here by the confident lyricism of the verse:

> All things that move between the quiet poles
> Shall be at my command . . .

At this point of the play at least, Faustus is shown proving that he can, and may perhaps continue to use his power for metaphysical and not paltry ends.

The reality of this momentary vision, set in verse of this quality, cannot entirely be destroyed. On the other hand its significance is – has already been – modified by the soliloquy from which it comes. Cunningly, before giving us the panegyric to magic, Marlowe has sounded obvious warning notes. In the first place, Faustus's chopping logic about divinity (Marlowe does not even give him the full Biblical quotation) is suspect:

> If we say that we have no sin,
> We deceive ourselves, and there's no truth in us.
> Why, then, belike
> We must sin, and so consequently die:
> Ay, we must die an everlasting death.

Unlike the concluding lines of the soliloquy, this is not the deep conviction of the atheist *persona*, but shallow, hurried reasoning given to a character deliberately in order to show that his pre-occupations are less with confuting divinity than with providing excuses to hurry on to his new toy, magic. To clinch the general impression the speech gives, there are confident pronouncements given to Faustus which, in the context of the later part of the play, turn ironically against him:

> Is, to dispute well, logic's chiefest end?
> Affords this art no greater miracle?
> Then read no more, thou hast attain'd the end.

In fact, however, his disputes with Mephistophilis immediately afterwards demonstrate undeniably the deficiencies of mere 'logic' itemized in this way. Mephistophilis has the better in all depart-ments of the debate, simply because his premises are sounder. Further, in the lines on physic and in the arrogantly turned though theoretically just condemnation of the law, Faustus again reveals his basic weakness in such argument – wrong premises and a fatal tendency to compartmentalize knowledge:

> The end of physic is our body's health.
> Why, Faustus, hast thou not attain'd that end . . . ?

A tendency to look at learning and knowledge in this way simply leaves Faustus open to the later accusations of the far less intelligent Morality Old Man who works by instinct and faith, not reason. The point is that Faustus's approach gives simple faith a far easier victory than it would otherwise have had. There is a restlessly, even vigorously enquiring mind behind Faustus's claims, but already Marlowe has begun to qualify some of his attainments and assump-tions. Even the famous

> Yet art thou still but Faustus, and a man.

is, for all its conviction and power, picked up and twisted fatally

later on when, in his last speech, Faustus is presented as wishing
desperately that he were something less than man:

> Oh, no end is limited to damned souls!
> Why wert thou not a creature wanting soul?
> Or why is this immortal that thou hast?   ll. 1488-90

Most, if not all, of these criticisms of the hero have been outlined in the play *before* the simpler, more confident praise of magic
in the concluding lines of the opening soliloquy: 'Oh, what a
world of profit and delight . . .' When we reach these lines, or
hear them, our minds have begun the to-and-fro journeying which
is to make up our reaction to the sum total of the play's appeal.
This is, therefore, no simple preoccupation with the limits of the
superman hero. The play, and the audience, are struggling with an
investigation of continually shifting emphasis and subtlety. At the
end of this particular soliloquy, we are holding in mind both the
freshness of Faustus's concluding appeal and the shiftiness of most
of his earlier reasoning.

In the great debates with Mephistophilis that follow, the play
becomes perhaps a little unbalanced in that the sheer orthodoxy of
Mephistophilis's position is given greater weight than we feel justified by the terms of the opening enquiry. Faustus is never a man of
straw in this play, but the position he represents tends, when con-
fronted with the calm assurance of Mephistophilis, to lack a little
of the substance it had earlier. More clearly perhaps than elsewhere
in the play, Marlowe impresses us here with the ease and unself-
consciousness with which he can bring into the dialogue familiar
Christian arguments ('Why, this is hell, nor am I out of it . . .') and
plain statements of belief, most significantly from Mephistophilis:

> *Faustus* Was not that Lucifer an angel once?
> *Mephistophilis* Yes, Faustus, and most dearly lov'd of God.
> *Faustus* How comes it then that he is prince of devils?
> *Mephistophilis* Oh, by aspiring pride and insolence,
> For which God threw him from the face of Heaven.   ll. 304-8

But if the balance is untrue here it is only slightly so, for where Faustus's intellectual daring is reckless it is also impressive – this word 'damnation' terrifies not him – and, more important, this play of Marlowe's is flexible enough for the whole range of action and structure to be constantly relevant. The scenes with Mephistophilis do not stand alone as they would tend to do in a play formed in the stiffer *Tamburlaine* mould. The pact with Lucifer looks forward to, and is in turn clearly incorporated in, the last scenes of the play when Christ's blood streaming in the firmament recalls the sinister earlier scene when Faustus's own blood would not run. Moreover, for all their general flimsiness, even the Wagner scenes are at their best quite lively and convincing enough to be incorporated in this telescoping of action and reference which is characteristic of the quicker moving *Faustus* dialogue. Constantly they pick up and develop points from the main plot, and gradually establish the robust world of the clowns as a value ⟨ which equivocation and magic cannot really shake. Significantly it is often Wagner's sheer stupidity which is given us as his strongest point:

> *Wagner* Alas, poor slave! see how poverty jesteth in his nakedness! the villain is bare and out of service, and so hungry, that I know he would give his soul to the devil for a shoulder of mutton, though it were blood-raw.   ll. 361-5

The cruder mind of Wagner, intent on hunger and the blood-raw shoulder of mutton, achieves a kind of immunity against the grim significance emerging from his own dialogue.

Admittedly the Wagner sections as a whole, and particularly the 'travel' sections that follow, present an obvious problem of intention poorly realized on Marlowe's part. The big point they are meant to establish – or one of the big points – is that, for Faustus, stealing the Pope's dinner and boxing his ears and setting crackers amidst the Friars is a game not worth the candle. Unfortunately, this particular episode is spoiled by Marlowe (or his collaborators) succumbing once again to the temptation of ridiculing established religions – his Pope and Friars are figures of fun merely – and too many of the central scenes are marred by the feebleness of the comic writing. The point is there, in intention, but the writing is farcically out of key and carries connotations of slapstick rather than pointed wit. It is amusing in a way to watch the horse-dealer's leg come off, but in context the impression left is only one of frivolity. The exaggerations are too often those of melodrama and farce; the texture of the writing loose and light rather than pointed and well-knit.

So much is obvious. Nevertheless important points are made in these sections. At its best the dialogue has a boisterous 'normality' which both mocks Faustus's plight and establishes as real the foolish, unimaginative solidity of Wagner's world:

> But that I am by nature phlegmatic, slow to wrath, and prone to lechery – to love, I would say, – it were not for you to come within forty foot of the place of execution, although I do not doubt to see you both hang'd the next sessions. Thus having triumphed over you, I will set my countenance like a precisian, and begin to speak thus: Truly, my dear brethren, my master is within at dinner, with Valdes and Cornelius, as this wine, if it could speak, would inform your worships . . .
>
> ll. 217 ff.

This is not unlike the rough, assertive comicality of some of Shakespeare's dialogue. It is certainly not *mere* dramatic irony and the points made are at least as substantial as Shakespeare's own in the low-comedy scenes of a play like *Much Ado*. After this, the travel sections follow, and Faustus's more intelligent interests in cosmography and culture are continually broken into by Mephistophilis who wishes to betray him deeper still into frivolity and futility:

Faustus   I swear
That I do long to see the monuments
And situation of bright-splendent Rome:

Come, therefore, let's away.
Mephistophilis Nay, Faustus, stay: I know you'd fain see the Pope,
And take some part of Holy Peter's feast . . .   ll. 860 ff.

All in all, I do not see why these middle sections of the play should
be seen as fatally interrupting the concentration established earlier.
The comparative shortness of the play is an indication that
Marlowe's span of attention, where complex matters are concerned, is not a great one; but in turn this helps to give consistency
and impact to such points as are in fact made. In this connection it
is very important to remember that the play is indeed short, and
that Acts I and II alone, even without Act V, would represent over
half the playing time.[1]

The final section, introduced by the debates between Faustus
and the Morality Old Man, returns quickly to the compressed
dialogue of the early part of the play. The speech to Helen is cast in
verse sometimes reminiscent of *Tamburlaine*:

> I will be Paris, and for love of thee,
> Instead of Troy shall Wittenberg be sack'd.
> And I will combat with weak Menelaus,
> And wear thy colours on my plumed crest.
>   ll. 1361-4

Once again, one can clearly sense Marlowe's own enthusiasm behind this. He is allowing – the feeling very strongly is that he cannot help allowing – his hero to assert up to the very last moment
the sense of energy and freedom which can come from emanci-
pation, from breaking the hold of traditional beliefs. For Marlowe,
the question is thus a far more difficult one than it would be for
anyone writing purely exhortatory Christian dogma. For the
confident lyricism, here as earlier, asserts genuineness and substance in the appeal of humanistic free thought:

---

[1] Act divisions based on Hazelton Spencer, *Elizabethan Plays* (London, 1934).

> Was this the face that launch'd a thousand ships,
> And burnt the topless towers of Ilium . . .

The verse here is not as substantial or rich as we feel, in terms of the developing drama as a whole, it should be. But on the other hand there is no possibility of reading the play as a simple condemnation of all that is not traditionally good (of all that the Old Man would condemn as unsafe or beyond the scope of 'sinful' man). Faustus is the centre of a struggle between the possibly valid (though here ill-used) claims of a new humanism and the too inflexible but very real authority of an older tradition. The result, though firmly based in Christian ethic and belief, is a challenge rather than a flat statement. Marlowe's position is one in which he asks: 'How can this new order of experience escape – as it must always attempt to do – the reality of conservative Christianity? For all its freshness, is it not doomed in the end to be self-regarding and sterile?' And in asking these questions he allows Faustus's humanism substantial scope and vigour, implies somehow that this is the beginning, not the end of a problem.

Thus, the speech to Helen for the most part holds the lyrical form of the opening, and indeed departs from or modifies this only with something of an effort. Yet on the other hand the lyrical confidence is firmly placed by interleaving irony. Immediately after the famous opening, Marlowe gives to Faustus the betraying lines:

> Her lips suck forth my soul: see, where it flies!
> Come, Helen, come, give me my soul again.
> Here will I dwell, for heaven be in these lips,
> And all is dross that is not Helena.
>
> ll. 1357-60

This is picked up all unconsciously, but with obvious inference, by the Old Man, tormented by devils. The Christian view of Faustus's pagan vision of the soul 'sucked forth' is rammed further home in turns of phrase which are almost an inversion of Faustus's own:

> Accursed Faustus, miserable man,
> That from thy soul exclud'st the grace of heaven,
> And fly'st the throne of his tribunal-seat!
>
> ll. 1374-6

And:

> Ambitious fiends, see how the heavens smiles
> At your repulse, and laughs your state to scorn!
> Hence, hell! for hence I fly unto my God.
>
> ll. 1380-2

By the last speech all doubt is ended and the play concludes on the reality and triumph, in the situation to which the action has now led, of traditional ethic and belief. At last even Faustus sees – we have seen it long ago – the full justice of Mephistophilis's early pronouncements and warnings:

> Ah, Faustus.
> Now hast thou but one bare hour to live,
> And then thou must be damn'd perpetually!

And the dialogue picks up and echoes, with new significance, the sinister early scene when Faustus's own blood would not run:

> See, see, where Christ's blood streams in the firmament!
> One drop would save my soul, half a drop: ah, my Christ! . . .
> Where is it now? 'tis gone: and see, where God
> Stretcheth out his arm, and bends his ireful brows!
> Mountains and hills, come, come, and fall on me,
> And hide me from the heavy wrath of God!

Marlowe's verse has here – and elsewhere in this play – a truly Elizabethan thickness of texture which permits statements on numerous levels. It easily presents the psychological reality of Faustus's faint-hearted appeals for pity. The hero, though sharply aware of his danger now, still has no conception of what makes the Old Man safe and himself damned; he can see the physical presence of salvation, but he cannot make any act of faith in God. Thus he gets no further than mentioning the name of Christ when, unlike the Old Man, he falls back in terror at what devils can do to him.

Yet this kind of insight by no means exhausts the total meaning and significance of the verse, for it takes us beyond Faustus's own mental and spiritual plight to establish, almost independently of the hero's own vision, the reality which condemns him. In the end we are as much concerned with the kind and nature of this reality as we are with the plight of the protagonist who has fallen short of it. The vision of Christ's blood in the firmament and God stretching out his arm is not merely Faustus's own but the play's and Marlowe's too. It is in fact the final achievement by Marlowe in this play of a position from which he can without further quali-fication or hesitation view the inroads made on Christianity by the confident humanism espoused by his hero early on. Intelligence of the kind Faustus has shown, however great, is barren. Marlowe's alternative (though this is really too simple a concept) to this, his 'affirmation' in the face of tragic impotence is, unlike Shakespeare's (and simpler than his), a specifically Christian one. His play as a whole, on the other hand, manages to remain a challenge or query (i.e. rather than simple dogma) at least to the extent that Shake-speare's plays do in works of the order of, say, *The Winter's Tale* or *The Tempest*. It is needless to add that these comparisons are rough ones and I have no intention of comparing the kind or quality of Shakespeare's achievement in his late plays with Marlowe's. The two writers arrived at widely differing conclusions about the nature of the Elizabethan tragic experience.

But the quality of Marlowe's achievement does mean that his play is in a position to deal more firmly than any twentieth-century play – or any other Elizabethan play for that matter – with the threaten-ing barrenness of humanist intellectualism. Our attitude, now, tends to be either one of grim acceptance of the tragedy of such sterility, as perhaps in some Ibsen; or acceptance blended with a self-conscious, over-specific symbolism which is intended to com-bat this (cf. O'Neill, Arthur Miller, and Ibsen himself in plays like *The Wild Duck*). Both Shakespeare and, for very different reasons,

Marlowe in *Faustus* easily transcend attitudes of this kind, and therefore, though plays like theirs could not be written nowadays (Middleton is here at once the barrier and the representative of a consciousness which recognizes this as inevitable), their work is doubly relevant to our situation. The texture of Marlowe's verse in *Faustus* demonstrates attitudes very different, in kind and quality, from Shakespeare's. Even with *Faustus*, it is still a matter of fairly simple concepts – like energetic humanism and conservative Christianity – being 'controlled'. But in this play, unlike *Tamburlaine*, the element of control inheres in the intelligence which juxtaposes the twin values, not merely in verse structure as such. Both cases – Marlowe and Shakespeare – represent playwrights discovering a flexibility of dramatic form and utterance which could bear on problems introduced by humanistic thought (of whatever age) and at the same time suggest possibilities which transcend humanistic thinking in ways beyond the grasp of most – if not all – modern playwrights.[1]

So far we have looked at two very different appraisals of the early Elizabethan situation. They are alike only in that neither leads on to future developments. *Tamburlaine* certainly does not. (It is in any case far too limited.) And even *Faustus*, exploratory though it is in its admission or contemplation of fresh experience, and fresh though it is in its treatment of this, ends very firmly on an old rather than a new position.

In the plays that follow – particularly Middleton's – there will be speculation and experiment of a kind Marlowe would never have contemplated. On the other hand, with a large group of these plays, there will also be a new orthodoxy of moral stand crystallizing around the apparently absurd Revenge plot. It is as if,

---

[1] The modern novel is affected by problems of this kind, but at its best it is clearly more vigorous, and more subtle, than modern drama. Here the obvious example is Lawrence's development of problems of intellectualism, and of the individual in modern society, in novels like *The Rainbow* and *Women in Love*.

with all their experiment and with all their individual diver-
gencies, most Elizabethan writers were beginning to feel the need
to cling, by whatever means and with whatever widely differing
results, to something that could represent what was in some degree a common enterprize in action and moral outlook. The comparatively simple and orthodox Christianity evoked by Marlowe
in *Faustus* was too static a concept to serve this need; and probably
it could not have been developed further, or even widely used,
once the complexities of the Elizabethan age reached the stage of
development they clearly did in Shakespeare. For reasons of this
kind – and unlikely though it seems at first glance – we will find
many later writers using and developing a Revenge morality for
the serious purpose of imparting order and stability to the changing
Elizabethan scene.

CHAPTER IV

THE MORALITY OF REVENGE: KYD AND MARLOWE

The Matter of *Tragedies* is haughtinesse, arrogancy, ambition, pride, iniury, anger, wrath, enuy, hatred, contention, warre, murther, cruelty, rapine, incest, rouings, depredations, piracyes, spoyles, roberies, rebellions, treasons, killing, hewing, stabbing, dagger-drawing, fighting, butchery, trechery, villany &c. and all kinds of heroyck euils whatsoeuer.

(John Greene, *A Refutation of the Apology for Actors*, 1615)

In spite of this, Revenge dominates Elizabethan play-writing as no motif has ever dominated a period of English literature after the mediaeval Romance. Metaphysical verse, Augustan moral epistles, nineteenth-century family romances – for better or for worse none of these has the unity and coherence given to a large group of Elizabethan and Jacobean plays by the Revenge plot. Even when, as in Webster and Tourneur, Revenge impinges on wider issues, it still manages to retain an almost separable identity. The nearest parallel to this situation would probably be with Restoration Heroic Tragedy, where the sense of structure, over a generation or so of writers, was almost as complete and as mandatory; but here the resulting product is irrevocably minor. The modern detective story, from the 'twenties onwards, is another comparison often cited, but it is one which, by virtue of its even more obvious limitations, only succeeds in demonstrating more clearly still the uniqueness of the position held by the apparently melodramatic Revenge plot.

Thus the period from Kyd and Marlowe to Ford produces a number of plays which stress – though admittedly in widely differing ways – the call to revenge an injustice inflicted by society, one's fellow human beings, the universe itself, or even, as in *Hamlet*, by something still less tangible and definable. Typically, the protagonist (villain or hero or both) is urged to action as much by a general *malaise* as by the specific wrongs he or his mistress has suffered; he is, like the contemporary Malcontent, isolated from and by a corrupt society, though in his isolation he nevertheless represents the human condition; and he is generally driven to act, not as Lear 'acts', in open rage, but rather with the cunning irony of a Vendice. The 'irony' of Revenge is indeed one of its most characteristic traits: in Revenge plots the hero must rely on his own wit to enforce his 'justice', and often he is in the end caught by the very cunning of his own plots. (Again, Vendice is almost a paradigm example.) A study of the melodrama of these plays – the biting out of tongues, the unnatural sex relationships, the general slaughter at the end which even the naturalistic Middleton could not quite avoid – all this will be one of the recurring problems of the chapters that follow. We are concerned with the ways in which melodrama of this kind merges into serious drama and what, once there, its new status is.

In particular, and as a first critical generalization, there is a marked and significant change in tone and attitude between the early Revenge plays, by Kyd and Marlowe, and the later ones. In discussing this I shall not be concerned so much with totting up points for and against individual authors, as with investigating the pattern of achievement that Elizabethan drama presents to us. The question is not which author is the best in the sense of exhibiting the finest literary talent, or even which author, in the simplest sense, most noticeably influenced Shakespeare and the rest. Rather, it is a merging of these two points into the final important question: What has Elizabethan tragedy to offer us now? At which points did the demanding questions of the age defeat dramatists and at which not? We have to disentangle questions of 'influence' momentarily, hold them up for inspection in the light of an enquiry which separates the valuable from the not valuable and demonstrates, firstly, what the achievement of the great Revenge plays was and was not; and, secondly, how, in this achievement, later authors both depended upon and at the same time were forced to change the original impetus provided by Kyd and Marlowe. Such an enquiry is in fact a two-way process rather than a simple matter of chronological development, and we might sum it up by saying that the questions we must ask about the early writers in particular are: In the light of what later writers did, what now is the worth we attach to the comparative clarity and simplicity of texture in the writing of Kyd and Marlowe? And, further, what light does their early vigour of simplicity (with all the limitations peculiar to each of them) throw on the divided aims of the disintegrating artistic and moral world which later on faced Webster, Ford and the rest? There are no easy answers to these questions. All that is possible at the moment is to raise them in such terms that a criticism of the plays will itself gradually outline or approach an answer.

First in this matter, Kyd's revengers – principally Hieronymo, Lorenzo, Bellimperia, Villuppo – like his play as a whole, have comparatively simple motives. In *The Spanish Tragedy* (*c.* 1589), and in Marlowe, Revenge is most clearly allied with motives of worldly gain (Villuppo, Balthazar, Lorenzo) or the eye-for-an-eye attitude summed up by the Ghost of Andrea at the end:

> Let me be judge, and doom them to unrest.
> Let loose poor Tityus from the vulture's gripe,
> And let Don Cyprian supply his room;
> Place Don Lorenzo on Ixion's wheel,
> And let the lover's endless pains surcease . . .

Similarly, in the wider context of the play as a whole, when issues like Hieronymo's concern for justice come in, they are clearly defined and limited. Whatever its limitations and crudenesses, Kyd's play has at any rate the characteristic advantages of the beginning of a literary convention. Obviously it does not range as widely as Webster; it has not the close-knit thickness of texture of Tourneur's verse; in sum, it cannot really be placed beside the best of the later Revenge plays. What it does have is simply the advantages of limitation. When it does manage to raise interesting or serious issues, they are clearly and sharply put. The best of the later Revenge writers, Tourneur, manages extraordinary clarity only in the face of mounting difficulty and complexity.

In a completely un-naturalistic context, this gives Kyd tremendous advantages. He can sketch in a 'motivation' – in the Elizabethan sense, and with due deference to Miss Bradbrook – for Villuppo, the Portuguese Machiavel, and a reader accepts this without protest, despite the fact that it must occur to everybody to wonder how on earth Villuppo could have imagined he could get away with claiming Balthazar was dead when he obviously wasn't! Again, Kyd (with the help of his collaborator) stage-manages the business of Hieronymo biting out his tongue – and doing so for no very obvious reason – simply so that he can finalize his picture of the revenger pleased with his own art, for its own sake. The closest scrutiny of the text doesn't seem to reveal anything further in the way of information that could have been got out of Hieronymo at this stage. And generally speaking, where Tourneur, and the far more individualistic Webster, dwell on and depend on the more intangible aspects of the Revenge idea, Kyd, by virtue of his position in the convention, is able to base his play more consistently on clear-cut issues. When dealing with Hieronymo, of course, he reaches out sometimes into the difficult and the intangible, but even here, and even if one includes the additions attributed to Jonson, the madness has a pre-Shakespearean simplicity about it. The rest of the play is resolutely un-Jacobean. Balthazar, Lorenzo, Bellimperia, Villuppo – all these are people more concerned with worldly gain or revenge in its most primitive and clear-cut form than with the groping after difficulty and complexity that fascinated Tourneur, Webster and their characters. Even when, as with Balthazar, Bellimperia and the rulers of Spain and Portugal, the business of revenge is based on contracted marriages, alliances between states, and revenge for the deaths of Andrea and Horatio (as Bellimperia's two lovers), Kyd is untroubled to keep the lines of intrigue, if not exactly simple, then at least clear-cut. There is as yet little tendency or temptation to involve a reader in dangerous complexities of the kind that arise out of speeches like Vendice's on similar topics.

The kinds of verse and dialogue Kyd uses define both the limitations and the interest of his attempt to deal with these matters at the beginning of what was to be a comparatively short but certainly important literary convention.[1] In the first place, Kyd is obviously experimenting widely. Stichomythia and patterned, near-Petrarchan verse stand out as the basis for a lot of the early acts at least. Often, the effect is ridiculous and poorly managed:

Bellimperia Why stands Horatio speechless all this while?
Horatio The less I speak, the more I meditate.   II, ii, 24-5

(Who was it suggested Hieronymo bit out his tongue because he was sick of stichomythia?) But it is probably a mistake to take this sort of writing as Kyd's main aim, or the basis of the play as a whole. He relies more on using whatever comes to hand than on any one or two main lines of attack. He is prepared at times to use the couplet form, or else the kind of balance that draws on but does not copy exactly sixteenth-century couplet writing. War, for instance, is often a matter of the picturesque, the neatly and, to us, rather amusingly dispassionate observation enclosed in stiffly

---

[1] For details of plays using the convention see F. T. Bowers, *Elizabethan Revenge Tragedy* (Princeton, 1940); and L. G. Salingar, 'Tourneur and the Tragedy of Revenge', in the Pelican Guide No. 2, *The Age of Shakespeare* (London, 1955), pp. 334-54. For an account of the technical advances Kyd made on earlier drama, see Wolfgang Clemen, 'The Uses of Rhetoric', repr. in *Shakespeare's Contemporaries, op. cit.*

moving, puppet-like images which remind one inevitably of early couplet writing (particularly translations):

> Here falls a body sund'red from his head,
> There legs and arms lie bleeding on the grass,
> Mingled with weapons and unbowell'd steeds,
> That scattering overspread the purple plain . . .
>
> I, i, 59 ff.

At other times, Kyd converts Elizabethan pastoral writing to grimmer uses. Compare, for instance, the following from Hieronymo:

> The blust'ring winds, conspiring with my words,
> At my lament have mov'd the leafless trees,
> Disrob'd the meadows of their flower'd green,
> Made mountains marsh with spring-tides of my tears,
> And broken through the brazen gates of hell.
>
> III, vii, 5-9

Or, again, he may decide that a Spenserian morality might be useful:

> There is a path upon your left-hand side
> That leadeth from a guilty conscience
> Unto a forest of distrust and fear,
> A darksome place, and dangerous to pass.
> There shall you meet with melancholy thoughts . . .
>
> IV, iv, 60 ff.

Much of this, of course, a reader dismisses as immaturity or conscious experiment, but the presence of so many kinds of verse is a sign at least that Kyd is not to be judged by first impressions and that he may possibly be performing a useful function, both for his own play and for others, in investigations of this kind. At his best, he has a surprisingly light hand at writing dramatic dialogue and there is life even in the extensive borrowings.

What of more consequence the play has to say than this must depend on how Kyd manages the two or three important sections

where he does move away from more or less deliberate experi-
mentation, or at any rate where he uses the experiments and the
borrowings for wider ends. One of the first important signs of a
widening and tightening of the play's field of reference is Act II,
scene iv, the wooing of Bellimperia and the death of Horatio. The
dialogue here is still almost embarrassingly patterned and self-
conscious; but it also both reaches out towards the sort of pointed
irony which will increasingly inform Revenge plays, and at the
same time exhibits a clarity of outline denied to Webster, and
even Tourneur. Horatio, we notice, is given lines the significance
of which he cannot possibly realize because Kyd is using the
mannered love-talk, which Horatio takes at face-value, for quite
other ends:

> Now that the night begins with sable wings
> To overcloud the brightness of the sun,
> And that in darkness pleasures may be done,
> Come, Bellimperia, let us to the bower,
> And there in safety pass a pleasant hour.
>
> II, iv, 1-5

Consistently, Horatio himself takes this as a sort of development of
the sonneteer's approach to love. To him 'safety', 'pleasant hour',
are merely polite compliments necessary in a romantic situation:

> Sweet, say not so; fair fortune is our friend,
> And heavens have shut up day to pleasure us.
> The stars, thou seest, hold back their twinkling shine,
> And Luna hides herself to pleasure us.   II, iv, 16-19

Actually, as the dramatic irony rather heavily but very clearly
points out, Horatio is being made to say precisely the wrong sort
of thing for this stage of the play. As Hieronymo and others later
make quite clear, and as indeed is clear on the face of it even here,
references to night, darkness, the action of the heavenly bodies in
carefully providing concealment for the two lovers – all these
things point to disaster, not happiness. As in much of the writing

for the Masque, for instance, darkness works here as a manifestation, embodiment, symbol of the opportunity nature gives to tragedy and evil. Horatio's blindness in not seeing the real import of his remarks, while not exactly causing or even actively contributing to his own downfall, is foolish because not sufficiently aware of the presence of forces of evil and destruction. His actions in courting Bellimperia in this way, and his speeches, are the trigger-action which, however well-meant, releases a destruction that was waiting for him anyway. The character of the world as Kyd sees it is pointed by the fact that Horatio must contribute, in however small degree, to his own murder by being unaware of the grimmer meaning inherent in what he is saying. On the discovery of the body, Hieronymo points the meaning again:

> O Heavens, why made you night to cover sin?
> By day this deed of darkness had not been.
>
> II, iv, 86-87

'Sin' here means, literally, the murder, but I think Kyd is sufficient of an Elizabethan to welcome the obvious echo of poor Horatio's own words and actions. In a conventional sense, at least, it was 'sin' that he and Bellimperia were flirting with, the more so as it was qualified by Horatio's dangerous insensitivity to the possibilities suggested by his love speeches. It is certainly no accident that Hieronymo here picks up the talk of day and night and makes specifically the point that Horatio failed to see consciously earlier on, though making it in fact by implication even then.

No-one could pretend that this was great dramatic verse. Some of it is downright childish:

> Ay me most wretched, that have lost my joy,
> In leesing my Horatio, my sweet boy! II, iv, 94-95

But *The Spanish Tragedy*, as well as being an interesting play, is a portent, and the fact that already the Revenge convention is using conventional writing for wider ends plays a significant part in one's vision of the whole range of Elizabethan writing. In the central acts, Hieronymo and others stretch the limits of the play beyond anything that could have been expected from earlier, surface impressions. Act III, scene ii, for instance, opens with the famous soliloquy 'O eyes! no eyes, but fountains fraught with tears . . .' Immediately, and largely, this is quaintly patterned verse of historical interest only. It even does its best to bury the perfectly valid complaint it is in fact making under the mass of patterning that culminates triumphantly in

> Eyes, life, world, Heav'ns, hell, night, and day,
> See, search, show, send some man, some mean, that may –
> (A letter falleth)

From beneath poetical exhibitionism of this kind, however, the point that the play is trying to make does finally emerge:

> O world! no world, but mass of public wrongs . . .

Characteristically, when the point is made, it is allowed a simplicity and a clarity of outline later writers simply had to sacrifice in favour of a richer complexity of meaning.

More interesting, however, than the famous speech itself is the extent to which the play as a whole does manage to make something of this embryonic tragic complaint. Immediately before this scene, the sub-plot – if that is what it can be called – has made the same point in a quietly effective way. Alexandro's trials are in fact happily ended by the arrival of the Portuguese Ambassador from Spain, but he too is very nearly destroyed by the workings of Machiavellian intrigue which blandly disregards natural justice and the innocence of individuals. With considerable imaginative insight, Kyd has used the limited, conventional plot of Villuppo to show how easily and how unjustly slander will stick, and the texture of the play is thickened by the parallels between Alexandro's complaints and Hieronymo's:

Alexandro But in extremes what patience shall I use?
Nor discontents it me to leave the world,
With whom there nothing can prevail but wrong . . .
As for the earth, it is too much infect
To yield me hope of any of her mold. III, i, 32–37

Already the Shakespearean tragic complaint is overshadowing the unstinted vigour of *Tamburlaine*!

More impressively – and even discounting the additions attributed to Jonson – Hieronymo, stilted though much of his dialogue and speeches are, focuses a complaint which later tragedy will develop more intricately but not always more rewardingly. Kyd's version, put largely through Hieronymo, is clumsy, but has the interest of freshness, forthrightness and clarity of outline that often characterizes the beginning of a literary theme:

Hieronymo [as the magistrate deciding others' causes]:
Thus must we toil in other men's extremes,
That know not how to remedy our own,
And do them justice, when unjustly we,
For all our wrongs, can compass no redress . . .
This toils my body, this consumeth age,
That only I to all men just must be,
And neither gods nor men be just to me. III, vi, 1 ff.

Kyd's verse, though not at this point literally in couplet form, is still bound to the couplet mentality which gives it, at its best, directness and point. Act III, scene vii develops this kind of attitude and hints broadly at the quizzical attitude to the justice of the heavens which Shakespeare, Tourneur and Webster later developed. Here, again, the outlines of the imagery are sharper and more uncompromisingly devoted to an obvious single point than in later writers, but by the same token Kyd's attitude is remarkably fresh and forthright. It's not that he's doubting the existence of the heavens, or that he's saying divine justice doesn't exist; only that in these circumstances it's difficult if not impossible

to see anything rational or humane in it. The heavens are strikingly
beautiful but unintelligibly aloof:

> Yet still tormented is my tortured soul
> With broken sighs and restless passions,
> That, winged, mount and, hovering in the air,
> Beat at the windows of the brightest Heavens,
> Soliciting for justice and revenge.
> But they are plac'd in those empyreal heights,
> Where, countermur'd with walls of diamond,
> I find the place impregnable . . .   III, vii, 10 ff.

This is the best of Hieronymo, and of Kyd. The play here is asking
the impertinent questions that great tragedy constantly asks, but
with Kyd they have a singleness of impact possible only to the
writer who does not see complications beyond the questions
asked. Thus Shakespeare is obviously an infinitely more complex
writer than Kyd, but on a simple level Hieronymo's concern with
justice is related to Lear's and is in any case impressive in its own
right. In particular, the personal directness of his final protest, with
only the faintest echo now of the affectations of 'O eyes! no eyes',
is admirable:

> I find the place impregnable; and they
> Resist my woes, and give my words no way.

Compared with the extreme patterning of many of Hieronymo's
more famous speeches the 'woes . . . words' balance here is barely
detectable and almost all a reader's attention is taken up with the
directness and frankess of his complaint.

The 'additions' develop both this and, of course, the questioning
madness which follows from it. Whether or not they are Jonson's,
they clearly represent both a more truly dramatic dialogue and a
freer and more flexible verse generally. Certainly, whoever wrote
them had his eye firmly on questions raised by Kyd himself:

> *Hieronymo* Light me your torches at the mid of noon,
> Whenas the sun god rides in all his glory;
> Light me your torches then . . .

> . . . Night is a murderous slut,
> That would not have her treasons to be seen.
>
> IV, vi, 28-32

And later there is a wilder version of Hieronymo's old point about the justice of the heavens:

> *Hieronymo* O ambitious beggar,
> Wouldest thou have that that lives not in the world?
> Why, all the undelved mines cannot buy
> An ounce of justice, 'tis a jewel so inestimable.
> I tell thee, God hath engrossed all justice in his hands,
> And there is none but what comes from him.
>
> IV, vi, 82-87

But clearly the Kyd of the main text could not compete with verse of this competence. The interest we have in his verse is of a more limited – and for the most part academic – kind. The additions, by keeping firmly to questions precisely raised by the original, give the play imaginative depth; at the same time they illustrate some of the directions in which the revenge play will be modified as writing closer to Shakespeare's in tone and idiom takes command. In particular, the idiomatic vigour of 'Night is a murderous slut . . .', and the almost Shakespearean ring of Pedringano's

> So that with extreme grief and cutting sorrow
> There is not left in him one inch of man.
> See, where he comes.   IV, vi, 14-16

– together with the more responsive, less patterned dialogue in the shorter exchanges between characters, all point away from Kyd towards the extreme flexibility of Jacobean and later Elizabethan writing. The uniqueness of Kyd's own section of the play is that it stands firmly off – often quite successfully – from this more mature writing and yet clearly provides the impetus and some of the cast of mind for later plays. It has the virtues of clarity and at the same time it is more representative and suggestive of future needs than, for instance, Marlowe's *Tamburlaine*.

The significant section of the Revenge tradition stretches from Kyd to Ford. The history of this development demonstrates both the customary thickening and softening of texture in the writing within a well-used literary convention, and also the movement of sensibility (clearly begun in the Jonson additions to the *Spanish Tragedy*) from Elizabethan to Jacobean writing. As is usual in these cases, the advent of sentimentality and the need to cultivate sadism and unnatural sex relationships of the kind Ford displays herald the exhaustion of the literary convention, the increasing temptation to re-invigorate it by concentrating more and more on the abnormal, the merely stimulating. Kyd's red-ink letters and bitten-out tongues are healthy melodrama compared with Ford's bleeding heart. It is the context that matters, more than the fact itself, and Ford surrounds his extraordinary scene at the end of *'Tis Pity* with a good deal of sentimentality and with the desperate lyricism of his attempt to turn morals upside down and justify Giovanni's praise of incest. He is forced to dwell far longer on his melodrama, make it a bigger issue than does Kyd, and the way in which he does this – particularly Giovanni's suspect lyricism – softens and blurs the impact of the dagger scene. In Kyd, it is a bloody moment which startles, but does not much affect the play. In Ford, it is an important and twisted climax. Before Ford, this danger had been lurking in and out of the Revenge play, particularly with Beaumont and Fletcher, though never fully taking command. In Tourneur, for instance, though much of the interest of the play depends on watching him balancing on the edge of dangers of roughly this kind, the important advance on Kyd lies not here but in the richness and, for all its control, the range of Tourneur's writing. Then, at the end of the convention, inevitably, the change towards sentimentality and a cloying softness of texture really takes command.

It is difficult and dangerous to state anything more definite than this in the way of description or explanation of the change from Kyd to Ford. Even short and widely accepted generalizations, such as most of these are, in fact are barely adequate, and then only for the most glaring cases. Because the progression is not, as it is all too easy to find oneself claiming, in a straight line. Webster's highly eccentric and loose use of revenge is an exception to all general rules, and Tourneur's one good play proves that any generalization based on a concept of 'the earlier, within a given convention, the better' will also at some stage or other break down. Tourneur's play is not only far more mature and far more significant than Kyd's – this in itself would hardly be surprising – but it is also, for all its thicker and more complex texture, a much more neatly constructed piece of Revenge work.[1] These two points are connected. Tourneur uses the convention more intelligently and more neatly than Kyd (whose politics of revenge are often very hard to follow) simply because, in his case, form and intelligence are now more closely linked. The 'conventional' aspect of the writing is helped by the author's attitude to wider questions, and these are wider questions defined and given form by the convention. This is an issue which is not *separated* from the development of a convention historically but one which proves that history, in these matters as in others, moves erratically. In the same way, sociological and historical explanations of the change in the convention must be treated as useful hints rather than rules of conduct. In some cases – Ford, possibly? – a hint of changing and unsettling social conditions may help, but the achievements of seventeenth-century poets like Donne and Marvell are a warning that there are no

---

[1] It is often claimed that Tourneur's plot is in places untidy and clumsy (cf. Bowers, *op. cit.*, pp. 137-8). Despite this, the neatness of his Revenge artistry seems to me to stand as an important fact (see Chapter VI below).

simple sociological reasons for the decay of the drama or even for its change in the directions taken by Webster and Tourneur.

Marlowe's contributions to the tragedy of blood are both more brilliantly individualistic and at the same time more fragmentary than Kyd's. In *The Jew of Malta* (*c.* 1589) the sense of elaborate, over-toppling stratagem as Barabas poisons or strangles one victim after another, weaves between Calymath and the Governor, leads his men through the tunnels into Malta's fort and, in the end, is seen busily at work at the top of the elaborate mechanism which closes the irony of the play – all this must have been a brilliantly significant lead to later writers who wanted to stress this aspect of Revenge. In some sense, of course, all did. The Revenger, particularly after Marlowe, is traditionally a scourge of God (or, as perhaps in Marlowe himself, of the author) against villains and sinners of all kinds. With Webster and Tourneur, the point that was implicit in *The Jew of Malta* comes more and more to be openly stated. The moral structure of the revenge play begins with the concept of irony stressed by Marlowe and to some extent Kyd. The revenger must destroy his victims in such a way that the manner of their deaths brings home to them and to us the peculiar irony of a universe which bides its time, often permitting all sorts of injustice to escape unpunished, until finally and effortlessly it catches sinners out in the most diabolically significant way. With Webster and to some extent with Marlowe this is so much an issue that it becomes a sort of game, very amusing, but tinged at the same time with undergraduate fantasy:

> To have poisoned his prayer-book, or a pair of beads,
> The pummel of his saddle, his looking-glass,
> Or th' handle of his racket, – O, that, that!
> That while he had been bandying at tennis,
> He might have sworn himself to hell, and strook
> His soul into the hazard! *The White Devil*, v, i, 71 ff.

With this compare the grim cynicism of Barabas's:

> As for myself, I walk abroad o'nights
> And kill sick people groaning under walls . . .
>
> II, 306 ff.

– or the delightful, cynical exuberance of Ithamore, picking up and further twisting the play's many references to religion:

> But here's a royal monast'ry hard by;
> Good master, let me poison all the monks.
>
> IV, 14-15

But the irony of revenge is, despite the flippancy of some of its most brilliant moments, a serious issue with all these writers, and I think it can be shown that suggestions thrown out by Marlowe are indispensable to the achievement of later writers (compare, for instance, Chapter VI on the interdependence of simple revenge irony and complex wit in Tourneur).

Apart from *The Jew of Malta*, one of the most impressive displays of Marlowe's genius in Revenge writing is the characterization of the Guise in *The Massacre at Paris* (1593) and the consequent development of the idea of the Machiavel in plays where, despite the melodrama, the overriding concern is moralistic and serious. In his attack on certain aspects of the tragedy of blood, far more even than Kyd, Marlowe is defiantly and refreshingly individual. In the minor plays, the individualism that characterized *Tamburlaine* gets freer rein. For instance a defiant carelessness turns the incipient Machiavellism of *The Massacre at Paris* almost into a personal pamphlet on contemporary issues:

> *Loreine* I am a preacher of the word of God;
> And thou a traitor to thy soul and him.
> *Guise* 'Dearly beloved brother,'– thus 'tis written.
>   (Stabs *Loreine*, who dies.) ll. 342-4

It's not so much that Marlowe is taking sides in these matters, though in a general sense (cf. the concluding lines of the play) he sometimes is. The main impression, especially from *The Massacre at Paris*, is of a young man using a conventionalized drama to express a sharply turned contempt for the respectable. In this play and in others, he rivals the Shakespeare of *Troilus and Cressida* as the angry young man of Elizabethan England. Henry's highly respectable concluding lines (1241 ff.) are for this reason rather a shock, though they act as a reminder that, like *The Jew of Malta*, the play has a refreshing carelessness about it. (Generally speaking, the touch is light enough for this to come off.) It is half a private manifesto, half a conventional piece of writing, tossed off carelessly and hurriedly. Kyd's solid worth could not rival the undergraduate brilliance and daring of this, though his consistency and seriousness of aim in some ways took him further and brought Revenge writing closer to the needs of Elizabethan tragic drama.

Both Marlowe's plays, then, go a long way towards expanding the formal, conventional aspect of Elizabethan and Jacobean Revenge drama. The next point to make is that there are times in these plays when Marlowe's brilliance looks as if it will carry him much further than this. *The Jew of Malta*, in particular, looks as if it very nearly could have been a much greater play than it is. The kind of verse typified by the 'two religious caterpillars' speech and the poisoning speeches of Barabas and Ithamore defines and uses conventional writing with brilliant individuality. On the other hand, Barabas's first speech promises a good deal more than this and a good deal more than the rest of the play performs. This opening speech looks as if Marlowe will go much further than he eventually does in this play. In the first place, as a dramatic triumph in the opening scene of a play it surely rivals the best of Elizabethan drama. Without as yet giving away anything of his wider intentions, or stating them too flatly and specifically, Marlowe, with a deadly accuracy of understatement, sketches in the Jew's regard for and contempt of mere money. The opening lines are dramatic in the sense in which the Elizabethans excelled:

they use language to embody the very gestures and action of the drama:

> So that of thus much that return was made;
> And of the third part of the Persian ships
> There was the venture summ'd and satisfied.
> As for those Scaenites, and the men of Uz,
> That bought my Spanish oils and wines of Greece,
> Here have I purs'd their paltry silverlings.
> Fie, what a trouble 'tis to count this trash!   I, 1-7

Money and wealth are physically present in the dialogue here, in a way of which even Middleton would have been proud. The actor's gestures are written into the dialogue for him, and thus embody all the more closely what he has to say. The result is that nothing could more precisely define at once the Jew's fanatical concern for money, and the carelessness – even contempt – born of habituation to wealth. (It is interesting that there are many speeches in *The Merchant of Venice* when Shakespeare's Jew, by comparison, seems more melodramatic, in context far less credible than this.)

The concluding section of the speech is distinctively Marlowe, and quite beyond both the convention that forms the backbone of the play and writers like Middleton and Jonson who triumphed over the miser in quite different ways. From the Jew's restlessness over mere money and goods, Marlowe leads on to the metaphysics of riches without possessions. 'Fie, what a trouble 'tis to count this trash!' – Barabas despises money, the laborious goal of Western mercantilism, and will emulate the Indian jewel merchant and 'the wealthy Moor' who deal in metal and stones whose value bears no relation to size or quantity. From here it is an easy step to the final conceit which, outdoing Jonson, definitively states the difference between the miser's wealth and his attitude to wealth. The ultimate value of riches is expressed in the idea of power divorced from bulk or numbers. Money and goods can be accumulated, but only in arithmetical progression which is limited because its end is vague and out of sight. Barabas's conceit expresses the infinite of wealth *in possession*:

> And thus methinks should men of judgment frame
> Their means of traffic from the vulgar trade,
> And, as their wealth increaseth, so inclose
> Infinite riches in a little room. I, 34-37

This combination of a subtly metaphorical outlook with a simple vigour and directness in the tone of the writing ('. . . so inclose / Infinite riches in a little room') is characteristic of Marlowe at his best. It is also characteristically early, rather than late Elizabethan or Jacobean writing. It would be surprising to find lines of precisely this *timbre* even in Shakespeare, and certainly they would have been beyond, say, Middleton, whose subtlety was of an entirely different and – if one can for the moment allow Marlowe his obvious limitations elsewhere in the play – probably inferior, less imaginatively flexible kind. The conceit of wealth and power increasing while the physical bulk of it decreases, might, ideally, have been something that Tourneur's particular genius could have dealt with, but in fact by the time Tourneur was writing other issues were crowding in and demanding most, if not all, of a playwright's attention. Marlowe's writing here demonstrates the uniqueness of the opportunities he and (given the limitations of Kyd) he alone had.

Unfortunately, nowhere else in this play, or in *The Massacre at Paris*, does Marlowe approach this ideal of imaginative objectivity. Had he done so, and held his focus for any length of time, he would have left Shakespeare's study of the Jew streets behind and eclipsed even the best of Kyd's dramatic writing beyond recognition. In many ways, perhaps he does so even as it is; but the bulk of his play rests on the brilliance with which he shapes the conventional element in Elizabethan tragedy rather than on the creative genius hinted at in the opening scenes. The careless ease with which, throughout the play, he drops hints of what was to come is at once admirable and tantalizing. More often than not in these plays, it looks as if Marlowe began a point and left it undeveloped simply because, unlike the lesser genius of Kyd, his was too often satisfied with the limited but clear brilliance of success in minor forms of literature. For instance, the barrenness of the Jew's life is obvious from the beginning, and could have been imaginatively developed from the point at which he begins to adopt Ithamore in preference to his own daughter. Marlowe is content to achieve the trite (because bluntly stated) moral that Barabas's 'love' for Ithamore is empty. Now that Abigail is dead, poisoned by her father, the Jew needs Ithamore, but the one corner of his emotional life not spent on wealth and power is wasted on a man who betrays him with the town prostitute. As Marlowe manages it, and taken on its own, this scene (the concluding one in Act IV) is certainly a more impressive attack on such problems than Tourneur's, for instance, in *The Atheist's Tragedy*; but in context it looks like an important point relegated to one item in the catalogue of hints for the future. In this scene, which obviously should have been central to the play's meaning, there is no power in Marlowe's writing, nothing really to pick up and expand or comment on the vitality of the opening speech by Barabas on the same subject, riches and possessions. Here, and I think too often elsewhere, Marlowe is content with flat statement which hints at a rudimentary sense of conflict on a simple, 'character' level, but goes no further:

Barabas (aside) I am betray'd –
'Tis not five hundred crowns that I esteem;
I am not mov'd at that: this angers me,
That he, who knows I love him as myself,
Should write in this imperious vein. Why, sir,
You know I have no child, and unto whom
Should I leave all but unto Ithamore? IV, 404-410

The Jew's love for Ithamore is presented as comically exaggerated, but even this fails to enliven the flatness of a scene which should have been more than comic.

One could add that the confusion of aim, the loosely held purpose in *The Massacre at Paris* reinforces the limiting judgment that Marlowe's technically brilliant and certainly influential Revenge writing nevertheless invites. Certainly, the Guise in this play is given an admirable clarity and vigour of statement. However, his various roles as Machiavel, cynic, the aspiring Marlovian hero of

> Now, Guise, begin those deep-engender'd thoughts
> To burst abroad those never-dying flames . . .
>
> ll. 90 ff.

– all these, clearly put in themselves, are difficult to reconcile and fit together. Even were the play complete, it is impossible to see how Marlowe could have cleared up the confusion engendered by placing a complex of this kind against his vacillating treatment of the kings of France, who appear first of all as mere shadows of the Guise, weak competitors in Machiavellism; then finally, in the person of Henry, as the martyr and virtual saviour of the Protestantism championed by Elizabeth. This is a truly disabling confusion of purpose because there is nowhere in it the sense of effort, the sudden moral awakening that enables Webster, for instance, to convert chaos into purposefully intelligent writing.

By comparison with these two plays of Marlowe, Kyd looks, at first glance, incredibly stilted. In his best scenes, he only just manages to struggle grimly out of patterned, mannered dialogue into something like tragedy. On the other hand, Kyd's contribution is to develop, within the most limited and conventional of all Revenge plays, material from which a Shakespeare could more consistently borrow than ever he did from the more brilliant Marlowe. That this leaves the status of *Doctor Faustus* untouched goes without saying, but it is interesting that, even if one leaves aside the specific question of *Spanish Tragedy* echoes in *Hamlet*, Kyd's questioning of the justice of Hieronymo's world opens up issues very similar to those that interested Shakespeare in *King Lear*. The toughness of Shakespeare's enquiry into the levels at which the word 'justice' means anything, and the sympathy he has for the humanity involved, are extraordinarily like the attitude of Kyd in the scenes of *The Spanish Tragedy* which break beyond the limitations he set himself in the beginning. Thinking in terms of early Revenge plays generally it is obvious that in *The Spanish Tragedy*, for all its patterned exhibitionism, there is a seriousness of purpose and achievement which Marlowe does not even seem concerned to rival. With Marlowe, at least in his minor plays, too often one finds oneself regretting the spectacle of talent – however distinguished it may look potentially – being used merely as talent.

Most of the later tragic dramatists rely on the concept of the Revenge plot, adumbrated by Kyd and Marlowe, in a sense which is certainly not purely formalistic but which has in each case something to do with a concept of form, of control almost. They obviously feel themselves to be writing in a tradition and they know that (even if, as in the case of Marlowe, the issues were at times irresponsibly dealt with) there was a clarity and simplicity of moral purpose in the early writers which is becoming increasingly difficult to recapture because, in the light of later developments, it is seen to be increasingly irrelevant or inadequate. Nevertheless, it is felt to be necessary in some sense, or at least admirable. Of all the later writers, only Middleton, by breaking new ground entirely, and Shakespeare solved this problem independently of the convention. All the others, in various ways, use the Revenge plot extensively, and all exhibit an uneasiness in dealing with it. It is seen as at once a constricting element, and a controlling form which is necessary in the face of encroaching complexity. In this connection the most interesting case is the greatest Revenge play of all: Tourneur's *The Revenger's Tragedy*.

PART 2
JACOBEAN
TRAGEDY

CHAPTER V

THE MORALITY OF REVENGE:
TOURNEUR'S CRITICS

In books and periodicals over the last thirty years there has been a closely sustained critical argument about the moral basis of the plays of Webster, Tourneur, Middleton and others. In this context *The Revenger's Tragedy* (1606–7) has more consistently drawn the fire of intelligent criticism than any other single play. Of all the Jacobeans, Tourneur is the one who most obviously and most literally is preoccupied with moral behaviour – it is not for nothing that he relies so heavily on a Revenge scheme – and he therefore conveniently and powerfully focuses our doubts about the legitimacy of an age of drama which ranks in English literature with Elizabethan Tragedy and yet seems so patently to rest on social and moral decadence. Most writers in this century have been fascinated by the paradox of the cynical Tourneur clinging fast to Mediaeval and Elizabethan moral maxims and – literally at the same time – launching forth into dangerously cynical comment on and about them. For clearly the central point with Tourneur is the combination of near banality on the one hand and, on the other, witty individuality in his comments on personal relations and the world about him. The 'jingling sententious couplets'[1] continually jostle against and merge into feelings which are experienced, detached, cynical. The overt morality in *The Revenger's Tragedy* is, for the most part, too immature to provide a firm moral basis for the play. The question is, has Tourneur provided anything else which would modify the surface impression of negativism and decadence?

[1] M. C. Bradbrook, *Themes and Conventions of Elizabethan Tragedy* (Cambridge, 2nd edn. 1952), p. 172.

97

Most critics see something of this, but make vastly different points from it. The two most influential I think have been Bradbrook and Eliot, and they crystallize the for and against pretty well. Eliot's too short and generalized pronouncement – it so notably lacks any sort of close contact with the text that one's immediate reaction is to disagree – is well known. The essay, or review, is of course mainly about authorship, and on the critical question he adds little or nothing beyond the following familiar passage:

> The cynicism, the loathing and disgust of humanity, expressed consummately in *The Revenger's Tragedy*, are immature in the respect that they exceed the object. Their objective equivalents are characters practising the grossest vices; characters which seem merely to be spectres projected from the poet's inner world of nightmare, some horror beyond words. So the play is a document on one human being, Tourneur; its motive is truly the death motive, for it is the loathing and horror of life itself. To have realized this motive so well is a triumph; for hatred of life is an important phase – even, if you like, a mystical experience – in life itself.[1]

It is a great pity Eliot was never tempted to expand this (and other) essays. As it is, for all the brilliance of the insight shown here, one is in considerable doubt as to how great a writer he thought Tourneur was and just how to balance the 'immaturity' and the 'importance' of the 'phase'. On the whole I would tend to assume an unwilling admiration behind this essay, but an admiration which starts, unfairly, by isolating a 'loathing and disgust of humanity' which does not in fact exist in the play.

Bradbrook's chapter on Tourneur is one of the most inconsequential and fragmentary in the whole of a book the brilliance of which obviously depends to some extent on its ability to suggest disjointedly rather than argue sustainedly. By the same token, Miss Bradbrook's suggestions on the difficulty of the mixture of

[1] T. S. Eliot, 'Cyril Tourneur', *Selected Essays*, 2nd edn. (London, 1934), pp. 189-90.

naïveté, subtlety and vitality in Tourneur are, if a little incon-
clusive for some tastes, obviously extremely valuable. I take it that
to most who read them they give at least the beginnings of a substantial answer to Eliot's brilliant, limited dogmatism.

The struggle continues in two important essays, by L. G.
Salingar in *Scrutiny*[1] and by John Peter in *Essays in Criticism*.[2]
These two rely on earlier critics but bring to a head certain matters
affecting one's whole approach to reading seventeenth-century
plays. Substantially, the issue between them by-passes Eliot's firm
stand for morality pure and simple. It is now – and rightly, surely –
a question simply of whether Tourneur's ironic detachment is held
with absolute surety, or whether he leans a little too far over the pit
he's contemplating. Both look in some detail at the text. It seems to
me that in the end Salingar (backed by Bradbrook) comes out as
clearly the more accurate: Tourneur is in fact not quite as surely
poised as Peter wants to make out.

I take it that Salingar's point, briefly, is that Tourneur, in *The
Revenger's Tragedy* at any rate, achieves a detachment which, in the
face of the imminent corruption of the Elizabethan world around
him, may fail to establish new, positive values to take the place of
the old, but does make an intelligent and powerful comment on
things as they are. He (Tourneur) avoids 'hysteria', manages an
'emotional equilibrium'. All is in negative terms as far as Mr
Salingar is concerned (so far at least Eliot is right), but the comment Tourneur makes, as Salingar sees it, is so intelligent, accurate,
vital, that this carries a value of its own for anybody, Jacobean or
not, to see.

This seems to me quite fair. It *is* rather a negative approach and
for this reason it does not, I think, say all that can be said for

[1] L. G. Salingar, '*The Revenger's Tragedy* and the Morality Tradition', *Scrutiny*, vol. VI,
No. 4, p. 402.

[2] John Peter, '*The Revenger's Tragedy* Reconsidered', *Essays in Criticism*, Vol. VI, No. 2,
p. 131. And compare Peter Lisca, '*The Revenger's Tragedy*: A Study in Irony', repr. in
Bluestone & Rabkin, *Shakespeare's Contemporaries*, *op. cit.*

Tourneur. But leaving the question of any more positive achievement aside for the moment, the first step in a true answer to Eliot is to say that Tourneur, considering the outlines of his subject, does remarkably well in not being swamped by horror and decadence of all kinds. Putting it slightly more accurately: it is necessary once again to distinguish between a playwright and his characters. Tourneur is not to be equated even with Vendice; and generally speaking in the play, where the characters wallow, Tourneur, in the tone of his verse and dialogue, takes the opportunity to comment on this. The result is a play which rightly stops short of constructing codes of conduct, but which certainly does, consistently, achieve moral comment of a subtler kind. Most often, with Tourneur, it is the vein of wit and conceit that seems to save him and to pave the way for positive rather than negative or purely cynical writing. The temptation of Castiza and her mother Gratiana, for instance, could easily have become an excuse for wallowing in sex. It looks, in a way, as if it very nearly did. In Act II Tourneur throws all he can muster into the role of the disguised Vendice. Even Vendice is half sure the impossible will come off and Castiza will prove 'a woman', and there is an eagerness in the dialogue which almost carries the author's persuasion behind it as well as the character's:

> I would count
> My yearly maintenance upon her cheeks;
> Take coach upon her lip; and all her parts
> Should keep men after men ... II, i (p. 367)[1]

This recalls the even clearer case of Act II, scene iii:

> Now 'tis full sea abed over the world ...

Here Vendice, and to some extent Tourneur through Vendice, are making a moral point, but it is in danger of turning out a negative one. They want to prove, not that good exists, or, even, that Castiza is innocent, but that the world is as bad as they think it is.

---

[1] Act, scene and page references throughout to Mermaid Edition.

In all passages of this kind from Vendice (and, significantly, it makes little difference whether he is in disguise or not) the verse hurries on with the sense of mixed alarm and admiration most convincingly illustrated by the brilliant end of this speech:

> Now cuckolds are coining, apace, apace, apace, apace!
> And careful sisters spin that thread i' the night,
> That does maintain them and their bawds i' the day. II, iii (p. 377)

No wonder Hippolito's admiringly trite little comment is brushed aside:

> *Hippolito* You flow well, brother.
> *Vendice* Pooh! I'm shallow yet . . . (p. 378)

Subconsciously Vendice realizes, or rather is painted as realizing, that he has a personal stake in the world's corruption; even, possibly, in Castiza's.

But Tourneur is not Vendice; or, at all events, not quite. The sense of hurry in the verse ('Nine coaches waiting . . .'), the occasional gloating over an image of evil ('This woman in immodest thin apparel . . .') places Tourneur, somewhat like Vendice, as an admiring looker-on in a world dominated by the frankly uncontrolled lust and corruption of the Spurios and the Supervacuos. At the same time the grotesquerie of the images, within that admirably controlled rhythm, is a plea for a quick intelligence which can rapidly, and fairly accurately, evaluate the situation it sees. To return to an earlier example: the temptation of Gratiana, seen properly in context, balances Tourneur's obvious sympathy for luxury and corruption with the objectivity of an intelligence neatly telescoping sex and the corruption that maintains it:

> No, I would raise my state upon her breast;
> And call her eyes my tenants; I would count
> My yearly maintenance upon her cheeks . . . (p. 367)

This speech has something at least of the intelligent oddity of Metaphysical wit put to the service of the drama. Significantly,

when Vendice attempts Castiza herself, the verse trades a little of
its objectivity for a richer, more dangerously evocative note:

> the stirring meats,
> Ready to move out of the dishes, that e'en now
> Quicken when they are eaten!   II, i (p. 370)

Even under the shelter of the disguised Vendice, Tourneur rarely
goes further than this in the deliberate relishing of allusion; yet
even here he is clearly protecting himself by the sense of the
curious, the witty, which keeps a reader's mind alive as well as his
senses. The speech ends with the compressed oddity of Vendice's
grim joke which looks like an alluring picture, but which works
also as a parody (surely not intended for Castiza's benefit!) of the
blindly self-destructive appetite Court life engenders:

> Banquets abroad by torchlight! music! sports!
> Bareheaded vassals, that had ne'er the fortune
> To keep on their own hats, but let horns wear 'em!
> Nine coaches waiting – hurry, hurry, hurry –   (p. 371)

The real Tourneur struggles in this way against encroaching
decadence. In this context, the very presence of those 'jingling
sententious couplets' that Bradbrook noted is a sign that he must
cling suspiciously hard to some sort of overt 'morality', however
crude. On the other hand a critical approach of the kind suggested
by Mr Salingar's article would clearly reveal a firmness and
subtlety in Tourneur's writing which ranges far beyond the
limitations of a couplet mentality:

> Advance thee, O thou terror to fat folks,
> To have their costly three-piled flesh worn off
> As bare as this: for banquets, ease, and laughter
> Can make great men, as greatness goes by clay;
> But wise men little are more great than they.   I, i (pp. 344-5)

In contrast, Mr Peter's attempt to prove Eliot almost completely
wrong seems strained. Much as one would like to agree that
Tourneur keeps a 'hovering distance' from evil all the way

through, it is not so, at least not quite in Peter's sense. Granted, as Mr Peter points out, that Piato, and even Vendice, are always in character, i.e. not to be identified completely with Tourneur, still Tourneur is there in the combination of characters and events, and the inescapable impression from the whole play is that, good as the ironic comment is for the most part, it occasionally slips. One line quoted by Mr Peter deserves comment. Spurio, tempted by his stepmother, succumbs, finally, with this line:

> Oh one incestuous kiss picks open hell . . .

Now there is, possibly, an 'intrusive moral comment' in this, though in a single line it's very hard to tell. But surely, anyway, it fights a hard battle with a leaning towards the delights of unnatural love? Peter's phrase, 'intrusive moral comment', suggests, I think, that Tourneur's share in the connotations of such phrases is one thing, Spurio's another. Or, if this is unfair: that Tourneur's comment is fairly securely placed and controlled. The fact would seem to be that the two are more thoroughly mixed than this and that Tourneur's attitude is far from clear. A 'hovering distance' from evil, in its more dubious sense, is indeed nearer the mark. Most notably, even where Vendice the moralist speaks, the verse admits a fascination in the prodigious sense of evil rapidly engulfing the world:

> O God! one,
> That has scarce blood enough to live upon;
> And he to riot it, like a son and heir!
> O, the thought of that
> Turns my abused heart-strings into fret. I, i (pp. 343-4)

Granted, as Mr Peter says, Vendice 'speaks arrestingly', as a revenger should, and this is partly the reason for such verse, it still depends on what kind of 'arresting' speech it is, and what are the implications of the tone. In fact, there is a kind of gloating satisfaction in the speech of many characters in Jacobean drama which satisfies not merely the demands of the action but the author's own feelings, as a private individual, into the bargain. An analogy that Mr Peter makes is important. Claiming that, to read this play, we must all be good Jacobeans and not moderns, he says that an audience then would have accepted Vendice's speeches in the spirit in which they accepted all homiletic attacks on cosmetics, and he quotes, as one instance, the following from Nashe's *Christ's Teares Over Jerusalem:*

> Theyr heads (women's), with theyr top and top gallant Lawne baby-caps, and Snow-resembled silver curlings, they make a playne Puppet stage of. Theyr breasts they embuske up on hie, and theyr round Roseate buds immodestly lay foorth, to shew at theyr handes there is fruite to be hoped. In theyr curious Antick-woven garments, they imitate and mocke the Wormes and Adders that must eate them . . .
>
> As many iagges, blysters, and scarres, shall Toades, Cankers and Serpents, make on your pure skinnes in the grave, as nowe you have cuts, iagges, or raysings, upon your garments. In the marrow of your bones snakes shall breede. Your morne-like christall countenaunces shall be netted over and (Masker-like) cawle-visarded with crawling venomous wormes. Your orient teeth Toades shall steale into theyr heads for pearle; Of the ielly of your decayed eyes shall they engender them young. In theyr hollowe caves, (theyr transplendent iuyce so pollution-ately employd,) shelly Snayles shall keepe house.

Now, the way in which one treats this sort of analogy is indeed crucial to the whole business of Jacobean moral writing. Peter calls it 'pure moralizing, the *vanitas vanitatum* of the homilist', and claims a seventeenth-century audience would have found Tourneur just as disinterested. This, it seems to me, is one very good instance of the dangers of the kind of critical approach which attempts to see the plays through Jacobean eyes. With purely period studies, and with second-rate authors, a relativistic approach of some kind may be a help; but not, surely, when judging an author of Tourneur's weight. Here, for instance, the attempt to import attitudes from outside has led Mr Peter to misread not only Tourneur but Nashe as well! I don't care how many other 'purely moralizing' preachers or writers there were at the time, surely this prose by Nashe is not disinterested. One cannot judge by other cases. In literature, the average is, if anything, even more meaningless than elsewhere. The relevant information is in the images Nashe uses and the way he treats them. The *bizarrerie* is funny, and intended probably as propaganda, but when a writer consistently uses, and lingers over, images of slime and horror, he has passed beyond the stage of merely warning or stating principles: 'Your . . . countenaunces shall be . . . cawle-visarded with crawling venomous wormes . . . Of the ielly of your decayed eyes shall they engender them young . . .' This sort of thing is suspect, whenever it was written, though of course it is by no means the worst the Elizabethans (or any other age for that matter) could produce.

Tourneur, so far from saying the same thing 'more passionately and memorably' (Mr Peter on Vendice), is actually much surer of his ground than Nashe, whose rhetorical play conceals an unhealthy interest in what he condemns. On the other hand, even Tourneur is tarred with the same brush to quite an extent. There is often a tendency, even if it is less marked than with any other major Jacobean except Middleton, to gloat over the thing he condemns.

One further argument I have with Mr Peter is, once again, on a point of great general importance in the study and reading of drama. (This is, in fact, the reason for looking at these articles in some detail.) To quote Mr Peter: 'What these climaxes (e.g. Vendice on 'silks, money, camphire and the rest') in the first half of the play are designed to convey is an atmosphere of evil which, far from being irrefragable, is already discounted and accordingly vulnerable, and what the second half of the play does is to consolidate and advance the ethical positives that the first half has implied.' This may be so, but *only if* the writing in the second half (or such of the second half as is relevant to Mr Peter's point) is as good as that in the first half. To put it with less emphasis on technique, Mr Peter's point is only true in so far as he demonstrates that Tourneur establishes the point he is trying to make in the second half, his 'positives', as well as he established the 'negatives' of Vendice's and Spurio's great speeches of the first. It is no good merely pointing to moral signposts. And the simple fact is that the specifically and literally 'positive' writing in this play is rather more general, rather more inclined, rhythmically and in every other way, towards the banal, than is the satirical, 'negative' writing. Mr Peter quotes (using the old spelling) Vendice's speech on his mother's tears:

> Yfaith 'tis a sweete shower, it does much good.
> The fruitfull grounds, and meadowes of her soule,
> Has beene long dry: powre downe thou blessed dew;
> Rise Mother, troth this shower has made you higher.

Certainly, this is not bad verse. It is in fact a good deal better than some of the 'positive' lines the play produces. But any comparison with the silkworm speech or any comparable one in the early half of the play is absurd. Vendice's speech here readily forsakes incisive individuality (in which as we shall see resides the truly positive side of the play) for the unobtrusive but unmistakable triteness of 'fruitfull grounds', the 'meadowes of her soule', and the metaphor of aridity and rain. All this, too, in Tourneur's strictest metre which here only clinches the dullness and dutiful obeisance to morality.

Mr Peter only worsens matters, I think, by recalling themes ('vegetable growth'!) abstracted from tone and attitude, and by referring to Castiza's 'implausible' behaviour at certain points in these scenes. He adds: 'Admittedly this is implausible, but one can see that the dramatist is hardly aiming at verisimilitude.' True enough, but verisimilitude or not, he should be aiming at accurate and positive writing, and this, for all his dutiful mentioning of positive values, he is not, or if aiming at it, he does not achieve it.

After referring once again to other favourite moral writers of the Elizabethans, Tertullian, Langland, Gascoigne, Mr Peter concludes his article: 'A critic must respond to what is before him, not import into it his eccentricities or preoccupations, and it is high time we judged Tourneur by what he actually wrote.' Or what Tertullian wrote, or Gascoigne, or Nashe . . . ?

All this does not destroy the kind of positive values which Tourneur actually has and which in the main have been pointed out by Miss Bradbrook and Mr Salingar. I pick out what seems to me, with all respect, a good article of its kind in order to attempt to show why its kind will not do. It is one thing to trace patterns, as Salingar does, and quote them in illustration of what is demonstrable by other means anyway. It is another to judge individual work in the light of what others were doing. In the mixture of sententious and witty writing that he achieves, Tourneur gives us all the information we need on the homiletic writing he incorporates in his play. What he actually says constantly modifies traditional attitudes, and though these may have been essential to his development as a playwright, we dare not take them as evidence by which to judge and interpret the delicate adjustment he finally achieved in *The Revenger's Tragedy*. This must stand as a play that clings to limited moral maxims simply because it is triumphing only precariously over incipient decadence. Its real strength lies in the consistency with which it achieves, not a moral superiority over lust and corruption, but an ability to realize and place its own attraction to them.

On the other hand, even Mr Salingar's thesis, though much more rewarding than most other approaches to Tourneur, still does not seem to me to offer a complete reading of the play. The attraction of Salingar's attitude is that it admits implicitly the force of Eliot's charges but offers a reasonable answer to them. Overtly, the only kind of 'morality' Tourneur has been able to give his Revenge figure is one of hatred for everybody, and as one element in the play – particularly in the important set speeches of Vendice – this, as Eliot saw, cannot be ignored. Salingar's thesis is an attempt to show that, for all the occasional wobbling of tone consequent upon this life-denying element in Tourneur, on the whole the writing is firmly poised. The implication is that Tourneur is prepared to expose Vendice as a sort of bastion to hold off the forces of sin and corruption at something like a decently poised, ironic distancing. So much is undoubtedly true of the play, and it makes interesting and lively reading on this hypothesis. The difficulty, however, is that concepts of irony and control alone, invaluable though they are as an approach to *The Revenger's Tragedy*, are essentially negative and do not of themselves satisfy our sense of what the play achieves or even of what, specifically, it is about. In particular there is surely, in the dialogue and verse dealing with sin and revenge, an *energizing* force which, though firmly controlled, is never destroyed or rejected by the irony. Tourneur is indeed in control of the attraction towards lust and sin his characters display; but more than this he also demonstrates energy and vitality in and emergent from the thing condemned. Any full answer to Eliot's charges must attempt to show in some detail what the play has to offer in this regard, and what relation the more positive achievement bears to the apparent negativism and hatred for life so compulsively expressed by most of the characters, not excluding the highly moralistic Vendice.

CHAPTER VI

THE MORALITY OF REVENGE:
'THE REVENGER'S TRAGEDY'

The energizing forces in Tourneur's play, the vitality that makes it more than a piece of nicely controlled irony, are centred on the sins condemned: murder, lust, gluttony, adultery, incest – the list is considerable, and a familiar one to readers of late Elizabethan drama. That Tourneur's attitude is not as healthy or as richly affirmative as Shakespeare's goes without saying. On the other hand Shakespeare himself, like all the major Elizabethan dramatists, saw the health and vitality of life most clearly and most richly when he was writing also about its tragic and chaotic possibilities. It is clearly basic to the Elizabethans that tragedy is a form which, leading to destruction and death, liberates at the same time life and energy. Rather than any concept of tragic loss or of the 'regenerative' force of love, it is this *paradox* of death and life, informing a given play from its opening scenes onwards, which is at the heart of the Elizabethan tragic vision.

Broadly, there are two aspects of *The Revenger's Tragedy* – related but also distinct – which display activating vitality and energy of a kind which offers something more rewarding than a mere sense of 'control'. The first is the treatment of traditional Revenge situations and themes; the second a movement away from comparatively simple moral attitudes of this kind towards the more complex, near-metaphysical wit we noted briefly in the last chapter. Certainly it is clear that Tourneur does not develop the traditional Revenge plot as Kyd tended to do – informing it at key points with a Hamlet-like introspection from the hero. His attitude is, rather, to make a substantial issue of the neatness and precision of the moralistic Revenge plot, but to lead from this at key points to attitudes and verse which are the reverse of simple and which rely, more clearly even than Shakespeare's commonly do, on a recognizably 'metaphysical' wit. The opening lines of the play, with their rapidly telescoping irony – 'grey-haired adultery', 'royal lecher', 'juiceless luxur'– are typical.

Tourneur relates these two strands of development in his play – clearly they are both kinds of 'wit' – though he keeps them at the same time recognizably distinct. The key to a true reading of *The Revenger's Tragedy* is in the movement of attention we are constantly forced to make between the almost naïvely simple clarity of Revenge morality on the one hand, and the richer, more complex wit of metaphysical or near-metaphysical verse on the other. Even within a single speech, such as Vendice's opening soliloquy, a couplet movement in the verse, re-enacting in smaller compass the simple structure of a Revenge morality, jostles up against and mingles with the more complex lines. Tourneur is a great dramatist in that, while he senses the limitations of the convention he is using, his wit is not dulled or bewildered by this (as Webster's, for instance, very often is) because at the same time he also sees firmly and richly areas of experience beyond the merely conventional. This I think is why the conventional side of his writing has a lightness, vivacity and precision which none of the other Jacobean tragedians – and hardly even Kyd or Marlowe – can achieve. If Tourneur had been merely conscious of rounding off an exhausted convention, or of seeing its limitations, he would have been either a much duller, or a much more confused writer than he is. As it is the vivacity of his Revenge writing both springs from, and in turn enables him to formulate more surely, his grip on experience outside the simple Revenge convention. Seeing Revenge clearly leads Tourneur outwards to 'metaphysical' writing; this in turn lends sureness of purpose to the Revenge structure itself.

For the sake of clarity I shall deal first with the guiding Revenge structure of thought in the play; initially, on this simpler level, Tourneur is summing-up, and relying heavily on, values implicit in traditional Revenge writing. Traditionally, the irony of Revenge poses the question: is morality something which the righteous anger of a Vendice must *impose on* a helplessly corrupt society? or, on the other hand, is the morality of Revenge, in which sinners are consistently caught in their own toils, a reflection of some deeper irony in the nature of existence (i.e. something which does after all represent a kind of 'justice' and which Vendice's schemes merely bring into the open)? Tourneur is clearly interested to some extent in the first proposition. That is to say he is interested in the assumption that a man with Vendice's overwhelming indignation at the spectacle of universal lust and corruption will be forced to try and impose his own justice on a society which is a mockery of justice. But most of the emphasis in Tourneur is given – more obviously I think than in Kyd – to the second proposition inherent in Revenge irony. The whole fabric of his plot in *The Revenger's Tragedy* is concerned with a villainy which, in promoting its own ends, inevitably furthers its own destruction. Vendice is a focal point for the grim justice of Revenge, rather than a character who creates and moulds his own justice by fighting a corrupt society (and certainly he is not, as Hieronymo in part is, a character who is deeply and personally concerned at his own failure to see Justice in the universe). In this connection the lightness of tone in much of the writing throughout the play is highly important and is in pretty marked contrast to plays of the Kyd-Hamlet type. In Tourneur, the tone of the writing is consistently directed towards a recognition that, if Justice nowhere exists in any clear and positive sense, there is nevertheless a sense in which the *comic* writer can see a kind of justice operating as Lussurioso, Supervacuo, Spurio and the Duke energetically cut each other's throats.

Indeed the potential life in Revenge writing is often – and certainly in Tourneur – rather one of comic assertiveness than of tragic power. As F. T. Bowers points out in his book *Elizabethan Revenge Tragedy* there was, in tales and *novelle* translated copiously from the 1580's onwards, a wealth of material available to the Elizabethan Revenge writer, and clearly it was of a kind which could be turned either towards the sadism and sentimentality of later Jacobean writing or towards a grim but distinctly lively tragi-comedy. Bowers describes a typical Italianate tale as follows:

> A horribly contrived and Italianate story of revenge, of a type popular with the Elizabethan dramatists, was contained in Rosset's eleventh history, 'De la cruelle Vengeance exercée par une Damoiselle, sur la personne du meurtrier de celuy qu'elle aymoit', in which Fleurie, to secure revenge for the murder of her lover, pretends that she will marry Clorizande, the murderer. She makes a secret assignation with him, and on his arrival he is entangled in ropes and securely bound. Fleurie then proceeds to cut off his nose and ears, to tear out his teeth and nails and to chop off his fingers; and at the end she cuts out his heart and throws it in the fire. On her return home she writes out the facts of the murder of her lover and of her vengeance, and swallows poison.[1]

Tourneur didn't pick stories quite as absurdly melodramatic as this one, but the basic situations of *The Revenger's Tragedy* (the poisoned skull dressed up as a country wench, the Duke caught in his own toils, and so on) are not as far removed from the flavour of the popular *novelle* as the term 'Tragedy' might seem to suggest. Tourneur was the only one who wrote a Revenge drama informed with comic sharpness and vivacity, but the raw materials were certainly to hand, and it is interesting that only one Jacobean play had the lightness and sureness of touch to use them successfully.

The strand of grim but lively comic writing that Tourneur sustains throughout his play is best suggested by his treatment of

[1] Bowers, *op. cit.*, p. 59.

Lussurioso's attempt on Castiza and the 'villains caught in their own toils' effect which the play catches so well here. For in most Revenge plays justice is only partly effected by the revengers. It is largely the villains' over-zealous prosecution of their own plans that brings about their confusion and downfall; and of course the revengers themselves suffer, in the end, from prompting destiny too readily. Thus, in *The Revenger's Tragedy* plot, Spurio abandons his plan to commit incest with the Duchess in order to catch Lussurioso with Castiza; but at the same time Lussurioso has abandoned *his* attempt on Castiza in order to catch Spurio with the Duchess. In the end Lussurioso bursts into the Duchess's room, but she is lawfully in bed with the Duke and so Lussurioso himself is arrested for what looks like an attempt on the Duke's life:

> *Vendice* His vicious purpose to our sister's honour I crossed beyond our thought.

He certainly did. Indeed practically every action the villains take in this story furthers Vendice's purpose and their own confusion. For instance Spurio, attempting to save the life of the (to him) harmless Younger Son, succeeds only in killing him and effecting the release of Lussurioso whose execution he had intended to ensure. The whole story is crowned later on by the Duke's kissing Vendice's poisoned skull, and the snowballing myth of the all-controlling Vendice is then used to set Vendice (in the character of Hippolito's malcontent brother) to kill Vendice (in the character of Piato). The fabric of the plot has consistently held more tightly and more neatly than even the revengers dared hope, and the only further irony possible to the play is the destruction of the revengers themselves. Right to the end they play with fire but seem safe until, acting in a way very like the villains they've executed, they become too proud of the artistry that was nevertheless essential to the ironic morality of Revenge. It is unsafe to tempt the universe too far, and when they boast openly of their part, in the concluding death-masque, they are themselves hauled off to execution.

In all this the tone has been – despite the incredible complications – one of comparatively simple comedy. The Revenge story itself is written simply – at least when we compare it with the 'metaphysical' writing which dominates the key scenes – and, more important still, the verse and dialogue have a sharply etched vivacity that Eliot, concentrating perhaps too specifically on the gloom of the *characters'* professed outlook, underestimated or missed entirely. For instance Tourneur often takes considerable pains over presenting Vendice as almost beside himself with joy at a simple piece of ironic justice that has been thrust into his hands, and the tone of the play at such points has a lot to say about the meaning and value of the Revenge plot in the structure of the whole:

> *Vendice* O, sweet, delectable, rare, happy, ravishing!
> *Hippolito* Why, what's the matter, brother?
> *Vendice* O, 'tis able to make a man spring up and knock his forehead
> Against yon silver ceiling.   III, iv (pp. 389-90)

When at last Vendice is able to express himself intelligibly again to Hippolito, it appears that all this is explained by the Duke's having hired him, of all people, to find a courtesan who will be suitably secret:

> In some fit place, veiled from the eyes o' the court,
> Some darkened, blushless angle, that is guilty
> Of his forefather's lust and great folks' riots . . .

Given the circumstances, this is certainly a telling irony, and the hint of grimmer implications still in the joke about Vendice knocking his forehead 'against yon silver ceiling' is not to be dismissed. But for all the acidity in the tone, this passage, and others like it, undeniably display *comic* values as well as darker twists of meaning. The whole Revenge story, even at its most complex, is informed with comic life which is more than simply a placing or

controlling agent, and which is certainly not the 'death motive . . .
the loathing and horror of life itself' of which Eliot complained:

> O, she was able to ha' made a usurer's son
> Melt all his patrimony in a kiss;
> And what his father fifty years told,
> To have consumed, and yet his suit been cold.
>
> I, i (p. 344)

Most of the key speeches and dialogue in *The Revenger's Tragedy*
have a crispness which successfully offsets ostensible decadence and
gloom. The very statements of corruption bristle with a vividly
evoked life and activity, as when Antonio describes his wife's rape
by 'that moth to honour', the Duchess's younger son:

> Last revelling night,
> When torch-light made an artificial noon
> About the court . . .
> . . . in the height of all the revels,
> When music was heard loudest, courtiers busiest,
> And ladies great with laughter – O vicious minute!
> Unfit but for relation to be spoke of:
> Then with a face more impudent than his vizard,
> He harried her amidst a throng of panders,
> That live upon damnation of both kinds,
> And fed the ravenous vulture of his lust.
>
> I, iv (p. 362)

But perhaps the most impressive display of Tourneur's sharply
etched vivacity is in the dialogue generally, the turn of mind
which can constantly enliven the Jacobean vision of lust and corruption. There are representative quotations from most sections of
the play. The important thing is that this attitude of Tourneur's is
pervasive and irrepressible, informing not merely the great
speeches, but also the rapidly conventional exchanges between
characters:

2nd Judge   Confess, my lord,
What moved you to 't?

Younger Son Why, flesh and blood, my lord;
What should move men unto a woman else?   I, ii (p. 347)

Dondolo Madonna, there is one as they say, a thing of flesh and
blood – a man, I take him by his beard, that would very desirously
mouth to mouth with you.
Castiza What's that?
Dondolo Show his teeth in your company.
Castiza I understand thee not.
Dondolo Why, speak with you, madonna . . .   II, i (p. 364)

And so on. There are some dull patches in *The Revenger's Tragedy*
dialogue (as there are in any English play outside Shakespeare's
great tragedies) but they are surprisingly few; and there is a great
deal which suggests comic vivacity rather than the indulgence in
gloom and horror, reflected in the softened texture in the writing,
of plays like Ford's and most of Webster's.

On the other hand, the simpler aspects of the play represent only
one part of Tourneur's position and achievement. The Revenge
story is on the whole good and important writing, but taken by
itself there is little in it which could be described in terms more
specific than 'liveliness', 'comic energy', 'witty and vivacious observation'. Tourneur's deeper vision depends on the movement of
our attention from these simpler Revenge ironies to a richer and
subtler note, though the guiding structure of Revenge morality –
sinners and revengers alike caught in their own nets – constantly
recurs as a dominant factor to the end. Thus the true moral centre
of this play shifts between the two main streams in the writing,
drawing something from each, and issuing finally as a complex in
which simple concepts of sin and salvation contribute substance to,
and are in turn reinvigorated by, and in, a metaphysical play of
mind.

The first speech of Vendice's provides clear evidence of what
Tourneur could achieve by his thickening of the poetic texture at

key moments in the play. With the famous skull in his hand, and meditating like many another on death and revenge, Vendice contemplates the oddness and conceit of lechery in old age, pleasure and lust capped by the death's head: 'Duke! royal lecher! go, grey-haired adultery . . .' Even within this one speech the sense of tension between the two basic elements in the play is marked. The opening depends heavily on conceit and moralistic couplet alike, but the difficulty of Tourneur's position is most clearly indicated by the straining away from the strongly marked rhymes of the beginning ('evil', 'devil') and also from their subsequent though far less obvious reappearance:

> Duke! royal lecher! go, grey-haired adultery!
> And thou his son, as impious steeped as he;
> And thou his bastard, true begot in evil:
> And thou his duchess, that will do with devil.
> Four excellent characters! O, that marrowless age
> Should stuff the hollow bones with damned desires!
> And, 'stead of heat, kindle infernal fires
> Within the spendthrift veins of a dry duke,
> A parched and juiceless luxur.   I, i (pp. 343-4)

By about the middle of the speech we are prepared for dialogue which will range widely from the couplet form and all it implies for Tourneur, but which will at the same time be unable to resist clinching a point or two, though far less noticeably than at the beginning, in just this way:

> And what his father fifty years told,
> To have consumed, and yet his suit been cold.

Finally in this speech, the complexity of tone and attitude is brilliantly demonstrated by the sardonic call to Revenge at the end. There is in this last passage a lightness of touch which would have been beyond almost any later writer in the Revenge tradition, but which here successfully anticipates the neatly etched ironies of Tourneur's plot ('Hum! who e'er knew / Murder unpaid . . .?').

At the same time there is a basically serious, in the sense of intelligent, wit and a final twist at the very end to a still stricter couplet
movement. The extraordinary richness and life of Tourneur at his
best is the richness of intelligence illustrated in those key images of
the 'costly three-piled flesh' and 'the uprightest man (if such there
be / That sin but seven times a day)'. In these more individualistic
sections of the speech there is just the kind of intelligent oddity and
rapid compression of images that one associates with the best of
the Metaphysicals; indeed the tone here is not far removed from
the sardonic gaiety of some of the early Donne 'Songs'. Donne, on
the other hand, whose larger preoccupations were far removed
from Tourneur's, would not have considered the easy but clearly
marked transition to couplet morality both within the speech and,
most notably, at the end. Tourneur's rhymes are often (somewhat
like Donne's in the *Satyres* for example) almost unnoticeable in the
midst of the general tone of conceit and oddity. At the end of this
speech, however, the tone is markedly, though smoothly, changed.
Without marking any separation from the rest of the speech by an
end-stopped line, Tourneur slips immediately and unselfcon-
sciously from the individuality of the conceit of the 'costly three-
piled flesh' to the final couplet:

> . . . for banquets, ease, and laughter
> Can make great men, as greatness goes by clay;
> But wise men little are more great than they.

But if subtlety and crispness of attack are the hall-marks of
Tourneur's dialogue here, what they yield is more interesting still
and far more substantial than these rather generalized critical
terms imply. The life of the verse is concentrated in the rapidity of
mind which gathers implications at once of richness (of 'apparelled
flesh', 'luxury', 'eager performance') and of the exhaustion, the
sterility of incontinence. In context, therefore, even in constantly
recurring words and phrases of an apparently negative kind, like
'parched', 'juiceless', 'marrowless' age, Tourneur is pointing both

to a rejection of sin and to suggestions that a kind of freshness (of 'juice' and 'marrow' in fact) is nevertheless attendant on its presence. A sense of life-in-sterility emerges from the rapid blending of what are perceived at once as separate and combining elements in the verse. For instance in the telescoping wit that 'melts' fifty years of usury in a kiss, we are conscious not merely of the sins of incontinence so vividly imagined, but also of the patient accumulation of solid wealth (the 'patrimony' that took fifty years of usury to build), and, finally, of the energy released by and in the glance of the mind that links the patient usury and the melting kiss. On top of this, the reserves of beauty Vendice is here building up around the figure-image of his dead mistress are extended infinitely by the conceit of the fifty years' wealth consumed *for nothing* ('. . . and yet his suit been cold').

Points like these are further developed in the ensuing dialogue between Vendice and Hippolito and, later, Gratiana and Castiza. Immediately after Vendice's speech, the play moves on in rapidly compressed dialogue which again borrows something of the speed and compression of the Metaphysicals. Tourneur's basic attitudes, on the other hand, are not simply those of any other poet of the time. In *The Revenger's Tragedy* the dominating impression is of an intense poetic energy feeding on and drawing substance from specifically identified sins of lust and policy. The following passage, for instance, produces, from the discussion about hiring villains, the grotesquely conceived but solid image of the row of 'built houses', and also the brief but crisply evoked suggestion that villainy relates to a kind of fertility, of 'unhusking'. The life and imagination of the conceits depend on and spring out of the desperate villainy discussed:

> Last evening, predecessor unto this,
> The duke's son warily inquired for me,
> Whose pleasure I attended: he began
> By policy to open and unhusk me

About the time and common rumour:
But I had so much wit to keep my thoughts
Up in their built houses ...   I, i (p. 345)

But this speech, compared with, for instance, Vendice's opening soliloquy in Act I, is rapidly evocative rather than definitive. Vendice's tongue-in-the-cheek fantasy to the Mother is more clearly revealing of the strengths – and also of the dangers – of Tourneur's view of the Jacobean world as it gathers depth and focus in the developing action of Act II. The central question, as always with Tourneur, concerns the life and energy released by the activities of sin and prostitution:

Would I be poor, dejected, scorned of greatness ...
No, I would raise my state upon her breast;
And call her eyes my tenants; I would count
My yearly maintenance upon her cheeks;
Take coach upon her lip; and all her parts
Should keep men after men, and I would ride
In pleasure upon pleasure.   II, i (p. 367)

Taken literally at face value, the life that Vendice so easily conjures up in his imagination here is disgusting, and Eliot was of course perfectly justified in drawing attention to this. And more important than this surface impression there is, in this and similar key passages, a sense of desperation in the verse, implying a kind of fascination for the possibilities of a world busy with decadence and sin, which, for all the correcting irony, involves Tourneur and the play as well as Vendice:

Now cuckolds are coining, apace, apace, apace, apace!
And careful sisters spin that thread i' the night,
That does maintain them and their bawds i' the day.
                                              II, iii (p. 377)

But combined with Tourneur's tough, witty cyncism, the crispness of movement and image here – one has only to think of the melting sentiment of Ford or Fletcher, for instance, to see the difference – imparts steadiness and control to the handling of what is certainly dangerously evocative material. To put it more accurately: a full response to the dialogue, while still recognizing the rather hectic quality in the verse which constantly threatens the rhythmic control, would add that the life and activity of and in such passages as this constantly works towards converting the horror of *situation* into poetry of imaginative possibility. Thus it is the desperate vigour of 'Now cuckolds are coining . . .', and the whole envisaged activity of prostitution, which finally yield the odd but surely imaginatively strong and stable image of the 'careful sisters' ('careful' in the sense both of 'wary' and 'providing for the future') spinning their thread in the night. There *is* a kind of strength and stability evoked, not merely in the prostitutes themselves, or in prostitution, but in the precision of verse which can borrow energy from the activity condemned in order to impart assurance to the conceit – here strength in the slender thread. Tourneur's mind turns very often towards this kind of wit – a wit for instance which balances the strength of the 'maintaining' activity against the slenderness of the maintaining thread – and this is one sign among many that Elizabethan drama is moving from its early vigour towards more sophisticated and self-conscious writing. Whatever the results of this shift of attention in later writers, however, with Tourneur the narrowing of focus achieves an unexpected strength and solidity. Later in the century the danger will be that irony will become *merely* irony – i.e. a detached comment on a life evoked in other terms – and therefore powerless in the face of the sort of sentimentality and melodrama which dominates writers like Ford, Fletcher and Shirley. Tourneur retains enough sense of the broadness and energy of life – of cuckolds 'coining' and prostitution 'maintaining' – to make his finely conceived wit a substantial thing.

The most impressive example of the *reality* of the connection between Tourneur's conceits and the life from which they spring

is Vendice's speech to the skull in Act III and in particular the
famous lines around which it is built:

> Does the silkworm expend her yellow labours
> For thee? For thee does she undo herself?
> Are lordships sold to maintain ladyships,
> For the poor benefit of a bewitching minute?[1]
> Why does yon fellow falsify highways,
> And put his life between the judge's lips,
> To refine such a thing –   III, iv (p. 392)

This is indeed a favourite Tourneur passage, but I think what most
people respond to in it is merely a 'poetic richness' which is felt –
often all too uncritically – to be characteristically 'Jacobean'. To
see and feel more than is implied in this rather generalized and
romantic attraction to Jacobean verse, it is essential to realize that
nowhere, outside Tourneur, is richness so crisply and so finely
evoked as here. The strength of the verse comes in the first instance
from the vividly created wealth of 'yellow labours', and also from
the sense in which that intense compression and concentration of
wealth also involves the expansiveness of the silkworm's endlessly
creative activity. The compression of the verse focuses an expan-
sive activity. Further, the same images link the concentration of
energy in the silkworm, and at the same time the pointlessness of
such labour, the uses to which it must be put. Thus phrases like
'*expend* her yellow labours' and '*undo* herself for thee' telescope the
two meanings of the silkworm's labour: she is at once 'undoing
herself' in the sense of creating, of spinning silk; and at the same
time 'undoing' in the sense of wasting herself, spinning to no
valuable end ('For the poor benefit of a bewitching minute'). This
is nowhere near Shakespeare's prolific sense for natural activity –
the sophisticated wit of Tourneur clearly has a much narrower
focus than Shakespearean verse – but it does evoke very strongly a
concentrated wealth in nature, even while it insists also on the

[1] The Mermaid text has 'bewildering minute'. Allardyce Nicoll gives 'bewitching,'
(*The Works of Cyril Tourneur*, p. 120).

grotesque disproportion between the 'labour' and the ends to which it must come.

From here the speech develops a further form of imaginative grasp and substance. The 'silkworm' lines have a rhythmic movement which is precise and clear, but which is also alive and urgent. It is an activating as well as a controlling force; and so from the silkworm lines onwards there is an impulse forward which takes in the 'bewitching minute' (itself alive and urgent for all the 'waste' involved) and yields finally that odd but in a way solid and substantial grasp of the *activity* of 'falsifying highways'. Here again Tourneur, in the act of seeing 'falsifying' for what it is, and placing it as clearly as any moralist could, has also gone further and built into his verse that image where our attention is gripped by the physical presence, almost, of the robber 'between the judge's lips'. This is of course not a literal picture, but the strange quality of the verse at this point rapidly and vividly incorporates, as part of its metaphorical insight, the solid fact of the judge's lips and the fellow between them. A sensuously conceived and imagined vision of sin is always crowding in on images of this kind in the play; where they resist it as successfully as they do here it is because they are also drawing strength and substance from it and from the Elizabethan vigour of life which still – in Tourneur – informs it. Thus the wealth of the spinning worms and the sustaining, physical solidity of the later image show Tourneur's art as stable, but as stable because its rapidity of thought is drawing substance from the activity in the life (of prostitution, sin, robbery) condemned.

In all this it is vital to recall again the lightness of tone and conception always at Tourneur's command and which he can rapidly bring to the fore, even in complex passages such as Vendice's address to the skull. The wit has a freshly personal stamp which informs the cynicism – undeniably present at all points of the play – with maturity, life, and imaginative vigour. Thus the 'jingling sententious couplets' almost always yield wit and energy which are in fact the reverse of sententious moral maxims:

> *Vendice* Art thou beguiled now? tut, a lady can,
> As such all hid, beguile a wiser man.
> Have I not fitted the old surfeiter
> With a quaint piece of beauty? Age and bare bone
> Are e'er allied in action. Here's an eye,
> Able to tempt a great man – to serve God:
> A pretty hanging lip, that has forgot now to dissemble.
> Methinks this mouth should make a swearer tremble;
> A drunkard clasp his teeth, and not undo 'em,
> To suffer wet damnation to run through 'em.   III, iv (p. 391)

It is not the overt morality itself that gives this sort of verse its authoritative ring. Tourneur is not saying: 'Look what happens to you if you drink or swear too much.' In fact, of course, the note is much more cynical than this. Even where a speech ends in simple couplets, or where something like a couplet movement has dominated the wit throughout, we are always aware that morality and precept have been qualified by an irony that says, in effect: 'This advice will not be followed except where death makes it a necessity.' It is more cynical than mediaeval morality, with which it is often compared, and which generally hoped more earnestly for, if not conversion, at least a salutary warning. But it is also as productive of imaginative life and vigour as anything in mediaeval drama itself. Certainly it holds its values, and its comment on them, too clearly in mind to be decadent or even, properly speaking, pessimistic.

There is one further point of great importance in the business of defining and evaluating the attitudes behind and in this play. Tourneur's ironic assurance is not merely centred upon Vendice (who would in this case tend merely to be propaganda for the author, with the other characters mediaeval vices and virtues illustrating a point that strictly needed further dramatic exploration), but is spread outwards into his contemplation of other characters and events as well. Most notably Spurio, far from being merely a butt for Tourneur's irony, himself focuses the imaginative vision of the author:

> Faith, if the truth were known, I was begot
> After some gluttonous dinner; some stirring dish
> Was my first father, when deep healths went round,
> And ladies' cheeks were painted red with wine,
> Their tongues, as short and nimble as their heels,
> Uttering words sweet and thick; and when they rose,
> Were merrily disposed to fall again.
> In such a whispering and withdrawing hour,
> When base male-bawds kept sentinel at stair-head,
> Was I stol'n softly.   I, ii (p. 354)

This fantasy of the 'whispering and withdrawing hour' rapidly and intelligently yokes together, just as many of Vendice's speeches do, the attraction and at the same time the dangerous instability of a world of sin as Tourneur sees it. With the exception of Castiza – and even she has her doubts[1] – most of the important characters, in different ways, feel and reflect the power inherent in these mediaeval-Jacobean sins; yet, even in the act of being attracted to them, they see their own danger. Or if they don't see it – and ultimately this does not matter – Tourneur's verse clearly does. A later, shorter example of Tourneur's own irony entering into and informing the mind of one of his named Vices comes from Lussurioso:

> (to Vendice) Ravish me in thine answer: art thou rare?
> Hast thou beguiled her of salvation,
> And rubbed hell o'er with honey? Is she a woman?
>   II, ii (p. 373)

---

[1] See her speech which opens Act II: 'How hardly shall that maiden be beset, / Whose only fortunes are her constant thoughts . . .'; also IV, iv (p. 417) to Gratiana:
> . . . are not you she,
> For whose infect persuasions I could scarce
> Kneel out my prayers, and had much ado
> In three hours' reading to untwist so much
> Of the black serpent as you wound about me?

The remarkable quality of this verse springs from the intelligent complexity of view that makes Lussurioso so mix the attraction and repulsion of sin. Throughout the play, Castiza represents the almost unbelievable essence of purity, so with the mention here of her salvation, heaven and hell are brought together – and enriched – in the paradox: 'Hast thou beguiled her of salvation, / And rubbed hell o'er with honey?' Thinking to forget sin, or disguise its harshness, Lussurioso only succeeds in reminding us once more that, to all these characters, the only attractions left are sins robed in holiness. And more, by choosing a paradox as powerful as this one, Tourneur has succeeded again, as he did so often in the key speeches of Vendice, in demonstrating the power and immediacy of a poetic imagination which is prepared to face the dangers of vice and sin as they are so energetically indulged by the people in this world.

Thus the full statement of Tourneur's meaning in this play involves a consideration of the impact he makes on two levels. It *is*, on the one hand, a brilliant statement of the simple morality of Revenge evolved from Kyd and Marlowe: on the other, Tourneur's final position is seen as a movement from this kind of morality to a more individual one. The resulting thickness of texture is beautifully controlled, and one of the delights of the play is the sense of watching a man handle such difficult transitions firmly – though not of course without being, in places, affected by the consequent dangers of instability and lack of focus. The very intensity of Vendice's preoccupation with his grotesque vision of a world of sin is a foothold for positive writing on Tourneur's part, provided, as is generally but admittedly not always the case, there is the necessary steadiness and control in the writing and organization of the play.

In the last analysis, few I think would want to call this play a tragedy. The point doesn't need enlarging, because it is not necessarily a limiting comment to make on a play. As much could be said, for instance, of *Antony and Cleopatra* which yields an inventive, comic richness probably as valuable as anything in the more purely 'tragic' *Lear*. But nevertheless it is clear that the particular kind of vigour centring on a figure like King Lear is something that later writers – even the later Shakespeare – will not readily be able to evoke, and it is probably truer to our sense of the directions in which Jacobean writing is moving to keep the term 'tragedy' largely for plays in which a powerful *human* sympathy and energy combine to give us a dominating central character. However, the loss of strength and directness of attack involved in the movement towards a wittier, more sophisticated vision of life is certainly not crippling for Tourneur; for one thing, as we have seen, he is by no means out of touch with the robustness of Elizabethan living. The real question at this stage is: What light does Tourneur's particular achievement throw on that of his contemporaries, especially Webster and Middleton?

A comparison between Tourneur's writing and Webster's places *The Revenger's Tragedy* as decidedly more self-assured than either *The White Devil* or *The Duchess of Malfi*.[1] Corrupt though the world is in *The Revenger's Tragedy*, the control in the writing itself, as well as in the outlines of the plot, prevents any sense of, for instance, the 'hideous rashness' of the beginning of *The White Devil*. Even in the earlier of the two great Webster plays, the crowding on of that scene with the carpet, the 'two fair cushions', and Vittoria's dream, sets the tone unmistakably. Despite Flamineo's interjections – more strikingly significant, actually, later on than here – the scene as a whole is not presented with any-

---

[1] In this respect the chronology of the three plays is interesting. In the short space of time that separates *The Revenger's Tragedy* and *The White Devil*, the crispness of Tourneur's writing seems to have vanished almost completely. E. K. Chambers, in *The Elizabethan Stage* (Oxford, 1923), dates the plays as follows: *The Revenger's Tragedy* 1606-7 (vol. IV, p. 42); *The White Devil* 1609-12 (vol. III, p. 509); *The Duchess o Malfi* 1613-14 (vol. III, p. 510).

thing like the correcting irony behind Vendice's and Spurio's lines
in the Tourneur play. Cornelia's morality is too limited and
dogmatic to make much impression on the rest of the scene, and
the verse, especially in the love scene between Vittoria and
Brachiano, lacks the controlling firmness of Tourneur's. In
Brachiano's speeches, in particular, there is a dangerously uncorrected lyricism to which it is difficult to give a meaning, unless
it be an unthinking abandonment on Webster's part to the joys of
the illicit grand passion:

> Sweetly shall I interpret this your dream.
> You are lodged within his arms who shall protect you
> From all the fevers of a jealous husband;
> From the poor envy of our phlegmatic duchess.
> I'll seat you above law, and above scandal;
> Give to your thoughts the invention of delight,
> And the fruition . . .

This is in fact an excellent contrast to speeches of Vendice,
Lussurioso, Spurio and others in *The Revenger's Tragedy*. The
speeches and dialogue of Tourneur's characters, when on ground
roughly similar to this, are almost always cast in a less solemn vein,
a vein, in fact, which is always on the edge of parodying itself –
thus establishing Tourneur's more distanced irony. With *The White
Devil*, had the Flamineo of the house of convertites scene been
present earlier, to pick up and underline the dangerous self-
centredness in lines like 'I'll seat you above law, and above
scandal . . .', things might have been different; though even then
it would be obvious that Tourneur's is the more mature dialogue
since it does not positively need the deflating comments of a
separate character. As it is, in Act I of the Webster play, that particular note from Flamineo is only hinted at, not strongly present
in the verse.

With *The Duchess of Malfi*, the comparison is different and much
more difficult to make. In the first place, the Duchess's essential

innocence (compared, at any rate, with Vittoria and Brachiano) is established early on, and the 'fearful madness' of Act I does not seem to need as much correction or comment as do the more lyrical passages of the early part of *The White Devil*. And then, too, the maturity of vision in Act IV and the commanding position this has over the rest of the material in the play give the whole work more authority than even the trial scene can give to *The White Devil*. Notably, there is a much clearer and more assured irony within Act IV of *The Duchess* than there is in either the trial scene or the scene in the house of the convertites in *The White Devil*. The point is not that one looks for irony in every play written; it should not become a collector's item; but when a play begins as *The White Devil* does, some correcting comment from the author is essential.

The Duchess of Malfi, despite its haphazard design, and its lapses of concentration, looks at first sight a more striking work than *The Revenger's Tragedy*. Certainly, the variations of attitude and tone in Act IV, at least, of *The Duchess* have a greater range than anything in Tourneur, and point towards levels of meaning that were beyond him. On the other hand, when we come to look at *The Duchess*, I think we will find that critical terms like 'pointing towards' a meaning overshadow any confident statements of 'achievement' of meaning and significance. It is very doubtful in fact whether Webster's apparently exploratory and original genius is, in most of his work, anything more than simply a hectic search for new sensations of whatever kind and at whatever the cost in terms of an organic relation of thought to thought, image to image. The only sustained stand of any kind that he seems able to make is in Acts IV and V of *The Duchess*, and the implications of this for the structural unity of the play are of such an unusual kind that we can make no estimate of their success until after looking at the whole matter in detail. I do not think, however, that, even granting *The Duchess* success of a rather unexpected kind, anything in Webster will challenge Tourneur's achievement in *The Revenger's Tragedy*. His represents by far the greatest and most intelligent attack on the old Elizabethan problem of a Revenge ethic. For anything rivalling this in importance in the age we will have to look again to Middleton.

Middleton quite clearly represents, after the definitive Revenge statement of Tourneur, a fresh start in Jacobean writing. Both his success and his comparative limitations are tied to this fact and there is nothing, I think, to be said for the many attempts that have been made to reduce Middleton and Tourneur to one dramatist or to claim any real homogeneity in their plays.[1] Tourneur's constant reliance on conceit, paradox, and moral epigram – this alone puts him in a world different altogether from that even of *The Changeling*, the most conventionally 'Jacobean' of Middleton's good plays. It should also be clearly realized that Tourneur's *involvement* in his world of sin, though it has its dangers, has also some advantages over the greater detachment of Middleton. Middleton could not have conceived either the dangerous attraction of, or the explosive energy in, scenes like Spurio's final yielding to the Duchess's advances: 'O, one incestuous kiss picks open hell ...' Yet on the other hand, obvious though this is, one can perhaps sympathize to some extent with the broad intentions of those who attempt the impossible task of proving Middleton and Tourneur one and the same man. Compared at least with the extravagant splendours of Webster, Tourneur's controlled cynicism looks nearer to Middleton than one might at first have thought. Of course the two men are different – the plays are certainly *very* different – but there is in Tourneur a certain economy in extravagance which gives the two something, at least, in common. Tourneur is nearer to Middleton,

[1] E.g. Samuel Schoenbaum, *Middleton's Tragedies: A critical study* (New York, 1955); and P. B. Murray, 'The authorship of *The Revenger's Tragedy*', *Papers of the Bibliographical Society of America*, LVI:2, 1962, pp. 195-218.

I think, than to Webster, and this note, as well as the clear outlines of his best play, makes him easier, probably, for a modern audience to read than any other Jacobean except Middleton himself. It is difficult to isolate the one element in Tourneur which does relate him to Middleton, because, whatever it is, it is invariably mixed with a grimly Jacobean turn of wit; but it comes out most clearly, I think, in Vendice's famous 'silkworm' speech. Here the balance within the tone is so much in favour of a quick intelligence, observing and grouping facts and fragments of experience, that Jacobean 'tragic' atmosphere is forgotten for the moment in the concentration that one must give to the oddness of these images: the tiny silkworm 'expending' her tremendous labours for women's pleasure, the robber putting himself 'between the judge's lippes', and so on. In most of Webster, the mind is not so constantly or so rapidly at work as this; and of course in Webster the control in the verse, the cynical detachment and assurance, are not nearly so evident.

The more one considers it, the more impressive a work *The Revenger's Tragedy* appears. Certainly its appeal to modern readers is greater and more immediate than anything in Elizabethan drama outside Shakespeare and Middleton. Before looking at Middleton, however, I should like to consider what seems to me the only Webster tragedy with claims to greatness, *The Duchess of Malfi*. The other Webster plays – including *The White Devil* – I shall leave until the final section of this book.

CHAPTER VII

WEBSTERIAN TRAGEDY:
'THE DUCHESS OF MALFI'

The most elusive case in all Jacobean drama is still Webster's.[1] True, thanks to Mr Eliot, Miss Bradbrook and others, a critic of Webster is no longer haunted by the ghost of William Archer. We no longer expect a play to show us pictures of ourselves and people we know. Yet, as Mr Moody Prior points out,[2] there are still difficulties. It is a useful thing to be able to show that the Elizabethans knew what they were doing, but we must be careful lest, by the same token, we succeed only in admitting that a given play lacks the realism (or better, the coherence) which, as a twentieth-century audience, we would normally demand. Or putting it another way, Webster must not merely prove that he was writing differently, but also that he was writing valuably. He cannot, as it were, expect us to take his own standards for granted, if they turn out to be his exclusively and not ours. In this case, then, what is there to be said about Webster's claims to greatness in English drama and about his claims to represent a key point in the developing Jacobean age?

First, it is to *The Duchess of Malfi* (1613-14), rather than to anything else in Webster, that we must turn. If anywhere, it is here that Webster succeeds in forcing his way beyond the pattern set by Tourneur and leaving something more than wreckage in its place. Certainly, the potentialities of Tourneur's beautiful proportion – his accurate sense of the fine balance between wit and simplicity

---

[1] Act, scene and page references to Mermaid Edition throughout.

[2] M. E. Prior, *The Language of Tragedy* (N.Y., 1947). The most telling attack on Websterian tragedy generally is L. G. Salingar's 'Tourneur and the Tragedy of Revenge', Pelican Guide No. 2, pp. 348-53.

– were limited. *The Revenger's Tragedy* was a very great achievement, but it was obviously the high point of an old tradition, not
the beginning of a new. It does no disservice to the play to say
that with no effort of concentration, however great, could its
success have been duplicated in Jacobean England. Its very distinction is that it succeeds in capitalizing on, bringing finally to a
head, the richness promised by the Revenge convention. Now
Webster's task in *The Duchess* is, virtually, to prove that the richness of the Elizabethan world is not yet – as Middleton, for instance, evidently felt it to be – virtually exhausted. If the wreckage
of Tourneur's cunning construction strews the pages of *The
Duchess* and makes them annoyingly untidy, can we yet find something in Webster's obvious vitality, some focusing agent, which
pulls the play together in the end? And if so, what exactly will be
the nature of his success?

I think undoubtedly there is a 'pulling together' in this play,
though it may be that in the end its significance is questionable
because nothing more can be said of it than this. But for the
moment it can best be described as an unusual and unexpected
sense of vitality and order, overtaking the play late in its career
and having nothing very specific to focus on; nothing more,
perhaps, than a tightening and ordering of previously scattered
threads. The key to this development – if it can be called that – is
in the kind of thing Webster pulls off in Act IV. There is not in
this play the continuously subtle intelligence of a Middleton or a
Tourneur; if Webster succeeds at all it is by a sudden and comparatively crude moral awakening, a pulling together of the play
by a massive concentration in the later acts and an effort of will
which as it were defies anyone to say that this is not a unified
work! One of the most important elements in this effort is
Webster's realization, in the very act of writing, that the chaos he
senses in the universe about him has almost destroyed the play
itself; so that there is in consequence, in Act IV in particular, a

sense of his attempt to say something about this, to make a last determined stand against it. Behind and in the closing stages of the play there is a comparatively clumsy but intense moral effort. It is a moral effort made by Webster in the full realization of the universal chaos he is in the act of describing and also in the realization that his own writing has been, up to this stage, brilliant but loosely inadequate.

The practical result of this sudden realization is, for me, the very unusual creation of a single, dominating image in the play; an image made up of the whole of the writing in and surrounding Act IV but having an internal consistency which enables it to be grasped virtually as a single whole. It is not entirely a pictorial image, though 'pictorial' elements (as of Bosola defying the Duchess's curse, the madmen asserting their claims against her, etc.) float to its surface here and there with more or less specificity. But as a whole it is an image felt to rely as much on a sudden concentration of forces as on specific pictures. A very rough analogy – before examining the relevant scenes – would be the kind of thing the classical French tragedy of Racine, at its best, seems to achieve and depend on. For all the obvious differences between the two, Racine and Webster both use, at times, what could be described as a *collective* image, something at once complex and yet massive enough to dominate, without as it were physically penetrating, surrounding action and dialogue. In Racine, I am thinking of images like those of Andromaque remembering her first view of the blood-stained Pyrrhus, wading from battle; or Hermione, pictured as caught in the labyrinth ('palace') of choice that the action has built up around her; or Phèdre's 'C'est Vénus tout entière . . .' Such imagery is obviously different from the penetrating subtlety of Shakespeare's, but it has nevertheless its own peculiar vitality, and its operation sheds light on the way in which an image of deliberate mass and weight can, without obscuring the complexity of a situation, suddenly crystalize issues and thought into a single, nearly *physical* whole. In Racine the concentration on these occasions is such that the resulting image has a sustained solidity, a quality almost of being touchable *as* a single image, and that of a kind that Shakespeare, for instance, would never have aimed at or felt necessary. With all this oddly physical solidity, Racine's imagery also springs from and is in turn anchored to surrounding dialogue and action, though again not in Shakespeare's way. There is no network of finely placed suggestion, leading into and out of the Racinian image. It arises from the action (e.g. of Phèdre drawn towards forces she does not always consciously recognize; of Hermione caught in the impossible choice of action) quickly and spontaneously, to remain a dominating factor in the mind for the rest of the play. It may be, and often is, repeated by the action later on, duplicated in various ways, but it is never seen as something constantly modified by or blended with other suggestions. With all this, the Racinian image is not a simple fact merely, or a static picture of action of the kind you find in, for instance, English Heroic tragedy. Indeed it is not felt as static at all, but rather as an intense concentration which, building up for the moment a kind of solidity, is at the same time seen and felt as an equilibrium, ready at any moment to break down into the threatening chaos never absent from the play's action.

While again disclaiming any parallel between Racine's writing as a whole and Webster's, I put forward this analogy as suggesting ways in which we can look at the relations between Act IV of *The Duchess* and the rest of the play. Another analogy – though for obvious reasons even less complete – would be the 'castle' image in *The Changeling*. In all these cases we are presented with a complexity which is a single image in the sense that we look down through its surface to an interior gathering of forces, focus complexity in one single and comparatively sustained act of the mind. Webster, I think, never rises to Racine's heights; but it is only in terms of an activity of the Racinian kind, representing for

Webster a late artistic and moral awakening, that anything at all can be made of the play's brilliant confusion.

Before trying to substantiate this in the detail of Acts IV and V, what of the earlier Acts? They represent a brilliant but brittle fragmentation of experience, and the danger obviously is that the fragmentation will be too complete for the concentration of Act IV to piece together. But on the other hand, and without denying what critics have repeatedly said about the unsatisfactory quality of these early acts, is there not occasionally, in their very instability, a sense of expectancy which may possibly be relevant to later developments – assuming for the moment that there *are* later developments? From the beginning of the play I think one senses the need for something which is certainly not yet there but which the urgency of the plot and the brilliant but scattered fragments of 'character' description from Bosola and others seem to expect.

The first two Acts take their tone in this matter very much from Bosola; and this not merely because he is an important character, but because the very writing itself seems to be cast in his mould. The play at this stage moves from one of his sardonic homilies to another and seems to halt there expectantly. In the very first scene, after Antonio's moral speech about the French court, Bosola takes charge of the action with his sketch of the Cardinal and Ferdinand:

> He and his brother are like plum-trees that grow crooked over standing-pools; they are rich and o'erladen with fruit, but none but crows, pies, and caterpillars feed on them . . .
>
> i, i (p. 135)

The speech develops into Bosola's conceit of the soldier's reward, a pair of crutches:

> . . . but for a soldier that hazards his limbs in a battle, nothing but a kind of geometry is his last supportation. . . . Ay, to hang in a fair pair of slings, take his latter swing in the world upon an honourable pair of crutches, from hospital to hospital . . .

In the play these speeches are too self-contained, too stiff in outline to allow of any developing dialogue. On the other hand, within each self-contained *sententia* there is, bottled up though it may be, a strong sense of life, of activity. In each case the general picture is one of decadence, but the *details* are alive with the paradox of richness fed upon by crows and caterpillars, of the precision of geometry brought alive by the movement to death. It is the same with Bosola's two speeches about women in Act II. The 'Old Lady' to whom these are addressed represents the high point of Webster's beautiful disregard for naturalism and 'functional' characters in the drama. She has no conceivable relation to the plot and her two appearances simply and frankly serve as cues for Bosola. And again, all is in the tone of the rapid grotesquerie of the malcontent; static in outline, though, within each self-contained homily, eagerly and restlessly searching out the oddities of the Jacobean vision of sex:

> Your wife's gone to Rome: you two couple, and get you to the wells at Lucca to recover your aches. I have other work on foot. II, i (p. 154)

During Acts I and II, everyone takes their cue from Bosola in this matter and gradually a sense of frenzied activity (if not yet of developing and expanding action) spreads from within the separate speeches to the field of the play at large. First Antonio, following his sketch of the French king and court, gives us his view of Bosola. Then Bosola himself enters, scattering pen-sketches of himself and others with every sentence. Often, indeed, a sentence is enough for Webster at this point of the play: 'I was lured to you.' There is no need to multiply examples further, or to worry over the old question of Webster's commonplace book technique which is said to have caused all this. The main point is to notice the restlessness of it all and how far into the very essence of the dialogue it extends in the early part of the play, covering a range from Bosola's long speeches to single phrases, and short pictures of the kind that spring constantly from the Cardinal and Ferdinand:

> Hypocrisy is woven of a fine small thread,
> Subtler than Vulcan's engine . . .   I, i (p. 144)

Thus the action, strung on a slender but rapidly moving plot, assumes the character of a swarm of grotesque visions or cameos, from various of the speakers, all vying with each other for the truth (e.g. who is right about the Duchess: Bosola? Antonio? Ferdinand?).

The deliberately slender action on which these early scenes and cameos are strung deserves special notice. It is of course intermittent and carelessly rapid: the wooing, the 'marriage', the birth of a son, and Bosola's intelligence reaching Rome all taking place before the end of Act II. Moreover all this seems to happen rather detachedly, hurried on in two or three scenes in the intervals of the grotesquerie introduced and led by Bosola. Even the Duchess's falling into labour, which is well on into Act II, is cast in terms of the 'apricocks' fantasy. In all, our attention is divided between a self-conscious brilliance from Webster which takes every opportunity to show itself, regardless of any continuing and co-ordinating action, and a sense in the story of the marriage itself of a desperate urgency which demands a resolution of some kind. Nothing has yet decided the play's course, or provided it with any integrating idea of substance. On the other hand, it is just possible that the restless jostling for position that Webster's images (held in this kind of action) exhibit may yet leave the door open for a later focusing agent, if such is to be provided. The nervous vitality of the writing, at present in danger of running to waste, is yet strong enough and rich enough not, perhaps, to be entirely lost.

I do not think there is much to change the texture of the dialogue or action from this point until at any rate the end of Act III (where

Bosola and the Duchess begin their debates). Clifford Leech[1] and others note, in the last scene of Act I and scene ii of Act II, the tentative introduction of a warmer and possibly more naturalistic tone into the writing. Personally, I don't see how it is possible to put so much stress on this sort of thing at this stage of the play. If warmth and humanity are there, it is generally only in a phrase or so, suddenly and clumsily introduced:

> *Duchess* Did you ever in your life know an ill painter
> Desire to have his dwelling next door to the shop
> Of an excellent picture-maker? 'twould disgrace
> His face-making, and undo him. I prithee,
> When were we so merry? My hair tangles ...   III, ii (p. 176)

This, at least, is very stilted. Webster is not finding it easy to extend the range of his writing. Like the following (from Act I) its importance is not that of achieved fact or attitude but rather of a portent: the task Webster is attempting is, it seems, not to write an academic exercise in horror, but to stretch the audience's attention from the brilliantly conventional to the more difficult and intangible world of naturalism or near-naturalism in feelings and emotions:

> *Duchess* Good, dear soul,
> Leave me; but place thyself behind the arras,
> Where thou mayst overhear us. Wish me good speed;
> For I am going into a wilderness
> Where I shall find nor path nor friendly clue
> To be my guide.   I, i (p. 146)

Later in the same scene the Duchess continues to use the Jacobean turn of phrase that Webster scarcely ever abandons, but gradually simpler feelings emerge as well, and there is indeed a sense that the dialogue is struggling, though as yet feebly, to do

---

[1] C. Leech, *John Webster: a critical study* (London, 1951). For a full study of the play, along lines which in many ways resemble Leech's, see Gunnar Boklun, *The Duchess of Malfi: Sources, Themes, Characters* (Harvard, 1962). See also Robert Ornstein, *The Moral vision of Jacobean Tragedy*, pp. 140-150.

something other than provide cues for the beautifully turned aphorisms which, otherwise, dominate the early part of the play. The most interesting passage begins with the by now familiar twists and paradoxes:

> *Duchess* Now she pays it.
> The misery of us that are born great!
> We are forced to woo, because none dare woo us;
> And as a tyrant doubles with his words,
> And fearfully equivocates, so we
> Are forced to express our violent passions
> In riddles and in dreams, and leave the path
> Of simple virtue . . .

– changes there to a tone that is simpler though still based on paradox:

>   Go, go brag
> You have left me heartless; mine is in your bosom;
> I hope 'twill multiply love there . . .

– and ends up, in verse that has abandoned almost all conceit, with a fresh and sincere (though significantly rash) appeal from the Duchess:

>   Sir, be confident;
> What is't distracts you? This is flesh and blood, sir;
> 'Tis not the figure cut in alabaster
> Kneels at my husband's tomb. Awake, awake, man!
> I do here put off all vain ceremony,
> And only do appear to you a young widow
> That claims you for her husband, and, like a widow,
> I use but half a blush in't.   I, i (p. 149)

The sense of 'hideous rashness' of the *White Devil* kind here very nearly cancels out the effect of any new development. Certainly I think it is too much to say that new values – of warmly felt humanity – have clearly and confidently entered the play. On the other hand there are signs of a more intelligent give-and-take in the dialogue, a deepening of the play's thought on central issues.

But signs only. For the rest of the first half of the play we return to the detached, expectant brilliance of the opening. There are moments so brilliant that a reader is almost prepared to forgive Webster no matter – one feels – how far he wants to go in the vein of Jacobean affectation. When Ferdinand, after his sadistic frenzies at the end of Act II, comes in, at first seemingly prepared to forgive or at any rate forget, the two juxtaposed sentences at the end of the exchange between him and the Duchess make the re- motely conventional world of Italian courts and intrigue spring suddenly and brilliantly to life:

> *Ferdinand* Go, be safe
> In your own innocency.
> *Duchess* (aside) O blessed comfort!
> This deadly air is purged.   (*Exit*)
> *Ferdinand* Her guilt treads on
> Hot-burning coulters.   III, i (p. 173)

Until Webster himself begins to have doubts, it is difficult to see any objections to this. On the other hand, once it becomes obvious, in Act III, scene ii, Act IV, and Act V, that he has doubts, the whole of the brilliant early dialogue falls into a different per- spective. Often, it is in fact not dialogue at all. The exchange quoted above is really an exception, in the midst of verse cut up into vignettes that seem to be there not because they have a dramatic relation one to another, but, almost, so that they can be lifted out of the text and admired for their own cunning:

> *Pescara* The Lord Ferdinand laughs.
> *Delio* Like a deadly cannon
> That lightens ere it smokes.   III, iii (p. 188)

Here the form of the dialogue is only distantly related to the real business of drama. For all its brilliance, the play still notably lacks the kind of continuously developing intelligence and order which are the mark of a dramatist's having something vital to say. At this stage of the play it is only possible to say, again, that the 'dialogue' is *so* restlessly brilliant that, given the hint of the closing scene of Act I, one would expect a great playwright to realize its deficiencies and at the same time its extraordinary, largely ill-directed vitality, and do something about this.

Act IV is the key to the precise kind of success this play can command. Up to now, the play has still lacked the organizing principles that its brilliance seems to demand. The looseness of texture is further marked, on a fairly superficial plane, by the offhand way in which Webster announces the Duchess's surprisingly enlarged family;[1] by Antonio's silly defence of a cowardice on his part which otherwise would have passed for what it is, a transparent device to get him off the stage; and by the clumsy business of the dumbshow in Act II, scene iv. Act IV changes this, and the point even of the unsatisfactory early scenes of the play begins perhaps to be established when, early in scene i, the Duchess is isolated in the midst of utter decadence and disorder. The point of Ferdinand's instability, Bosola's gloating over corruption, the Cardinal's venality, is now seen to be that Webster is asking, or, to put it more accurately, has at last got round to asking, what of the person who, surrounded by all this, *has* some individuality, integrity, wholeness? It is not, as perhaps putting it this way might suggest, a simple question of the Duchess (and us) *versus* the rest. With the entry of the madmen, in particular, Webster's ability is seen to be one which can move the Duchess in and out of the world of chaos and fantasy which surrounds her. She is of it and not of it. Part of Webster's real point, obscured in the beginning of the play, is now becoming clear. It is another twist to the problem familiar to the Shakespeare of *Much Ado* and the last plays: What is, after all, the status and nature of 'innocence' in a guilty or disorganized or stupid world? It can hardly stand alone – it must in

[1] Bradbrook, *Themes and Conventions of Elizabethan Tragedy*, pp. 209-10.

some sense derive from the world it lives in: what then of Hero, Imogen, Hermione, the Duchess?

These, it may be said, are Webster's general preoccupations, or some of them, in the play. To see the real nature of his achievement, and place it precisely, we must go deeper into the dominant Act IV and watch the new alertness in the writing and the tautness that begins to gather up images that were previously only barely related to each other. With a new give-and-take in the dialogue (perceptible also in Act III as it builds up towards the 'prison' scenes of Act IV) it becomes in fact suddenly possible for Webster – where before he had been content with fragments of experience jostling for position – now more clearly to conceive of action in terms of a developing scene. There is still a brittle quality about some of the dialogue – its very life and liveliness come partly from this – but the new sense of developing action has relaxed and softened its texture considerably. One speech leads more easily now into another; the edges of what previously tended to be self-contained pronouncements from characters are now sufficiently yielding to fit into each other and facilitate a play of mind over a developing situation:

> *Duchess* . . . and yond's an excellent property
> For a tyrant, which I would account mercy.
> *Bosola* What's that?
> *Duchess* If they would bind me to that lifeless trunk,
> And let me freeze to death.
> *Bosola* Come, you must live.
> *Duchess* That's the greatest torture souls feel in hell,
> In hell, that they must live, and cannot die . . .   IV, i (pp. 199–200)

If some of this reminds us still of the quality of self-containedness in, say, Bosola's brilliant early dialogue, there is nevertheless plenty to re-establish quickly the relaxation and flexibility essential to the play's new developments:

Duchess Portia, I'll new kindle thy coals again,
And revive the rare and almost dead example
Of a loving wife.
Bosola O, fie! despair? remember
You are a Christian.
Duchess The church enjoins fasting:
I'll starve myself to death.
Bosola Leave this vain sorrow.
Things being at the worst begin to mend . . .
Duchess Good comfortable fellow,
Persuade a wretch that's broke upon the wheel
To have all his bones new set . . .   IV, i (p. 200)

The flexibility in this dialogue is important. What it yields in
the way of a developing imagery-in-action is far more so. Bosola's
opening speech in Act IV begins the snow-balling process which
gathers to the tautness of Act IV seen as a unified whole: we are
now being presented with a series of consistently held pictures of
the Duchess imprisoned by, and taking part in, a world of precisely defined violence and horror:

Bosola . . . I'll describe her.
She's sad as one long used to't, and she seems
Rather to welcome the end of misery
Than shun it; a behaviour so noble
As gives a majesty to adversity:
You may discern the shape of loveliness
More perfect in her tears than in her smiles:
She will muse four hours together . . .   IV, i (p. 197)

This romantic image of the Duchess is never allowed to rest unqualified (Bosola's next speech is on 'those pleasures she's kept
from' and the English mastiffs 'grown fierce with tying'). But on
the other hand it is important to see that neither is it developed
quite in the way made familiar by Shakespeare (for instance in
plays like *Macbeth* and *Antony and Cleopatra*). Instead of changing
and developing with a flood of rapidly assembling images of the
Shakespearean kind, it bobs to the surface of the dialogue again

and again in Act IV, and the amount of correction or modification we are forced to make to it each time is small. Rapidly it assumes a very familiar outline in our minds, and we build up a composite notion or image of the 'imprisoned' Duchess, an image which almost always includes Bosola, or other of Ferdinand's agents, acting on and confronting her strongly asserted attitudes:

> *Duchess* If they would bind me to that lifeless trunk,
> And let me freeze to death.
> *Bosola* Come, you must live . . .

> *Duchess* What are you?
> *Servant* One that wishes you long life.
> *Duchess* I would thou wert hanged for the horrible curse
> Thou hast given me: I shall shortly grow one
> Of the miracles of pity. I'll go pray; –
> No, I'll go curse . . .   IV, i (p. 200-1)

> *Duchess* I am Duchess of Malfi still.
> *Bosola* That makes thy sleeps so broken . . .   IV, ii (p. 207)

This is not to say that Act IV is *literally* one single image; rather, as we read it through (and it includes a variety of material ranging from the presentation of the lunatics, to Bosola's doggerel speeches, and the psychological oddity of Ferdinand's behaviour) gradually and all the time this dominant, repeated image of the Duchess imprisoned in horrors grows on us as a single experience. It is never in abeyance, but with us all the time we are reading of other events, waiting for a further assertion, a further clarification. We see it, I think, partly in pictorial terms (mainly of the Duchess striking attitudes: 'What do I look like now . . .'), partly in less tangible terms – focused on but not limited by the pictorial – of effort and the force of assertion necessary not only to confront chaos, but to take an active part in it. The process is one of sharper and sharper definition; a series of visions of the Duchess's splendour and singular force, held in deliberate poses ('I am Duchess of

Malfi still') but twisted inevitably slightly out of focus by the chaos surrounding *and invading* the picture ('That makes thy sleeps so broken . . .'). It is indeed something like the twisted magnificence of Phèdre, driven by forces she cannot control but which she, embodying the action of the play, must both battle against and rely on (simply because, however dangerous, they are the forces underlying action). In Webster the picture – in so far as we have a specific picture – of the Duchess changes slightly with each renewed assertion in Act IV, but the basic idea remains, and it is not far from Racine's own: a figure or personalized image, asserting itself against the engulfing chaos, failing to struggle free, indeed on the contrary deriving (as a total image rather than merely as a person or character) great force and power from the twisting violence of the 'background' (Ferdinand, Bosola, the madmen, etc.). And all this, present throughout Act IV, is brought to sudden focus and sustained by the repetitive nature of the image, gathering the figures together into an increasingly familiar *scena* (e.g. of the Duchess responding to Bosola's jeers, or surrounded by the madmen, or presented with her 'tombmaker').

It is very necessary I think to see the issues thus in terms of a sort of collectivized imagery. Otherwise we are reduced to seeing the Duchess as a simply heroic figure (which she is not); or, as Clifford Leech more subtly puts it, seeing her as the representative of humanity, driven, in the face of a chaotic universe, to 'boasting', for she is so alone that nothing else is possible. Certainly, this is one of the constant suggestions in the play; but putting it in terms like these of purely personalized endeavour – man *versus* the universe – is I think to limit and sentimentalize the play's achievement. In fact the chaos and the individual are never separate and consequently they are never simply chaos or simply individual man. We see the total situation as a dominant image in which the figure of the Duchess, posing in familiar attitudes, is both tainted (or twisted) by the bitterness of Bosola and at the same time borne up, heightened in significance by a kind of sympathy with the violence she opposes:

> I'll tell thee a miracle;
> I am not mad yet, to my cause of sorrow;
> The Heaven o'er my head seems made of molten brass,
> The earth of flaming sulphur, yet I am not mad.
> I am acquainted with sad misery
> As the tanned galley-slave is with his oar ...
>
> IV, ii (p. 203)

Putting the position now in terms of the development of Act IV as a whole, there is a central sequence of scenes which presents us with the figure of the Duchess contacting and focusing certain closely allied elements in the Websterian world; elements, that is to say, both of the 'real' or normal, and of the unstable or chaotic. That this story is seen on an imagistic as well as a personal level, so far from worrying us, should be the source of the play's interest.

First, the Duchess's famous curse and Bosola's ironic reply give us a typical and vivid picture of her function as a personalized image-in-action, sharpening and deepening Webster's vision of the dominating issues in his play:

Duchess I shall shortly grow one
Of the miracles of pity. I'll go pray; –
No, I'll go curse.
Bosola O, fie!
Duchess I could curse the stars.
Bosola O, fearful.
Duchess And those three smiling seasons of the year
Into a Russian winter: nay, the world
To its first chaos.
Bosola Look you, the stars shine still.
Duchess O, but you must
Remember, my curse hath a great way to go, – IV, i (pp. 200-1)

If there is sympathy for the Duchess here – sympathy for the 'lonely representative of mankind'– it is a severely qualified one.

Indeed, 'sympathy' and 'pity' seem quite the wrong terms to apply to the Duchess in this scene. For the one thing Webster seems concerned to stress as far as the Duchess is concerned is the energetic violence of her behaviour at this particular stage. She is infected, 'possessed' (almost in the Racinian sense of the term) by the chaos which she, therefore, partly represents. The posing, 'theatrical' attitude at the heart of the image of the Duchess helps to display her as not only protesting against chaos but also as representing it, enacting it; and that, at times, with relish:

> And those three smiling seasons of the year
> Into a Russian winter: nay, the world
> To its first chaos.

It is important to see that Bosola's reply ('Look you, the stars shine still') is represented only as a partial truth in this situation, a correction to the Duchess on a purely personal level. It places but does not go anywhere near destroying the powerful vision of the 'Russian winter' and the 'first chaos' which the verse – remarkably firm and clear at this point, and in the sudden ironic shift to 'O, but you must remember . . .' – has established. The wildness of the Duchess's gestures and actions, for which she is rightly rebuked by Bosola, is one aspect of the scene; touching this, indeed overreaching it in general significance, is the image of violence at the heart of things, rapidly but very sharply painted in that other aspect of the Duchess's behaviour now constantly before us, her *participation* in chaos.

Perhaps this will be made clearer if we look at Webster's rapid introduction of the next picture of the Duchess, grouped this time with the madmen. Again, she introduces the scene herself:

> *Duchess* Who do I look like now?
> *Cariola* Like to your picture in the gallery . . .
> Or rather like some reverend monument
> Whose ruins are even pitied.
> *Duchess* Very proper;

And Fortune seems only to have her eyesight
To behold my tragedy . . . IV, ii (pp. 203-4)

Immediately after this, the madmen enter ('Your brother hath intended you some sport . . .'!) and the Duchess is surrounded by
still further representatives of chaos and instability. It is important
to realize just how closely the chorus of madmen touch the
Duchess. They are not merely a Jacobean divertissement to amuse
the audience in a way the audience expected to be amused. Their
speeches are in fact an accusation. They challenge the Duchess on
whether or not she can escape being in a sense one of them. All
their talk is a fantasy of lust and sin. Webster's point I think is this:
The Duchess has certainly not committed the sins of defilement of
which the deranged Ferdinand accuses her. She is rash – what else
could she be in the face of Ferdinand's and the Cardinal's attitude? –
but she is innocent of these crimes. Yet (Webster seems to be saying)
so all-embracing and inevitable is the corruption with which she is
surrounded that in a sense she belongs to the brothers' world –
certainly to no other – and some of the mud must stick. It has
now become impossible to disentangle the image of the Duchess
from the images of surrounding chaos on which she, indeed, has
come partly to depend. The lunatics are of course innocent of any
premeditation; they are symbols of what motivates, or what may
motivate, the unconscious:

> Hell is a mere glass-house, where the devils are continually
> blowing up women's souls on hollow irons, and the fire never
> goes out. IV, ii (p. 205)

It is a questioning process, in fact: Does not this fantasy of the
unconscious apply to everyone in the world as it has been consistently, if untidily, presented in the play? Like the Duchess, the
madmen too suffer, probably for no real cause. Is her pillow, too,
stuffed with a litter of porcupines? Again, and more obviously
now, this is the figure-image of the Duchess immersed in the
violence – and energy – at the heart of this play.

149

The final development is a renewal of the problem in terms of the Duchess-Bosola configuration. Initially, and immediately after the dance of eight madmen ('with music answerable thereto'!) the image of the Duchess reasserts itself with the by now very familiar theatrical pose:

I am Duchess of Malfi still.

But Bosola again reminds us (and her) that she cannot escape being a part of the chaos that surrounds everyone in this play; and, most significantly, his cutting reply brings even the Duchess to a quieter acceptance of this fact. The scene as a whole, indeed, emerges here briefly from the mist of sin and error, places this quickly in the light of a new directness of tone, and then, as quickly, relapses into fantasy. Much of the remainder of Act IV depends on a movement of this kind, though focused still on the figure of the Duchess herself. She moves in and out of the horror-fun world presented in the main by Bosola, now relying on it for some temporary refuge and support, now repudiating it and accepting, in quieter tone, the inevitability of destruction:

> *Bosola* Glories, like glow-worms, afar off shine bright,
> But looked to near, have neither heat nor light.
> *Duchess* Thou art very plain.
> *Bosola* My trade is to flatter the dead, not the living:
> I am a tomb-maker.
> *Duchess* And thou comest to make my tomb?
> *Bosola* Yes. IV, ii (p. 207)

The note of acceptance, of looking directly at and grappling firmly with the shifting horrors that the Websterian world can so effortlessly create – this note is shared now even by Bosola: 'My trade is to flatter the dead, not the living . . .' The final scene of the Duchess's life is therefore played out as one which shifts between (and in doing so yokes together) the calmly real and the violently fantastic in Webster's world. At times the fantasy lifts slightly, and the new note of directness and acceptance underlines Webster's firm rejection of any evasion, any sentimentality:

Bosola This is your last presence-chamber.
Cariola O my sweet lady!
Duchess Peace; it affrights not me.
Bosola I am the common bellman,
That usually is sent to condemned persons
The night before they suffer.
Duchess Even now thou said'st
Thou wast a tomb-maker.   IV, ii (p. 208)

Certainly Webster's manipulation of tone is not faultless here; but at last it is possible to say that the mistakes, like the Duchess's 'syrup for my children' speech, are corrected by the clear-sightedness with which Webster constantly surprises. The horror invading the Duchess's image is never forgotten, but is now firmly controlled:

Cariola Hence, villains, tyrants, murderers! alas!
What will you do with my lady? – Call for help.
Duchess To whom? to our next neighbours? they are mad-folks.
                    IV, ii (p. 209)

After this, as protective colouring, the Duchess reassumes some of her old theatricality and blends with the frightening, irresponsible world of conceit around her ('What would it pleasure me to have my throat cut / With diamonds . . .?'), and the scene, or the Duchess's part in it, closes with a slightly defiant acceptance of death. To the end, Webster's attitude is surprisingly detached. Ironically anticipating Ferdinand's repentance, the Duchess dies with a message to the brothers:

Go tell my brothers, when I am laid out,
They then may feed in quiet.   IV, ii (p. 210)

And after her death suggestions of greatness and ironic qualifications continue inexorably to mingle. They comment on and modify each other, as Bosola with grim irony comments on Ferdinand's beautiful but inaccurate epitaph:

> *Ferdinand* Cover her face; mine eyes dazzle; she died young.
> *Bosola* I think not so; her infelicity
> Seemed to have years too many.   IV, ii (p. 212)

Thus the concentration of Act IV completes its task of attempting, by a singular effort of will and imagination, to pull together the nervous fragments of the earlier sections. The image of the imprisoned Duchess is now established and at this point joins with a brilliantly written last act in an attempt finally to sum up the play's shifting attitudes.

Like the rest of the play, Act V depends upon the dominating and organizing impact of Act IV. With the death of the Duchess, the disintegration of the brothers' world is absolute. The play then resumes the tone of impressionistic horror of the opening scenes, but now with more direction and purpose behind it. For one thing, the writing is now less coldly brilliant than it was, in Acts I and II especially. There are not so many long set speeches and the dialogue consequently has more flexibility and power. Enough of the spontaneity of IV survives to give, quite rightly, a deal of sympathy for all the figures mixed up in the falling apart of whatever unity there was in Webster's world. Early, Webster was only half sure of what he wanted to do with the brilliant evocation of decadence he could so easily command. Now, having got where he did in Act IV, he can simply state the fact of complete disorder, and state also his feeling of pity for almost everybody involved. For instance, whereas earlier a speech like the Cardinal's at the beginning of scene v would have been longer and more inclined to indulge bravura and conceit, here, for all its brilliance, there is somehow a simple directness, even in the middle of the Jacobean horror:

> I am puzzled in a question about hell:
> He says, in hell there's one material fire . . .

The Cardinal is alive here, in a sense in which he wasn't earlier. He speaks personally, not merely with depersonalized brilliance, and he really is puzzled in a question about hell. The impact is the greater because, looking at the nihilism that follows Act IV, so, indeed, is everyone else, including, notably, the mad Ferdinand:

> Strangling is a very quiet death . . .

Included in the beautifully Jacobean horror of this, there is a grimly striking note of genuine feeling. This is, in fact, the play's and Webster's most urgently terrifying discovery: poetic horror-fun of this kind *can* uncover real emotions and attitudes. In this way, again, Act IV has given the play a moral point of reference it would otherwise have lacked.

All this is clinched by the deaths of Bosola, Ferdinand and the Cardinal. Bosola's view of the world as a 'general mist of error . . .' is at last recognized to be correct by the survivors. All of them recognize failure, weakness, extinction, and recognize it, if anything, with clearer sight than Bosola himself originally did. There is less fantasy now. When the Duchess died, many questions were left open. In a sense they still are: What is after all her particular status and worth in this kind of situation? But in the case of the other three, some termination, some finality is there. Within the often fascinating Jacobean irony, there is with each of them a recognition of the rightness and accuracy of the way the action of the play has finally developed. The Cardinal is clearest and simplest of all:

> And now, I pray, let me
> Be laid by and never thought of.

In terms of the emptiness that is awaiting people like the Cardinal, the play here achieves a pretty clear-sighted statement of the emptiness of Webster's world in its entirety. The irony and clarity of the verse raise the whole thing above the pessimism that has been lying in wait for Webster all through Act V (if we believe Eliot, all through the play).

In the most general terms, one could say that the problem of Elizabethan tragedy up to and including Webster has been the relation of order to chaos, of life to destruction. Taking this one step further, I think it is also true that all the plays we have considered so far accept as a matter of course, though in varying degrees, the complexity of this relation; that is to say none of them – except possibly *Tamburlaine* – states the problem simply in terms of a 'mankind *versus* the universe' or 'man *versus* the irrational' formula. It seems basic to the Elizabethans that the world against which the heroes struggle is also and at the same time the world that nourishes and supports them, even if only by a tide of violence and destruction. Thus there is a sense in which Hieronymo, Lear, the Duchess and others are possessed by, activated by a 'madness' which is surely revealed as an energizing force in the universe:

> . . . And thou, all-shaking thunder,
> Strike flat the thick rotundity o' the world!
> Crack nature's moulds, all germens spill at once
> That make ingrateful man!

And at its best, as here and in *Macbeth* for instance, the richness of the dramatic verse is in no way limited to the effect it has on us through the protagonist. Nature is alive, a force on its own, as well as something channelled through character. We respond to the thing itself as an active substance in the drama, one particular manifestation of which is seen and felt on the plane of people or characters submitted to the probing action of the play.

Now I think a true measure of a dramatist's importance would be the degree to which in each play he can bring these issues to the point of a fresh evaluation and definition. They will never, of course, be 'defined' in the logical sense – the very attempt would be absurd. On the other hand, we do expect more of a great drama than that it should simply express or dramatize 'conflict' and 'storm'; more, even, than that it should simply 'explore' or 'probe' a given problem. Admittedly the drive towards destruction, the urge to strip mankind of all its old values does indeed seem to be an essential part of tragedy, especially of a tragedy like *Lear*: but even in plays of this radically enquiring kind – plays which we may feel are at the furthest remove from the more all-embracing activity of comedy – this urge to annihilation is still not 'the whole truth'.[1] A great dramatist, in short, always takes an evaluative attitude, and this to particular issues and problems. A full reading of *Lear* or *Macbeth* reveals not a sense of 'purgation' or 'ennoblement', but a fresh and particular set of values in living which were not there before. They did not, in fact, exist, in or out of our consciousness, though of course they are in part the result of a playwright's observing and collating things which did.

The Duchess of Malfi is a key point of reference with regard to this distinctive quality in Elizabethan and Jacobean plays. It seems to me the only Webster tragedy which clearly escapes the charges of decadence so often levelled against the Jacobeans generally. 'Decadence' proper is the result of dramatists thinking of themselves merely as lesser copies of a Shakespeare or a Marlowe, content therefore to play upon worn-out Elizabethan themes and attitudes; content also to allow any and every pattern of emotions suggested by the social milieu to subjugate their awareness of the changing demands life makes on writers. *The Duchess* is substantial and individual *enough*, I think, to prevent our seeing it as merely a lesser play cut in the Shakespearean (or any other) mould. In *The Duchess* Webster has something to say, and it is still – as it is not, for instance, in Ford – something of value. Generally speaking

---

[1] The phrase is taken from A. Huxley, who was applying it differently: 'Tragedy and the Whole Truth', *Music at Night*.

that decadence of tragedy which we shall be discussing in the final section of this book hovers around *The Duchess*, but doesn't actively invade the play. On the other hand, after *The Duchess*, only Middleton presents experience freshly enough to stand against what has now become a pronounced softening of the core of English drama. Indeed, as I hope to show, Webster's earlier tragedy, *The White Devil*, fascinating though it is, points all too clearly the way things were to go.

The case for *The Duchess of Malfi*, then, is simply that, centring as it does on the 'prison' image of Act IV, it succeeds in presenting a new and particular attitude to living, a fresh statement of the familiar Elizabethan problem of clarity in chaos, vitality in destruction. Moreover Webster's success comes because of, not despite the decadence and disintegration that threaten him at every turn. If we see him merely as clinging to his place on a slippery ladder of decadence, however *high* a place beneath Shakespeare we accord him, we will miss the individuality to which he was led by very force of circumstance. The success of his play lies in the fact that the disintegrating forces at work on and in the early scenes, appearing there as restlessness and energy fragmented, are challenges to Webster, manifestations in fact of the same energizing violence on which he later has to rely in order to build and focus the dominant image: the image of the Duchess placed as both fighting against and responding to her environment. A cruder (and a vaguer) point than any of Shakespeare's, this is nevertheless more than a simple warding-off of decadence, or a point made *faute de mieux*. For his final view of the Duchess image, Webster draws on the very forces he is also seeking to control: the shifting horror of Bosola's 'mists of error'; the madmen's vivid and alive presentation of lust and sin; the Duchess's own sense of immediate response to the 'heaven' of 'molten brass'. The result is an image of impressive greatness, but greatness defined partly in terms of anarchy and violence.

Nothing else in Webster is as good as this; nothing else is as clearly a valuable and evaluating statement about the Elizabethan world order. On the other hand, even Webster's best play scarcely competes, I think, with the best of Middleton. Even granting Webster's success in *The Duchess of Malfi*, it is Tourneur and Middleton, writing almost at opposite extremes of the Jacobean age, who dominate drama of the period. Webster wrote one great play, but its structure and development betray too much strain at key points – i.e. even at the points which define its success – for it to carry real weight in the Jacobean era. Before attempting to justify this statement further, I should like to consider in more detail the kind of drama that Middleton wrote.

CHAPTER VIII

NATURALISTIC COMEDY AND TRAGEDY 'A CHASTE MAID IN CHEAPSIDE' AND 'WOMEN BEWARE WOMEN'

Middleton's comic world is not far removed from his tragedy, especially the kind of tragedy represented by *Women Beware Women*.[1] In fact a good part of his genius and appeal lies in having the kind of vision that needs to make so little adjustment between a play like *A Chaste Maid in Cheapside* (1611) and *Women Beware Women* (1625?–7),[2] the sparest and most direct of his good tragedies. In his writing in these plays there is no more than an occasional hint of the usual divisions between tragedy and comedy. The deliberate flatness of tone so important to his tragedies (especially *Women Beware Women*) is also the core of the best of the comedies. To some extent this sort of thing is true of any writer of domestic tragedy – he must be nearer comedy than people like Shakespeare, Webster, Ford – but then the simple fact is that, before Ibsen and Chekhov, nobody but Middleton wrote domestic tragedy worth serious and sustained attention. It is this complete absence of any sense of the literary, or any feeling that tragedy is the preoccupation of the dedicated bard, and hence written about figures who stand outside their society, that makes Middleton such an invaluable figure in English literature. In a very real sense the naturalism in *Women Beware Women* is purer even than in Ibsen and Chekhov.

[1] Act, scene and page references to Mermaid edition throughout.

[2] G. E. Bentley, *The Jacobean and Caroline Stage* (Oxford, 1941–56), vol. IV, pp. 905-7, says the date of *Women Beware Women* is 'highly speculative'. Some put it earlier than 1622, the date of *The Changeling*.

The two plays put together in this chapter represent about the best of Middleton's comic writing and one of the two kinds of tragedy, allied but slightly different, that he virtually initiated. In both plays, marriage as a bourgeois contract for the exchange of people for money, goods, or land predominates. There is usually a superficial attraction which works at least for one of the parties (the women are always genuinely attractive, the men only sometimes so), but with one or two exceptions affection *is* superficial because it is either greedily jealous, like Leantio's in *Women Beware Women*, and Sir Walter Whorehound's in *A Chaste Maid*, or easily destroyed, like Bianca's love for her husband. The exceptions to this rule are, most notably, the romantic couple in *A Chaste Maid*, Touchwood Junior and Moll, and perhaps, in the early stages of the play, Isabella (who does not know she is committing incest) in *Women Beware Women*. (Her coolness in the matter of contemplated adultery is, however, something akin to the single-minded obtuseness of Beatrice-Joanna.) Bianca's love for the Duke is a difficult case. It is certainly genuine enough, but of course it began, when forced on her, in the hard-headed way that predominates in the play and, anyway, it is mixed up with the rather melodramatic ending the play has.

This, then, is the area of experience that the two plays have in common. They both represent a world where daughters are quite openly bargaining-counters in the business of acquiring money and goods, and where even 'genuine' love like Leantio's is constantly weighing the cost against the profits of 'factorship' – talks, indeed, of its conquests and losses in marriage in terms of theft of goods. The sphere of reference is only slightly, but quite pleasingly enlarged by the presence, occasionally, of the kind of sentiments represented by Moll and Touchwood Junior. Middleton, for the most part, is not bitter or angry or even 'understanding' about this. The only trace of bitterness comes in with his crushing contempt of fools like the Ward and Sordido. He is nowhere near as vehement, for instance, as Jonson in *Volpone*, nor as sarcastic as Jonson in the *Everyman* plays. Rather, the tone is one of accurate observation and, it follows, condemnation of all this. And the condemnation exists not in anything that could normally be called satire, but simply, or largely, in the presentation of the facts. Even the irony of marrying Tim to a penniless whore, or of presenting Livia as caught in love by the man she betrayed for the Duke's money, is still rather in the vein of handing us the facts with just the barest of underlinings and no open comment. The characters, especially in *A Chaste Maid*, have names like Yellowhammer, Touchwood, Whorehound, but these are merely signposts for the reader. There is a pretty large gap between the obviousness of names like these and the calmness and realism of most of the actual text:

> *Allwit* The founder's come to town: I'm like a man
> Finding a table furnish'd to his hand,
> As mine is still to me, prays for the founder, –
> Bless the right worshipful the good founder's life!
> I thank him, has maintain'd my house this ten years;
> Not only keeps my wife, but 'a keeps me
> And all my family; I'm at his table:
> He gets me all my children, and pays the nurse
> Monthly or weekly . . .   I, ii (p. 182)

If bitterness at the sordidness of City life is somewhere behind all this, it is never allowed to be present specifically. Despite the twists of irony which provide the author's comment we need, naturalism is so much the predominating tone that, coming from an age given largely to boisterous satire in these matters, the plays are uniquely lasting.

The comparison with Jonson is important. As Professor Knights points out,[1] Jonson writes under the threat of the new capitalism.

[1] L. C. Knights, *Drama and Society in the Age of Jonson* (London, 1951). On the 'bourgeois' world of Middleton see also R. B. Parker, 'Middleton's Experiments with Comedy and Judgement', *Jacobean Theatre: Stratford-upon-Avon Studies I* (London, 1960).

Volpone is the most interesting case, because here he is at once re-
pelled and powerfully attracted by the acquisition of enormous
wealth. The play is bursting at the seams with a vitality Middleton
could never allow himself. Volpone delights not merely in the
hoarding of money, but in the gulling of others who desire it even
more strongly than he does, and in running bigger and bigger
risks in order to fool more and more people. The edifice of luxury
he builds thrives on the ever-present danger of toppling over if, as
it surely must, one of his tricks fails. There is nothing of this in
Middleton, least of all in *A Chaste Maid in Cheapside*, the comedy
most obviously concerned with greed and wealth. Nevertheless
Middleton can put in its place a detachment that, in *A Chaste Maid*,
is extremely telling, and in *Women Beware Women*, the subtler play
of the two, is I think at least as impressive as Jonson's extraordinary
vitality. Jonson's play (cf. the importance in it of the mountebank
speech) is just verging on the *tour de force*. For all its vitality, it is,
compared with Middleton, just a little bit operatic, a shade inclined to the magnificence of hyperbole. Middleton's naturalism,
the more powerful because it approaches a bitter denunciation
without ever actually stating it, is in fact one of the best critical
comments available on the exuberance of *Volpone*.[1]

Considered in more detail, the two plays modify slightly the
general remarks above. The road from comedy to tragedy is short
in Middleton, necessarily much shorter than for anybody else
writing at the time. Within Middleton's own sphere, however,
there is one important distinction which holds the two sets of
contiguous plays slightly apart: in comedy, his concern for the
new bourgeois values of living is focused more specifically than in
tragedy. *A Chaste Maid in Cheapside*, for instance, has just slightly
more of the Jonsonian concern with city wealth than has *Women*

---

[1] The *Everyman* plays lack the organizing vitality of *Volpone* and hence cannot come near
the status of Middleton's best writing. They are not only different in kind, but too loosely
written to compare.

Beware Women (for all its careful investigation of Leantio's bargains and of the contractual basis of marriage). In *Women Beware Women* these issues are held just below the level at which they could dominate the wider concerns of establishing and criticizing the new values of middle-class life in general. *A Chaste Maid*, on the other hand, begins specifically with the detailed preoccupations of getting a husband or wife with money and, preferably, lands as well. Yellowhammer's wife, Maudlin, and his daughter Moll open with an argument about the way to get a husband, and consequently, the way to add to the Yellowhammer gold. Maudlin's speech is a little spoilt perhaps by rather heavy Elizabethan puns on the word 'bord' (probably 'bore' or calibre as in gun!) but generally it is neatly precise. Middleton is pleased with his character's charmingly unaffected greed:

> *Maudlin* . . . when was the dancer with you?
> *Moll* The last week.
> *Maudlin* Last week? When I was of your bord
> He miss'd me not a night; I was kept at it;
> I took delight to learn, and he to teach me;
> Pretty brown gentleman! he took pleasure in my company . . .
> You dance like a plumber's daughter, and deserve
> Two thousand pound in lead to your marriage,
> And not in goldsmith's ware.   1, i (pp. 173-4)

The air of amused observation from the author is completed with Yellowhammer's entrance and, particularly, with his delightfully offhand remark about Tim and the news of the Welsh girl's arrival:

> Had word just the day after, when you sent him
> The silver spoon to eat his broth in the hall
> Amongst the gentlemen-commoners.   1, i (p. 175)

After an introduction of this kind in the opening scene of Act I, the play concentrates on the bringing in, one after another, and then the grouping and re-grouping of the important related idea-characters: Touchwood Senior, the Kixes, Allwit, Whorehound, plus the romantic leads Touchwood Junior and Moll, and Moll's commercially-minded parents, the Yellowhammers. In all this, the Yellowhammer household, with its opposition of the commercial and the lightly sketched but quite satisfactory romantic love theme (it could not in this play stand heavier treatment) from Moll and Touchwood Junior, provides the main thread of the story. Around these characters are grouped the rest in ways that comment on each other's positions and on the whole.

The first of these we meet is the extraordinary cuckold Allwit. Middleton's presentation of this man's utterly barren, parasitical existence is beautifully effortless. He allows neither Allwit nor his wife a single scruple of conscience about what they are doing. They spend almost the whole play in a daze of self-satisfaction that needs no overt comment from the author at all. Again, this can hardly even be called anything as usual as satire. Together, these characters represent that aspect of the general bargaining and buying which is completely sterile, completely devoid of anything approaching ordinary humanity, and no anger of Middleton's ruffles the surface of what is simply handed to the reader. The high points of their activity and function in the play are, first of all, the extraordinary self-satisfaction of Allwit's first long speech (Act I, scene ii; p.152) and then, what this ultimately leads to, the dialogue between Allwit and his wife towards the end when they have finally got rid of Sir Walter. This sort of dialogue is very characteristic of Middleton in this play, and, to a lesser extent, in *Women Beware Women*: there is as it were a savouring delight that he gives his characters in the meanest and most ordinary objects of possession. The verse lingers over cloths, furnishings, possessions so cheap and ordinary they cannot possibly stand for anything beyond their own limited and worldly significance. It's as if Volpone had abandoned his huge delight in the power of gold and turned to worship chairs and tables:

Allwit What shall we do now, wife?
Mistress Allwit As we were wont to do.
Allwit We're richly furnish'd, wife,
With household stuff.
Mistress Allwit Let's let out lodgings then,
And take a house in the Strand.
Allwit In troth, a match, wench!
We're simply stock'd with cloth-of-tissue cushions
To furnish out bay-windows; pish, what not
That's quaint and costly, from the top to the bottom;
Life, for furniture we may lodge a countess:
There's a close-stool of tawny velvet too,
Now I think on it, wife.   v, i (p. 246)

Immediately opposed to the Allwits, in Acts I and II, are Whorehound, Touchwood Senior and the Kixes. Whorehound's entrance follows on from Allwit's first big speech and is in fact the
subject for it. Right up to the last act, Whorehound is only very
lightly sketched in, but he does represent, after Allwit, something
just barely human, even if his appearances are so brief that he can
be little more than a fairly conventional gamester in love and
property. Characteristically, Middleton gives him enough shrewd-
ness and bite to fill in the picture as much as is necessary for (at this
stage) a minor character:

> Let me see, stay, –
> How shall I dispose of these two brats now
> When I am married . . . ?   i, ii (p. 185)

With the brief first appearance of Sir Walter over, Middleton
follows up immediately with the remaining figures he must establish early in the play. In fairly rapid succession we have already
seen the Yellowhammers, the Allwits, Whorehound, and, now,
the Kixes and Touchwood Senior. Like Allwit, Kix is barren, but
this time for natural and not voluntary reasons. Touchwood, of

course, is the reverse. (Act II also has one of his apparently count-less victims, the country girl.) Amidst the slightly grotesque attempts all these people make to deal with the problem of money and wealth, Touchwood's fecundity is as fatal as Sir Walter's carelessness, the Yellowhammers' greed, and the others' barren-ness and sterility. This group of people, with the Yellowhammer plot providing most of the links between them and also the sheer story interest, makes up the substance of what Middleton has to say about commercial values in living.

And it is this kind of organization in the play which provides the only sure lines of demarcation between the London comedies and *Women Beware Women*. In the tragedy, the flat, naturalistic tone, with comment from the author implied as much by what charac-ters don't say as by what they do, is continued, even intensified; but the deliberate grouping of so many characters (types, though certainly *not* humours) has gone. The two plays are extraordinarily alike in tone – again, I would claim this is a sign of Middleton's rare success – but the organization is slightly different. In the tragedy, the evils of London life are less in the foreground.

The ending of *A Chaste Maid in Cheapside*, like the ending of *Women Beware Women*, is a little difficult to take. In both plays, Middleton suddenly moves into a different key, abandons naturalism for, in the one case a supposedly death-bed repentance bordering on the cliché, and in the other a conventional revenge masque. In the case of *Women Beware Women* the change is obviously unfortunate. With *A Chaste Maid*, I think it almost comes off. Here the realism has been constantly moving towards, though never quite reaching, the type-characters of conventional Jacobean comedy, and Sir Walter's change of heart, combined as it is with a touch of the string-pulling and 'magic' of Shakespeare's last plays (cf. the 'death' and mock funeral of the lovers), does not jar so much. The Morality-play tone of Sir Walter's 'I am o'er-grown with sin . . .' (Act V, scene ii *passim*) is certainly a mistake on Middleton's part;[1] but apart from this, the change of heart is nicely balanced by the continued utter lack of sentiment in the picture of Allwit's callousness, and by the beautifully right ending with Yellowhammer planning to make 'one feast . . . serve them both'. (Just prior to this, in the midst of Sir Walter's recantations, he had shown his only comment on the supposed death of his daughter to be a plan to save what he could of his fortune by marrying Tim to the Welsh 'heiress'!)

Women Beware Women is the one play in the history of the English stage that puts beyond any shade of doubt the great possibilities of domestic tragedy. It has not got the immediately obvious vitality of *The Changeling*, but the sequence of Leantio's oddly nervous verse in Act I, followed by the seduction scene, and then the banquet scene, should have assured it a much more prominent place in stage history than it has had. This uncompromising clear-sightedness is a side of the Jacobeans that should consistently be stressed in face of the abundant and occasionally confusing rich-ness of tone by which they are more usually known and, it must be admitted, more widely represented.

In this connection, the first and third scenes of Act I deserve the closest attention. Once the significance and tone of these scenes is established, the rest falls easily into place. In this play there is not the strong and symmetrical outline of *The Changeling*. The order and significance behind the writing are more difficult to grasp because they depend more simply on Middleton's maintaining with absolute accuracy the tone and key in which he starts. Apart from this, the structure and meaning of the play rests on the high points of Act I, on the seduction scene, and on the banquet. The sub-plot of Isabella and Hippolito moves a little away towards a more conventional Jacobean theme of guilty love, but it is linked with the

---

[1] Cf. the *Faustus* echoes. Middleton is like many of his contemporaries at least in that he often cannot resist borrowings.

rest in tone and by the commanding fact that Middleton makes both the women, Isabella and Bianca, the subjects of various of his commercial transactions.

Leantio's verse in Act I establishes at once the firm links that this play has with Middleton's writing in the London comedies. There are no Touchwoods, Allwits or Whorehounds, but Leantio's nervous garrulity springs straight out of the world of *A Chaste Maid* and *A Trick to Catch the Old One*. At first sight, the text of the first scene looks operatic in a sense that Middleton's plays rarely are. It is filled with long speeches from Leantio, often punctuated only by an occasional remark from the Mother. Before the sense and tone of the verse are taken in, this looks strange in a naturalistic play. In fact, the speeches are a beautifully correct statement of Leantio's weakness. He is one of the people in Middleton who, for all their careful 'factorship', simply cannot stop talking. The first speech, for instance, keeps going for so long simply because it cannot be stopped. One idea leads to another and, making all allowances for the excitement of the moment (Bianca is clearly quite something!) it must be that Middleton is commenting on the gap between the almost puritanical control in business affairs (nothing must interfere: Act I, scene iii) and the rather irresponsible chain-of-associations reasoning on marriage and private affairs. These are people who place great faith in commercial prudence ('and the long warehouse cracks . . .'), but in the very act of doing so reveal that they have not managed to carry this over to other matters. Leantio thinks the connection is well established, but his way of stating it betrays him.

Leantio's introduction of Bianca to his mother is the first clear sign of what is coming. He starts (Act I, scene i; p.264) with a conventional hyperbole:

> O, you have named the most unvaluedst purchase
> That youth of man had ever knowledge of!

This continues for four or five lines, ending with 'It joys me that I ever was ordained / To have a being, and to live 'mongst men'. At this point, Leantio's mind shoots off on the first and neatest of its digressions in this long speech. It is not the sprawling Jacobean excitement you get in Webster and some others; it is simply the self-satisfaction of a very dull, insensitive man who has for once done something far beyond the bounds of his normal, very limited activities. He has committed theft of goods, and the goods is Bianca! Thus the '... live 'mongst men' suggests the fatuous cliché:

> Which is a fearful living, and a poor one,
> Let a man truly think on't.

From here his talk spins on, through the parody of Jacobean Death's-head verse

> To have the toil and griefs of fourscore years
> Put up in a white sheet, tied with two knots ...

(somehow the 'two knots' is too pedantic to be anything but a parody of the real thing); then moralizes about the sins of adultery, finally on to the self-congratulatory aphorisms:

> I find no wish in me bent sinfully
> To this man's sister, or to that man's wife;
> In love's name let 'em keep their honesties,
> And cleave to their own husbands ...

Already this sounds dangerously insensitive and (compare here Beatrice-Joanna) dangerously unaware of the gaps in its own logic and maturity. Why on earth *should* he feel the need for anyone else's wife on such an occasion? And, why, therefore, the need to congratulate himself in quite this way on not feeling the need for it? It might be merely a young man's foolishness, were it not for Leantio's fantastic self-satisfaction, his extraordinary inability to see through the moral clichés with which the verse is packed. Once again, all this is sealed by Middleton's just barely excited (or, to put it another way, almost aggressively flat) blank verse. The verse here is to be taken, I think, as noticeably *ordinary*, displaying the bourgeois values of caution and self-withdrawal; at the same time it comments on these by revealing the betraying excitement beneath Leantio's factorship-in-marriage. The 'ordinariness' is made to look distinctly odd in the face of what Leantio is actually *saying*. Certainly the acuteness of the verse here has no dealings with the richly poetic overtones of the usual Jacobean play; it is even more uncompromisingly naturalistic than the bulk of the verse in *The Changeling*.

The next step away from apparent security follows almost immediately. Leantio is going to shut his wife up, like merchandise that must be hidden from thieves, and set his mother to watch while he is away on business. This is a very familiar move from Jacobean jealous husbands, but here, as hardly anywhere else, the whole affair is scaled down right away from the hyperbole and grotesquerie of plays like (to take examples which are very different from each other) either *Volpone* or *The Broken Heart*. And it is much more literally related to real life. For instance: part of Bianca's imprisonment is to be the metaphorical one of keeping ideas (i.e. as well as princes and courtiers) out of her mind. In the face of Leantio's earlier protestations of romantic love (albeit they *were* slightly alloyed with talk of 'treasure', possessions, goods, etc.) selfishness as stupidly blind as this is amazing; but Middleton's touch is so sure that it always remains literally credible:

> I pray do not you teach her to rebel,
> When she is in a good way to obedience;
> To rise with other women in commotion
> Against their husbands for six gowns a-year,
> And so maintain their cause, when they're once up,
> In all things else that require cost enough.
> They're all of 'em a kind of spirits soon raised,
> But not so soon laid, mother; as, for example . . .
>
> I, i (pp. 265-6)

To end this opening section, scene iii gives us Leantio on wisdom in marriage. Nothing he has yet said has been raised more than a degree above a sort of dangerous insensitivity; yet his farewell is interspersed with reflections on wisdom and the absolute need to see clearly the proper perspectives in love and business (again, the talk of wisdom and reason is like Beatrice-Joanna's):

> Get out again, for shame! the man loves best
> When his care's most, that shows his zeal to love:
> Fondness is but the idiot to affection,
> That plays at hot-cockles with rich merchants' wives;
> Good to make sport withal when the chest's full,
> And the long warehouse cracks. 'Tis time of day
> For us to be more wise, 'tis early with us . . .
>
> I, iii (p. 277)

The Middleton suggestive economy of phrase makes us believe in part of Leantio's speech, that is to say in his (or rather Middleton's) evocation of bourgeois values ('. . . when the chest's full, / And the long warehouse cracks'), but this is cunningly set off against the alarming meanness of spirit the *character* Leantio has and against his incredible insensitivity. The play postulates bourgeois values (and other values too, such as Bianca's initial love for Leantio), but constantly plays these off against bourgeois behaviour. In the face of the wildness and strangeness of much of Jacobean tragic drama, it represents, therefore, an acceptance of the need for a new kind of investigation. It doesn't solve any questions; doesn't establish new values as positively as Shakespeare, at least, established his. What it does do, with firmness and absolute clarity, is establish the solid presence of new modes of living, and in the same breath reveal tendencies which are working to unsettle this very solidity. Middleton sees the new accumulation of middle-class attitudes – the rapid crystallization of all sensibility around thought and image of contracts for merchandise – as exciting because extraordinarily powerful and concentrated. At the same time, in the very act of showing this, he allows, at certain key points, the very slightest blurring or twisting of the apparently calm surface of events – the suggestion, for instance, of a bewildering and unsettling excitement in Leantio's very spurning of the game of 'fondness', of playing 'at hot-cockles with rich merchants' wives'– and by this means, without unsettling his own control, he radically criticizes the stability this new world gives every appearance of achieving. The bourgeois gains in wealth and security are real gains, until one puts them – as their own tendency to transfer the terms of bargaining in goods to the business of love and marriage itself puts them – into a context of personal living. Here their claims to exclusive control over life break down. It's not that there is anything inherently mean or evil in middle-class attitudes; indeed Middleton, for all his apparent calm, shows more interest and excitement in them than many later writers, including perhaps Shaw and Ibsen. The trouble, rather, is that the very concentration they are shown to have achieved is so exclusive of other aspects of life – so clearly wishes, for instance, to ignore the irrational hopes and fears that continually break out from Leantio's apparently 'logical' discussions of marriage – that its firmness rapidly becomes unstable. As an investigation and evaluation of attitudes that were increasingly to dominate modern living, the tautly controlled excitement of Middleton's dialogue, playing on these issues, is an unrivalled achievement.

Middleton has put a lot of his comment on the kind of world he's describing into this first view of Leantio with his bride. A full examination of it is therefore important, and the more so as it also serves to lay another ghost in Middleton criticism, viz., that it is the women who hold the key to these plays. Certainly they hold one of the keys, but the *exposé* of Leantio at the beginning of *Women Beware Women* is as important as anything else, in this play at any rate; further, it is of a kind which should dispose of any suggestion that Middleton was interested in drama merely on a 'character' level. He is a brilliant psychologist, certainly, but he is also concerned, both in the comedies and in *Women Beware Women* (this is at the core of their similarity), with exploring and commenting on the entry of the commercial values and modes he has been talking about into the business of living and loving, in and out of marriage. Roughly, his comment is turning out to be that City life is stupidly limited and dull in its values, but that these values have their importance; and, further, that this is because values of this kind and traditional human values rub shoulders in the world as he sees it. In his plays the attempts to combine the two areas of experience – the personal and the public – always end disastrously, but the process is fascinating and important not least because it is, Middleton finds, devastatingly common.[1]

The end of Act I, catching up suggestions thrown out in the earlier speeches of Leantio, drives home again the further sense in which the 'commonness' of this bourgeois world is important: like Leantio's speeches, the concluding dialogue stresses – even while it criticizes and places – the solid actuality of experience. To put it more accurately: the power of this play is generated by the emotions that constantly threaten the calm surface; but the fabric of this surface – the fabric, that is, of ordinary living – has a kind of stupidly real quality which is part of the very substance of Middleton's total vision. The focal point of this quality as it is given us in Act I is the full chest and the long warehouse of Leantio's early speeches; the end of the Act is a lightly comic re-

---

[1] Again, a comparison with Jonson is interesting. Middleton's calm, for the most part unaccentuated dialogue illustrates that he – more clearly than Jonson or any other Elizabethan or Jacobean playwright – sees the bourgeois world as, by the time he was writing, long *established*. Indeed his calm clear-sightedness about it is so remarkable that one might confidently say that the world he is writing about must have had its roots much earlier than the beginning of the Jacobean age.

On this question I should add that it has always seemed to me possible that some of the dialogue in *Women Beware Women*, now printed as verse, might have been conceived originally by Middleton as prose. I know of no direct evidence on this point, however. It is merely a personal impression (cf. sections of Leantio's speeches in Act I).

assertion of the same attitudes and values. As the Duke's procession takes the stage, Bianca's nicely intimate 'What's the meaning of this hurry?/ Can you tell me, mother?' produces the Mother's unconsciously pointed reply ('See, if my dull brains had not quite forgot it!/ 'Twas happily questioned of thee . . .') and Bianca artlessly supposes that the Duke has looked up and seen her. The Mother's discounting of this is well-intentioned but, again, ironically wide of the mark:

> That's every one's conceit that sees a duke;
> If he looks steadfastly, he looks straight at them,
> When he, perhaps, good, careful gentleman,
> Never minds any, but the look he casts
> Is at his own intentions, and his object
> Only the public good.

And from Bianca, simply:

> Most likely so!   I, iii (p. 280)

Before this, amid the hurry and bustle, Middleton inserts a neatly trivial and utterly real conversation between the two:

Mother I hear 'em near us now: do you stand easily?
Bianca Exceeding well, good mother.
Mother Take this stool.
Bianca I need it not, I thank you.
Mother Use your will then.

Given this air of detached observation from Bianca, her pointedly revealing though, at this stage, entirely innocent observations about the Duke, are beautifully placed (cf. 'Is he old, then?'). Middleton can always command writing of this kind and it is important not merely as 'atmosphere' but as part of what he has to say in this play. For instance, again, towards the end of Act IV, when the slightly unreal turmoil of the masque is being foreshadowed, he effortlessly recalls the solid, unambiguous world of reality by the conversation between Livia and Hippolito about the

Duke's marriage. There is no need, in this dialogue, Middleton's writing being what it is, to mention names or facts that would not have been specifically mentioned in actual conversation:

> *Livia (pretending a reconciliation with Hippolito).*
> 'T has pleased the duke so well too, that behold, sir, *(Giving paper)*
> Has sent you here your pardon, which I kissed
> With most affectionate comfort: when 'twas brought,
> Then was my fit just past; it came so well, methought,
> To glad my heart.
> *Hippolito* I see his grace thinks on me.
> *Livia* There's no talk now but of the preparation
> For the great marriage.
> *Hippolito* Does he marry her, then?
> *Livia* With all speed, suddenly . . .   IV, ii (pp. 352-3)

Even after the change of subject in the conversation, neither of the two characters needs to mention what marriage it is or who is concerned. Even admitting Shakespeare, few writers at that time would have bothered or would have been able to pare that part of the dialogue down to the simple 'Does he marry her, then?' It would not even have been important for the average (or even the unusual) Jacobean playwright. Middleton, on the other hand, is both changing the sensibility of the age and at the same time representing a tendency in it for change and for concentration in a new direction.

The rest of the play, simply, parallels Isabella and Bianca; at the same time, and in the act of doing this, it widens and deepens the sphere of Middleton's enquiry. In different ways, both these characters are the objects of commerce (respectively, for Fabricio and Leantio). Both change from this to adultery, actual or intended. Isabella, of course, is seduced by Livia's worldly generosity (Livia – of all people – as the Marriage Goddess almost redeems the Revenge masque at the end!), but her extraordinary, Beatrice-like obtuseness in the business of arrangements for a life of adultery

puts her very much into the same world as Bianca and Leantio. [1]
Guardiano, Fabricio and the Ward complete the picture as set by
Middleton's dialogue generally. On these lines, the play moves
fairly rapidly to the two great scenes which, building on earlier
ones, finally establish and define the new values which Middleton,
the uncharacteristic Jacobean, sees in the Jacobean world. These
scenes are the 'game of chess' and the banquet.

The game of chess brings the play very rapidly to a much
greater intensity of feeling and tone than anything so far in Acts I
and II. In particular, with Bianca's entry after she has been seduced,
the issues Middleton is presenting take on a fresh and more urgently
personal dimension:

> I'm made bold now,
> I thank thy treachery; sin and I'm acquainted,
> No couple greater . . .   II, ii (p. 305)

On the other hand, whatever he does later on in Act V, Middleton
is conscious that he must allow no break here in the *kind* of writing
he uses. The great moments follow naturally from the clear-
sighted cynicism of what has gone before. Thus the seduction (including the rather conventional part given to the Duke: 'I can
command . . .'etc.) is continually placed against the tough, worldly
realism of the dialogue in the game of chess:

> *Livia* Alas, poor widow, I shall be too hard for thee!
> *Mother* You're cunning at the game, I'll be sworn, madam.
> *Livia* It will be found so, ere I give you over. – [Aside]
> She that can place her man well –
> *Mother* As you do, madam.
> *Livia* As I shall, wench, can never lose her game:
> Nay, nay, the black king's mine . . .   II, ii (pp. 299–300)

Middleton uses the old Elizabethan gallery scene to get the closest
integration between two parts of a scene in almost any seventeenth-
century play outside Shakespeare. Right up to and even including

[1] Cf. her absolute lack of comment on her mother's supposed adultery.

the great intensity of Bianca's entry after the seduction, the realistic dialogue in the scene below comments on the scene above and places it as, in a sense, ordinary. No hint of scruple or even worry on Livia's part, no melodrama or hyperbole anywhere from Middleton disturbs the correctly sustained tone of the dialogue. The point Middleton is making is this: seen through Livia's eyes – or rather, seen as controlled by Livia's personality – the whole affair with the Duke has been so convincingly usual and common that in part we must share her view. It has its validity: this seduction isn't as overwhelmingly destructive of all certainty as Bianca at first thinks. For one thing it produces, later on, Bianca's own perfectly genuine and convincing love for the Duke, her seducer. Also, in this scene itself, seduction destroys the fatal complacency of Bianca's early insularity and in so doing liberates the tougher, more energetic realism of 'sin and I'm acquainted . . .' Livia's part in this juxtaposes the sordidness of her (and The Mother's) unfeeling commercialism, against the rightness of her stand – all unconscious though it is – for common experience. The very vulgarity of the world Livia represents has a toughness and actuality which we accept – repellent though it is in some of its aspects – as a necessary and valuable contribution to experience. Indeed throughout the rest of the play, Livia is given a much more sympathetic appraisal by Middleton than, for instance, The Mother, who reflects simply the sordid and unpleasant side of factorship in love and marriage.

On the other hand, what has happened to Bianca in this game of chess is not merely 'ordinary'. It is for Livia, and in part we share her view. But with Bianca's entry after the seduction the tough, worldly realism of the dialogue is deepened to incorporate the personal tragedy of Bianca's sudden realization of sin. In the play so far, Bianca has been the unthinking accomplice of Leantio in his treatment of love and marriage as a matter of commercial practice and commercial greed. Her seduction is in fact the logical outcome of his 'zealous' care in keeping his personal life (Bianca) locked up and out of sight until trade flourishes ('. . . when the long warehouse cracks'). But trade flourishes with others sooner than with Leantio, and Livia's 'factorship' in procuring Bianca for the Duke destroys at one blow the division between merchandizing and living that Leantio had attempted to enforce early on. This is not merely a matter of Leantio's own personal deficiencies; the whole substance of commerce and factorship, as Leantio consistently represents it, contains inevitably a tendency to force the personal (like his love for Bianca) into a separate compartment in living. Livia regards such a separation as perfectly ordinary, and up to a point the dialogue endorses her stand; on the other hand the tragic impact on the life of an individual is given us in the power and intensity of Bianca's awakening to experience:

> Now bless me from a blasting! I saw that now,
> Fearful for any woman's eye to look on;
> Infectious mists and mildews hang at's eyes,
> The weather of a doomsday dwells upon him:
> Yet since mine honour's leprous, why should I
> Preserve that fair that caused the leprosy?
> Come, poison all at once. [Aside] –

In this speech Middleton converts the very clichés of Jacobean moralizing into dialogue which is urgently alive. Thus Bianca follows up her 'aside' by addressing Guardiano directly in these terms:

> Thou in whose baseness
> The bane of virtue broods, I'm bound in soul
> Eternally to curse thy smooth-browed treachery,
> That wore the fair veil of a friendly welcome,
> And I a stranger; think upon't, 'tis worth it . . .

– where the 'bane of virtue' is indeed a cliché, but one which, in context, enlivens her contemptuous dismissal of the whole society Guardiano represents. She thinks half in terms of conventional morality (cf. the later 'Beware of offering the first-fruits to sin') but her personality, as given us in this scene especially, is one which makes the conventional suddenly meaningful. Indeed the point of the clichés is to show what happens to conventional morality when it is acting upon and through a personality which is notably alive and fresh. Thus, in particular, the bane of virtue 'brooding' leads to the much more imaginative vision of 'smooth-browed treachery', and then to the direct, insistent note which rams the 'moral' home: 'think upon't, 'tis worth it'. Similarly, the rest of the speech blends convention with an inescapable frankness and directness ('I give thee that to feed on') and with Middleton's (and Bianca's) imaginative realization of the power of a true 'acquaintance' with sin:

> Beware of offering the first-fruits to sin;
> His weight is deadly who commits with strumpets,
> After they've been abased, and made for use;
> If they offend to the death, as wise men know,
> How much more they, then, that first make 'em so!
> I give thee that to feed on. I'm made bold now,
> I thank thy treachery; sin and I'm acquainted,
> No couple greater . . .   II, ii (pp. 304-5)

The two simple terms in the Middleton world – love and commerce – have been forced apart, only to clash together again in what is now the only way possible: Bianca's seduction through the activities of the commercially minded Livia.

At the same time it is a characteristic strength of Middleton that even at such moments in the play he is never tempted – as many 'realists' are – by the romantic fallacy of isolating personal anguish from the experience in which it is grounded, or valuing the personal at the cost of rejecting the common or vulgar. Bianca's is a personal tragedy, but it incorporates also a new toughness of mind culled from the very 'game of chess' attitudes which originally placed her seduction for what in part it was: a commercial transaction. The very lines she speaks on her re-entry after the seduction

give us something more solid and substantial than a *mere* sense of
unrelated personal anguish or loss; they are sharply turned to remind us of – and incorporate within themselves – the broadly
comic talk earlier of *what* it was Bianca 'saw':

> *Guardiano* . . . the gentlewoman,
> Being a stranger, would take more delight
> To see your rooms and pictures.
> *Livia* Marry, good sir,
> And well remembered; I beseech you, show 'em her,
> That will beguile time well; pray heartily, do, sir,
> I'll do as much for you: here take these keys;
> > (*Gives keys to Guardiano*)
> Show her the monument too, and that's a thing
> Everyone sees not; you can witness that, widow . . .
>
> II, ii (p. 299)

After the seduction, Bianca herself partly takes on the colouring of
her new habitat and her dialogue mingles a comic 'acceptance' of
the whole affair with a directness of response of a kind beyond
The Mother and even Livia. The phallic comedy of 'the monu-
ment' recurs:

> *Mother* You have not seen all since, sure?
> *Bianca* That have I, mother,
> The monument and all: I'm so beholding
> To this kind, honest, courteous gentleman,
> You'd little think it, mother; showed me all,
> Had me from place to place so fashionably;
> The kindness of some people, how't exceeds!
> Faith, I've seen that I little thought to see
> I' the morning when I rose. II, ii (p. 305)

The Act concludes with Bianca's energetic personality freed from
the seclusion carefully provided for her by Leantio, and now
thoroughly immersed in the real world. She can now answer
Livia in Livia's own terms and give as good as she gets:

179

Servant Supper's upon the table.
Livia Yes, we come. –
Will't please you, gentlewoman?
Bianca Thanks, virtuous lady. –
You're a damned bawd. (*Aside to Livia*)   II, ii (p. 306)

Immediately after the game of chess, the return of Leantio from business, with a nicely inappropriate moral soliloquy ('When I behold a glorious strumpet . . .'), leads up to the banquet scene where plot and sub-plot mingle. As Miss Bradbrook notices, the departure of Bianca and The Mother for the Duke's banquet gives Middleton the opportunity for the telling lines which finally bring The Mother herself into the general buying and bargaining:

Bianca Come, mother, come, follow his humour no longer;
We shall be all executed for treason shortly.
Mother Not I, i' faith; I'll first obey the duke,
And taste of a good banquet; I'm of thy mind:
I'll step but up and fetch two handkerchiefs
To pocket up some sweetmeats, and o'ertake thee. (*Exit*)
Bianca Why, here's an old wench would trot into a bawd now
For some dry sucket, or a colt in march-pane. (*Aside and exit*)
III, i (p. 316)

Middleton is of course fond of this imagery of eating (cf. *A Chaste Maid in Cheapside* and the gossips at the funeral breakfast). It is used constantly in *Women Beware Women* and provides one of the important elements in the lust for possession of things and people which dominates this play. However, the comment given here to Bianca reminds us again that Middleton's attitude, like Shakespeare's, is something to be gathered over and above the mere sum of image-pattern or character portrayal. There is in fact a kind of intensity, a bitterness in Bianca's lines which represents the closest Middleton ever comes to an explicit statement of his own attitude to the life he is so accurately portraying.

The banquet scene itself is supremely important here. It has a few flat, because merely conventional lines –

O hast thou left me then, Bianca, utterly?

– but in the main the controlled clarity that has informed Acts I and II is sustained with admirable precision. Once again, the accuracy and energy with which it is sustained help to outline a moral attitude to the situation described. Livia's punishment (falling in love with one of the objects of her own particular brand of factorship), and her success in buying her way out of it by offering Leantio the use of all her wealth, seem absolutely right here. And for Leantio himself, who returns at this point as a major character, there is a very intelligent blend of a new clear-sightedness and the old egotism. Bianca's behaviour has given him the only kind of shock that could have jolted him out of the pleasant dream he was in before, and the result, surprisingly, is one of the very moving scenes that Middleton can rise to in this play:

> She's gone for ever, utterly; there is
> As much redemption of a soul from hell,
> As a fair woman's body from his palace.
>
> III, ii (p. 329)

A controlled sympathy from Middleton in this play is surprising but, in context, surprisingly correct.

Correctly again, this turns quickly back towards the profit-and-loss attitude of the Leantio we knew in Act I:

> ... then my safest course,
> For health of mind and body, is to turn
> My heart and hate her, most extremely hate her; –

There is a directness and conviction here, but poor Leantio doesn't realize that at the same time he's being forced to use the terms of business and merchandise which set the limits of personal response for so many of the people involved in Middleton's world:

> I have no other way; those virtuous powers,
> Which were chaste witnesses of both our troths,

> Can witness she breaks first. And I'm rewarded
> With captainship o' the fort; a place of credit,
> I must confess, but poor; my factorship
> Shall not exchange means with 't . . .
>
> III, ii (pp. 329-30)

The blend of the two attitudes – commercial bargaining and a new freshness of personal response both from Leantio and the rather engaging Livia – is utterly convincing. To all this Middleton adds Bianca's hard cynicism of acceptance and, later, her genuine and quite acceptable love for the Duke. (It is only suspect because placed in the middle of the unconvincing banalities that go to make up the Revenge-masque.[1]) The true values of the play have now fully emerged. There is, most clearly of all, the absolutely uncompromising Middleton clear-sightedness. Implicit in the strictness with which he observes this throughout – the clarity with which he sustains the tone of his writing – there is a comment, a controlled protest against *what* he observes, against the turn he sees events must take. Finally, in the sudden tautness and energy of much of the dialogue – even for Livia and Leantio – there is a clear realization of what is involved in the forcing apart of commerce and living, factorship and love.

The rest of the play is a mixture of the finely controlled writing we have enjoyed up to now and the slightly unfortunate resolution in the masque. Act IV, notably, contains the magnificent scene of Leantio, unable to keep away from Bianca, coming to her lodging at court, 'richly dressed', to show off his new finery and prove to her that he doesn't miss her after all. Very soon the comedy of manners is too much for him and he breaks out again with the passionate resentment of the earlier banquet scene:

---

[1] Even on the simple level of characterization, Bianca's new love for the Duke is convincing. She has always had at least something of the single-mindedness and at the same time the strength of mind that Beatrice-Joanna had, and this is undoubtedly what such a character would do: fall in love with the Duke, her seducer. No further explanation of the change is necessary in the play.

Leantio 'Tis a brave life you lead.
Bianca I could ne'er see you in such good clothes
In my time.
Leantio In your time?
Bianca Sure, I think, sir,
We both thrive best asunder.
Leantio You're a whore!
Bianca Fear nothing, sir.
Leantio An impudent, spiteful strumpet!
Bianca O, sir, you give me thanks for your captainship!
I thought you had forgot all your good manners.
Leantio And, to spite thee as much, look there; there read,
  (*Giving letter*)
Vex, gnaw; thou shalt find there I'm not love-starved . . .
                                        IV, i (p. 338)

These last two lines for Leantio in particular are brilliantly done, and characteristically Middleton.

Shortly after this, however, the Cardinal enters and Middleton gives the first clear sign of the moralistic and conventional Revenge ending. Admittedly, the Cardinal's first long speech, steeped in the Seven Deadly Sins and the mediaeval torments of Hell, is surprisingly good.[1] It is probably both good enough, and conventional enough, to fit on to the end of this otherwise highly naturalistic play simply *as* a purely conventional ending, drawing things quickly and neatly to a close. But his second entry (Act IV, scene iii) is somehow much duller and the change of key therefore less forgivable. And the Revenge-masque itself jars badly. It begins to take shape as early as Act IV, scene ii, and at this early stage it is all still in the naturalistic tone we have been used to. Guardiano hands out the roles and Livia is to play Juno Pronuba, the marriage goddess ("Tis right indeed'), Isabella the Nymph

---

[1] In tone it is reminiscent of Tourneur. Further, the Duke's reaction to the Cardinal's moralistic warnings carries something of Tourneur's wit: in answer to his brother's condemnation of adultery, the Duke plans to murder Leantio so that he may marry Bianca 'lawfully'.

183

who offers sacrifice 'to appease her wrath'. This is all plain enough and witty enough to be promising. But the masque itself, heralded by the Cardinal's second (and far inferior) outburst, is too long, too conventionally literary and too lacking in the customary hard-headed insight of the rest of the play to satisfy any but the most critically unaware. A modified form of the familiar Revenge holocaust might have done, but this has so many bodies, so many artfully contrived deaths and weakly ironical misunderstandings that it appears irretrievably banal. It is also, of course, highly moral, with the sinners all caught in their own nets. There is enough moral intention behind the play to make it quite right that Bianca and the Duke, for all their by now quite genuine love for each other, should be separated at the end, but not in quite this way.

Thus, a little unfortunately, ends what is almost a very great play indeed. It is certainly unique in Jacobean drama and quite good enough, up to the last Act, to be highly important in any scheme of the drama of that period or of any other. Its severely uncompromising attitude – and this includes, where necessary, a precisely controlled sympathy from Middleton – almost, but for the end, rivals the similar but more richly flexible attitude of *The Changeling*. Both plays, or rather the two plays taken together, outline an attitude which both recognizes and hastens the end of the Shakespearean age. In the same breath, they also outline new possibilities which gain more from their inevitability, as recognized facts of experience, than any plays – even Webster's and Tourneur's – could have gained at that time from any attempt further to extend and capitalize on earlier (Shakespearean) tragic attitudes. In the comparative inflexibility of Middleton's writing, gain and loss are clearly balanced.

CHAPTER IX

POETIC NATURALISM: 'THE CHANGELING'

The ghost of William Rowley troubles readers of *The Changeling* (1622). There is no need for this at all. The play is obviously richer in texture, more imaginative in outline than any other of Middleton's, and indeed this may be Rowley's doing in part. But *The Changeling* is also sufficiently a triumph of naturalism to make it a key study in that part of Jacobean tragedy which is virtually Middleton's own preserve. Beatrice-Joanna, at least, would find herself thoroughly at home in the world of hard-headed commercialism constructed by Middleton in *Women Beware Women*! The two plays – to take a wider view – are sufficiently alike in tone to be in the same line of succession, and to be grouped together apart from almost anything else in Jacobean tragedy. They are also both good enough to rank with Tourneur; and they are very clearly more intelligent, and richer, than any plays of Webster's or Ford's. However, with the exception of the Pelican *Age of Shakespeare* (which is notably clear and firm on this point) and Miss Bradbrook's *Themes and Conventions*, no modern surveys of the field that I know stress or even allow a comparative evaluation of this kind, and I am certain that most readers of the plays would find it strange. In the chapters that follow I hope to justify further Middleton's superiority over Webster, and most certainly over Ford, and to show what the significance of this is for our total view of Elizabethan and Jacobean drama.

But first, I want to examine the character and quality of the Middleton world as it is given us in his best play, *The Changeling*. Here Middleton is clearly in touch with material of a kind that older tragedy – even Shakespeare's and Tourneur's – was not concerned to touch; and yet at the same time he writes with a depth of focus and a richness unique within the range of his own plays. Indeed the play develops a single dominating image (Vermandero's 'castle') in such a way as to achieve a structure and meaning unique in the whole of English drama; in many ways the most fruitful comparisons are between *The Changeling* and plays of Racine's like *Phèdre* and *Andromaque*.

As a first generalization, and before examining fully the significance of the 'castle' image, we could I think say that *The Changeling* is, outside Shakespeare, the most obviously *intelligent* play in English. Others deal intelligently with comparatively simple material, or sporadically with complicated material, but Middleton in *The Changeling* deals with complex ideas and feelings in such a way that the whole structure appears to rely on a sustained sureness and quickness of mind. It is almost as if, in the face of the terrifying certainty of Beatrice-Joanna's fall, this were a virtue in itself. There is as it were a moral strength in the clarity and precision with which Middleton's mind looks at these people and these events. At all events, the feeling that you always get from Middleton of an uncompromisingly clear intellect behind the plays is there, made more intense in this case by the dangerous complexity of the issues at stake. Compared with it, Webster's admittedly fine intelligence seems continually in danger of being swamped by muddle; and even Tourneur, at times, seems dangerously poised over the abyss his own characters so persistently contemplate.

The story of *The Changeling* would apparently have been familiar to Jacobean readers.[1] On a simple level, Middleton uses it to make a characteristically modern and un-Jacobean point. Rather like an Ibsen showing us not the tragedy of great men and great actions, but the tragedy of a world where, with every step forward, people are further caught up in the past, he gradually

[1] G. E. Bentley, *The Jacobean and Caroline Stage*, vol. IV, p. 863.

presents the real affinity between Beatrice and the apparently utterly dissimilar De Flores. All the action focuses on this image of the refined, apparently unimpeachable Beatrice gradually being brought back to the commanding obsession that underlay all her earlier calm and reason. This means, not that her character deteriorates (or as Eliot says, that she 'becomes damned')[1], but that any move forward (or downward!) in the action is also a reference backward and qualifies the ostensible calm and reason of the opening. The shape of the play presents us with Beatrice 'changed' from her contracted husband, Alonzo de Piracquo, to a lover of her own choice (i.e. not her father's choice), and then, because she must use the terrible De Flores to get rid of Alonzo, changed finally to him. Thus at the end of the play we are in a sense back where we started, with the fear of De Flores – always pathological, and now fully revealed for what it was from the beginning, a fear based on a real affinity too frightening to be dealt with and controlled at a conscious level. The parallel but franker and more sordid lust and bargaining of the sub-plot emphasizes or rather

---

[1] *Selected Essays*, p. 163 ff. Eliot's insight into Middleton's 'unprejudiced' view of human nature and human problems is of course invaluable. However, his analysis of *The Changeling* seems to me to suffer from attempting to divorce 'dramatic technique' and 'poetry' (in both of which, he says, Middleton is inferior to Webster) from what he calls 'the moral essence of tragedy' (in which Middleton is superior to Webster).

Eliot also tends to consider Beatrice's 'character' as the centre of the play. He talks in terms of her 'habituation . . . to her sin' and claims, rather enigmatically, that 'she becomes moral only by becoming damned'. The objections to this approach are, first, that there is no mention in this play of 'damnation' (certainly not in the *Faustus* sense). More important, the whole question of Beatrice-Joanna's character is part of a wider problem, the nature of which I think Eliot does not see. The whole structure of the play depends upon rapid changes from one point of view – or one vantage-point – to another. Thus, illusion and reality, public honour and private lust, interchange so quickly that they are seen, in the course of the play, both as different things and as parts of the same thing. Beatrice herself is a focal point both of this process and of the 'castle' image. She is drawn quite deliberately as a single-minded and in that sense comparatively uncomplicated person. Her personality does not try to include all possible varieties of experience as, say, Flamineo's does. She is much more like the Racinian heroines – especially Hermione – who switch from one position to another without any pause for reflection, much less any mature understanding of why they do so. As such she focuses on a personal plane the wider implications developed in the switch between the outside and the inside of Vermandero's castle.

further defines Middleton's point. There is in this drama a terrifying gap between the apparently impeccable processes of reason and the intellect (cf. Beatrice-Joanna's early speeches) on the one hand, and on the other, the world of sex and the passions which keeps breaking in. Those early speeches of Beatrice, Alsemero and Vermandero look so calm and controlled, but as the action goes forward it becomes clearer and clearer that it was a calm that was maintained, for a while, only because it ignored a good half of the problems which even then were present. It is the oddity and danger of this gap between two worlds which cannot afford thus to ignore each other that Middleton is exploring. He chooses an action with a constantly shifting focus because, though the concepts of reason (or 'judgment' as Middleton more usually puts it) and love look at first sight quite stable, it is in the end their very stability which is seen to be wrong. In a healthy society they should, presumably, be related; here they circle around each other, and Beatrice-Joanna in particular is capable of seeing only one at a time. Middleton, of course, sees the whole and sees it clearly. His placing of points of view, at odds with each other, results in a combination of clarity and depth of focus unique in Jacobean drama. The constantly shifting set of relationships provides a much more difficult and complicated play than anything supplied by the usual tragedy of blood; the clear, dispassionate and stable intelligence which is always sensed to be behind this gives direction and clarity to difficulties which enrich but at the same time confuse writing from other Jacobean authors.

The clarity and depth of Middleton's enquiry depends principally upon certain key points of the action. First, in this respect, Act I as a whole in a packed, Ibsen-like beginning to the play presents us with Vermandero and Beatrice-Joanna already trapped in the equivocations of seeing and not-seeing that dominate the play. They, and other characters at this stage, are convinced that they are living and acting in a world dominated by the virtues of clarity and good sense. Everything they say hints that they are drastically mistaken in this belief. We shall see that later in Act I this kind of dilemma is enriched by Middleton's exploration of the castle image that Vermandero and others insist on.

The opening scenes, as Miss Bradbrook points out,[1] depend on an enquiry into the dangerous inadequacy of reason as a guide to conduct. There is here a good deal of talk, especially from Beatrice and Alsemero, about eyes (the organs of sight which give you the outward and apparently obvious view of things) and judgment (the faculty which should tell you the true value of what has been presented by the sight). Here already the themes of the play are first stated:

> *Alsemero* I love you dearly.
> *Beatrice* Be better advis'd, sir;
> Our eyes are sentinels unto our judgments,
> And should give certain judgment what they see;
> But they are rash sometimes, and tell us wonders
> Of common things, which when our judgments find,
> They can then check the eyes, and call them blind.
>
> I, i, 74 ff.

This is small talk between lovers, and were it the only example of its kind, it would be rash to take it too seriously. However, Middleton's method in this play, very often, is to qualify apparently innocent remarks by giving them later on an ironic significance, and here this is very much the case. Beatrice herself takes up her own phrase in a more serious way in an aside which follows immediately. It is almost as if she were surprised that anything she said could be so true:

> *Beatrice (aside)*   For five days past
> To be recall'd! Sure mine eyes were mistaken;
> This was the man was meant me.   I, i, 86–88

And the whole sequence is given its true significance by De Flores's

---

[1] *Themes and Conventions*, p. 214 ff.

entrance which follows immediately. Beatrice has advised judgment – more seriously than she at first intended – and it must be
pointed on Middleton's part to bring in then, within a few lines, the
very thing that removes her judgment entirely. First, the father's
approach, bearing the news of Piracquo's arrival, is announced by
De Flores, whose words unconsciously echo the strain of the previous conversation and in particular of Beatrice's aside, with its
suggestion that her 'eyes' had seen wrongly in the case of Piracquo:

> *De Flores* Your eye shall instantly instruct you, lady;
> He's coming hitherward.   I, i, 98–99

It is at this point that De Flores's presence throws Beatrice immediately off balance:

> *Beatrice*   What needed then
> Your duteous preface? I had rather
> He had come unexpected; you must stall
> A good presence with unnecessary blabbing;
> And how welcome for your part you are,
> I'm sure you know.   I, i, 99–104

This is the earliest statement in the play of how all or most of these
people go wrong in the business of living. Already Middleton is
juggling the concepts of reason and irrational love or hate, showing
them at times as separate; at others as seriously in danger of
clashing; at no time properly and stably united. There is, in fact,
too wide and too sudden a gap between the talk of reason and the
presence of passion, and this, simply, is what the play is about. The
bewildering irrationality of passion in a world otherwise dominated by reason yields a concept very like Racine's: love is a
'possession' in the Racinian sense ('C'est Vénus tout entière à sa
proie attachée').

The whole sequence between Beatrice and De Flores is repeated
and extended later on in Act II. Before looking at this, there are
added complications, widening the sphere of Middleton's enquiry,
in those opening scenes in Act I. In fact it is the complexity and

wide scope of the opening scenes that make it very necessary for
Middleton to restate the simple basic problem, between Beatrice
and De Flores, in Act II.

The Ibsen-like opening, with dark hints of more beneath the
pleasant naturalistic surface than would at first appear, is brought
into focus and widened in scope by two things: the beginning of
the series of puns on the word 'changeling', and the introduction
of the image of Vermandero's castle. The changeling image I need
hardly more than mention at the moment. It is obviously very important and I cannot see how critics could have so long assumed
that it referred simply to the characters in the sub-plot.[1] Here, right
at the beginning, it announces the way in which characters in the
play as a whole, particularly, of course, Beatrice-Joanna, 'change'
from one kind or sphere of significance to another. The lovers in
the sub-plot are 'changed' by lust and the disguises they adopt into
madmen (love is a 'tame madness'), and Beatrice is changed from
the sphere in which we first see her (public respectability) to that
dominated by De Flores and the sub-plot. On a more general
plane, the image of the changeling juxtaposes the two worlds,
Vermandero's and De Flores's, which both have a claim on
Beatrice. More particularly, the temple image in the first scene,
from which Alsemero will not change, but from which Beatrice
fears she may, opens up the whole business of being a changeling
and this then continues through the bargain with De Flores and the
sub-plot to the open statement at the end:

> *Alsemero* What an opacous body had that moon
> That last chang'd on us! Here's beauty chang'd
> To ugly whoredom; here servant-obedience
> To a master-sin, imperious murder;
> I, a suppos'd husband, chang'd embraces
> With wantonness – but that was paid before.
>
> V, iii, 197-202

[1] E.g. Hazelton Spencer, *Elizabethan Plays* (London, 1934), p. 1016.

The image of Vermandero's castle is the really important focal point which both widens and sharpens Middleton's investigation of his theme. The meaning of the play as a whole, and its significance, can perhaps most easily be seen in terms of this image. I had nearly called the theme of the play, as Bradbrook tends to do, that of appearance and reality, or sight and judgment. But this will not do because it is too schematic to fit Middleton's play. Some such phrase as this might work as a summing up, or a temporary reminder of the outlines of the action, but the ironic balance of the appearance of reason against the reality of lust needs a more extended statement than that given by any single phrase, and the temptation to over-simplify must be avoided. All I can say at this stage is that these two images, of the changeling and the castle, are part of the action as outlined so far, part of Middleton's investigation into the gap between intellect and the passions, and so into the various worlds between which Beatrice-Joanna moves.

The image of the castle is rather like that of the temple. It stands for something which looks, and in a sense perhaps is, firmly irreproachable. In a limited way there is a stability behind Alsemero's worshipping at the temple and, also, behind Vermandero's concept of a stronghold which must be jealously guarded, simply because it is a position of strength and order. But Middleton sees these images *both* as admirable in themselves *and* as modified, even endangered, by their position in the action as a whole. The first important mention of the castle image is in Act I, scene i, 160ff. It comes in the middle of an admirably controlled dialogue between Alsemero, Vermandero, and Beatrice which culminates in the beautifully naturalistic maunderings of the old man about his youth with Alsemero's father. The surface – again as in certain important Ibsen passages – is unruffled, and this reinforces Vermandero's estimate of himself and his household; but the reinforcement is ironically twisted because Vermandero has not the faintest conception how far his remarks really reach into the depths

of the circumstances that even now surround him. The key speech
is in answer to Beatrice's request that Alsemero be shown over the
castle; Vermandero is terribly proud, and terribly cautious of his
castle:

> With all my heart, sir.
> Yet there's an article between; I must know
> Your country; we use not to give survey
> Of our chief strengths to strangers; our citadels
> Are plac'd conspicuous to outward view,
> On promonts' tops, but within are secrets . . .
>   I, i, 168 ff.

'Within are secrets' indeed. A little later, after the talk of
Alsemero's father, the same note of curious foreboding returns,
this time firmly based on one of the equivocations of 'changed'.
Alsemero, realizing that Beatrice is contracted to Piracquo, suddenly decides to leave and is rebuked by Vermandero:

> How, sir? By no means;
> Not chang'd so soon, I hope! You must see my castle,
> And her best entertainment, e'er we part.   I, i, 207-9

The exchange concludes with an aside from Alsemero, who, alone
with Beatrice, has recognized the likely implications of Vermandero's innocent insistence on his daughter's marriage and the
arrival of Alonzo:

> How shall I dare to venture in his castle,
> When he discharges murderers at the gate?
>   I, i, 229-30

At this stage, of course, nobody has the faintest conception of what
the 'best entertainment' will turn out to be, and the dramatic irony
is doubly enhanced by the wonderfully real heartiness and insensitivity of Vermandero, completely unconscious alike of what his
castle will provide and of what his daughter is thinking, indeed of
what she is really like inside. The sort of slightly stupid or blunted
calm of mind that Vermandero is given here is one of the best

examples of Middleton's ability to introduce the naturalistic solidity of common life into tragedy which reaches beyond naturalism to a poetic ordering of experience.

Here then is a statement on yet another plane of what the play is getting at. The image of the castle is established as something fair and publicly acceptable on the outside; within, unstable and tortuous in some way as yet undefined. By this, Middleton cuts far deeper than the merely psychological level of the ins-and-outs of his extraordinary, fascinating heroine and juxtaposes the appearance of things and the inner 'reality' (if that is what it will turn out to be) on a more general and more significant plane. The play takes on a new dimension here, a new thickness of texture, without losing the intelligent clarity of outline essential to Middleton's point. Indeed, together with the story of Beatrice and De Flores, this image of Vermandero's castle supports and governs the whole play (much as, for instance, Racine's palace-labyrinth image supports and governs *Phèdre* and, to a lesser extent, *Andromaque*). I think it is not too much to say that, right up to the end, the plan of the action in a general way is that the main plot takes place on or near the 'outward view' of the castle, either in the open or in rooms like Alsemero's apartments recognized, by the ethos of the play, as having an official status in the well-ordered living of the household; the sub-plot, on the other hand, is deliberately placed in the asylum kept, at Vermandero's pleasure, by Alibius. This may or may not be specifically placed in some remote part of the castle, but the point is that, by the character of the dialogue, especially Isabella's, the asylum takes on the character of a labyrinth, a section within Vermandero's apparently straightforward castle which will have a comment to make on the quality and worth of the outside:

> *Isabella* Stand up, thou son of Cretan Daedalus,
> And let us tread the lower labyrinth;
> I'll bring thee to the clue.

Of this, more presently. The main point here is to establish the action as depending to a very large extent on this image of Vermandero's castle, apparently straightforward and publicly acceptable (cf. again the naturalistic tone he uses when talking about his affairs generally), but 'within are secrets'. The duplicity of the castle image (like the temple, it betrays all the main characters by its seeming self-sufficiency) sharpens and extends the dichotomy in the character of Beatrice-Joanna (who turns out in the end to be very like it) and points the way in which she moves from Vermandero's world to that of De Flores and the sub-plot where, in a sense, she always belonged. Vermandero's remarks at the beginning, with unconscious irony, refer to his daughter as well as his castle: 'We use not to give survey / Of our chief strengths to strangers . . .'

The only possible exception to the general rule of the main plot in the public, official portion of the castle, the sub-plot 'below', or in the asylum, is the murder of Alonzo. This is strictly part of the main plot and has nothing directly to do with Isabella's plotting; yet it takes place, not, of course, in the open, but in its own kind of labyrinth, parallel, obviously, to the labyrinths of sex Isabella enters in the sub-plot. However, this only means that one portion of the main plot has borrowed something of the structure and location of the sub-plot, in order to bring the two closer together still. Like Isabella, De Flores is at this moment working up to his bargain with his lover, or the woman he hopes will be his lover, and so the action descends from the public plane to the fortifications hidden beneath the battlements. Appropriately, all the imagery in this murder scene recalls earlier talk about the structure of the building. Apart from a slight hint of a more conventional Jacobean wit in De Flores's *double entendre* here, even the prevailing naturalistic tone of the opening scenes is repeated:

Alonzo De Flores.
De Flores   My kind, honourable Lord.

Alonzo I am glad I ha' met with thee.
De Flores   Sir.
Alonzo   Thou canst show me
The full strength of the castle.
De Flores   That I can, sir.
Alonzo I much desire it.
De Flores And if the ways and straits
Of some of the passages be not too tedious for you,
I will assure you, worth your time and sight, my Lord.
II, ii, 157-62

Middleton is clearly enriching his 'castle' image and building up to
a scene which will combine a view of the strength and prosperity
of the outside with the dubious fortifications underneath; and in
Act III, scenes i and ii, it follows:

De Flores All this is nothing; you shall see anon
A place you little dream on . . .
My Lord, I'll place you at a casement here
Will show you the full strength of all the castle.
Look, spend your eye awhile upon that object.
Alonzo Here's rich variety, De Flores . . .   III, ii, 1 ff.

Alonzo is being conducted 'within', but he doesn't see just how
different from the 'rich variety' of the public appearance of the
castle this will turn out to be. Middleton is fairly launched on his
investigation of the various worlds into which Beatrice-Joanna
must move.[1]

I have commented at length on the details of the imagery and
tone of the verse and the movement of the dialogue in the opening
scenes of the play because *The Changeling* is both so complicated

[1] There are times in the play when Vermandero's castle is seen merely as a citadel commanding a town in which minor incidents in the action take place. But despite Middleton's
naturalism, there is a lot in the play which is not to be taken literally. Citadel or castle, the
image takes on, poetically, the character I have ascribed to it above.

Furthermore in scenes like the ones discussed here (Act III, scenes i and ii) the sexual puns
Middleton constantly uses enforce the suggestion that the 'castle' itself is an image con-
ceived at least partly in sexual terms. On Middleton's puns see Christopher Ricks, 'The
Moral and Poetic Structure of *The Changeling*', *Essays in Criticism*, July 1960, pp. 290-306.

and so consistently intelligent a play that, more obviously even than other great Jacobean plays, its full meaning and worth emerge only from such an examination of detail. It has, on the other hand, a story. I should like now to notice how, at various key points, the plot and sub-plot change character and are modified and extended as they become involved in the kind of very subtle and complex writing that characterizes the opening scenes.

As early as Act I, scene i, we are beginning to realize that the mind will be constantly cast backwards and forwards over the extent of the whole play. The final effect is a sort of pun on the word 'change'. People do change, relationships change, but often they only change towards something that was in a way as real as their first, i.e. their outward, appearance. It is not a simple change from one state to its opposite only; the opposite was in a sense there all the time: compare the betraying vehemence of hatred – quite inexplicable on rational grounds – that Beatrice has for De Flores all through. What follows is, in a way, a change, but also it merely proves what was so in the first place, though disguised then.

As the action unfolds, early references to this sort of thing are picked up and the movement forward becomes also, as in Ibsen, a movement backwards. First of all, in Act I, scene ii, the perfectly well-meant remarks of Vermandero about his castle spring back to mind when we begin to see what in fact is 'within'. This scene presents us with the first display of madmen. The general talk in the scene runs on jealous husbands (a theme dear to the heart of Jacobean playwrights but also, perhaps, related here specifically to Vermandero's paternal despotism) and, more particularly, intro-duces Antonio, disguised as an idiot so he can win Alibius's young wife. This fills out considerably the fairly simple statement of the castle image in scene i, because, though no direct comparisons have been made yet, this *is* the inside of the castle and it is given over to the frank pursuit of lust, accompanied by the lewd chorus of

madmen: 'Cat whore, cat whore! her permasant, her permasant!'
Beatrice has earlier been specifically connected with the fair outward view of the castle, and though she has done nothing yet
beyond disobeying her father in the matter of marriage, or
wanting to, the parallel between her actions and Antonio's (and
hence the inside of the castle) is the more significant. A hint of
relationships not yet fully worked out can be far more telling than
a direct statement.

Parallels of this kind continue as the play proceeds. Meanwhile,
there are also many references backwards to specific phrases and
turns of speech. For instance, moving to the first scene in Act II,
there is Beatrice's extraordinary speech about loving now 'with
the eyes of judgment' (lines 6-26). This picks up her earlier dialogue
with Alsemero on judgment and sight which, however, has since
proved intensely suspect. (The very first thing she did was to act
unreasonably towards De Flores.) Here, the remarks themselves
sound unexceptionable on the face of it:

> He that can choose
> That bosom well who of his thoughts partakes,
> Proves most discreet in every choice he makes.
> Methinks I love now with the eyes of judgment,
> And see the way to merit, clearly see it.
>
> II, i, 10-14

The sentiments themselves are fine, but there is the feeling of a
dreadful gap in the woman's logic, and this makes her reaction to
the horrid De Flores (repeated again here), and the whole business
of the outward and the inward castle, gradually more pointed.
She's no more acting by reason than flying to the moon – she
scarcely knows either Alsemero or his friend, let alone whether
they're reliable – and, by giving De Flores another entrance at
this stage, Middleton must again be pointing this gap between her
absolute conviction of reason and the, in fact, shaky reasoning that
went to make it up. In the circumstances, the suggestion of couplet

form enhances the dangerous self-sufficiency of her thought-processes. One is inevitably reminded of Vermandero's complacent praise of his well ordered and defended castle, and his ignorance of what the inside of it is really like. And in both scenes, the irony depends as much on the unruffled naturalism of the dialogue as on any other single aspect of the writing:

> *Vermandero* Oh, sir, I knew your father;
> We two were in acquaintance long ago,
> Before our chins were worth iulan down . . .
>   An unhappy day
> Swallowed him at last at Gibraltar,
> In fight with those rebellious Hollanders.
> Was it not so?   I, i, 180 ff.

In this context, the absolute irrationality of Beatrice's loathing for De Flores is doubly alarming and significant. Beatrice shares her father's vein of complacent reasoning and rationalization, but Middleton, right from the beginning, couples this fairly consistently with language reserved for De Flores: 'This ominous ill-faced fellow more disturbs me / Than all my other passions'. In context I think it is fair to suggest that the phrase 'all my other passions' implies that De Flores – and all he comes to stand for in connection with the inner forces of Vermandero's world – disturbs Beatrice more even than her accepted lover, Alsemero. In fact the energy of the play consistently comes from the *un*-reasonable and the irrational, which therefore appears as twisted and destructive not because it is *in essence* evil, but because somehow the gap between reason and passion has grown too large. The energetic forces of the play are the 'secrets within'; the focus of Middleton's dramatic structure allows them to contribute depth and strength to the poetic image (the castle), even while they are presented as inevitably destroying the people in their power.

The next scene that, as the action unfolds, presents itself as an important key to Middleton's meaning is De Flores's killing of

Alonzo, the man Beatrice no longer wants. I have already looked at this and it only remains here to stress again the way in which De Flores's irony develops and deepens the image of Vermandero's castle. Middleton is now fairly launched on his artistic task of uniting the story of Beatrice's attraction to De Flores with the more subtle and generalized implications of that image.

And indeed, the murder scene is followed immediately by a return to the madmen and the scheming over Isabella. On the one plane, there is a simple parallel between the people involved: Lollio, like De Flores, puts in for his share; Isabella, like Beatrice and unlike her, appears to grant it, but willingly this time.[1] On the other plane, this comparison is widened by the fact that, again, this asylum is the reality that Vermandero had so innocently referred to as the 'secrets within'. Middleton is further exploring his identification of the apparently impeccable Beatrice, the image of the well-brought-up young girl (though the asides to her father in Act I have already been disturbing), with the dubious irrationality of the asylum and the fortifications.

This brings us pretty well to the centre of the play and to a further and stronger statement still from Middleton on Beatrice's extraordinary blindness to things she doesn't want to see; again it is a statement in terms of an apparently reasonable judgment which appears flawless but in fact misses the obvious. The importance of this scene (Act III, scene iv) lies as much in the lateness of its appearance in the action as in anything else. De Flores's point, that his bargain is in fact a just one and must be carried out by someone who is his partner in murder, is stated by Middleton in the clearest and most literal terms, simply in order to demonstrate that

[1] Many commentators would disagree with my emphasis on Isabella's apparent 'willingness' to grant her lovers' demands. Admittedly, she does not *actually* 'fall'; but it seems to me that the implications of her speech 'Hey, how he treads the air . . .' (for discussion of this, see below) and of her frank replies to Lollio ('The first place is thine, believe it, Lollio . . .') are that there is a serious intention beneath the comedy. For a contrary view, see Bradbrook, *op. cit.*, p. 222; William Empson, *Some Versions of Pastoral* (London, 1935), pp. 49-51; J. D. Jump, 'Middleton's Tragedies', in the Pelican *Age of Shakespeare*, p. 367.

Beatrice, even as late as this, has got nowhere in her attempts to
see 'reasonably'. Deliberately, she is presented, not as a character
who 'develops', but as someone who, unless she sees a point or
argument wholly (which she does not, until the end), sees none of
it. And in all this, the sub-plot and its implications are again
brought to mind both by De Flores's bargaining, akin to Lollio's,
and by specific remarks such as Beatrice's unconscious echo of
Isabella:

> *Beatrice (aside)* I'm in a labyrinth;
> What will content him?   III, iv, 73-74

One important qualification to these remarks on Act III, scene
iv: though, as the dialogue demonstrates, Beatrice is almost unbelievably ignorant of her guilt –

> Why, 'tis impossible thou canst be so wicked,
> Or shelter such a cunning cruelty,
> To make his death the murderer of my honor!
> Thy language is so bold and vicious,
> I cannot see which way I can forgive it
> With any modesty.
>
> *De Flores* Push! you forget yourself;
> A woman dipp'd in blood, and talk of modesty!
>
>   III, iv, 121-7

– nevertheless Middleton wants us to feel that honour is not
merely a word to Beatrice and to others in this context. There are
times when the tone of the verse and dialogue changes slightly.
Just occasionally, Beatrice is allowed to drop the tone of cold,
frightened rationality which so far has been the only modification
of the calm of the opening scenes, and Middleton borrows a little
of the richer, more lyrical note of her last speech (Act V) to point
out that her protests are, in fact, perfectly sincere. Honour is more
than simply the 'fair name' implied by the speech quoted above,
and the labyrinths within have not the monopoly of truth in this
play. They share it with a deeply felt concern by Beatrice for the

virtues rather stupidly espoused by her father. In this passage, for example, the tone of the verse is unmistakably more heartfelt, less coldly distant than before:

> *De Flores* Justice invites your blood to understand me.
> *Beatrice* I dare not.
> *De Flores*   Quickly!
> *Beatrice*   Oh, I never shall!
> Speak it yet further off, that I may lose
> What has been spoken, and no sound remain on't;
> I would not hear so much offence again
> For such another deed.   III, iv 101-106

Both views of Middleton's castle have their own validity. The final truth resides with neither alone, but in the juxtaposition of the two.

Beatrice's blindness itself is not finally cleared away until the last scene of the play. Meanwhile, one other important scene takes us back once more to Alibius's house and gives the last and most authoritative enlargement of the depth of the puzzle within the castle image. Here it is, in Act IV, scene iii, that Isabella dresses up as a madwoman in order to meet Antonio (also disguised) and, possibly, submit to his proposals. The implied comment is divided between the by now familiar idea that we must assume changeling shapes, shapes other than our own, in order to bring out and define something that is in a sense in our natures anyway (the whole sequence recalls Beatrice's 'I shall change my saint, I fear . . .' Act I, scene i, 162 ff.), and the idea that in the madhouse or labyrinth 'below', and in the language and thought used by madmen, lust that would otherwise be repressed by respectable society has free rein. The many references in the dialogue to 'lunatic lovers' and love as a 'tame madness' refer, I take it, both to the present situation and to the link that has been built up between the 'tame' loves of Alsemero and Beatrice and the madness in the sub-plot.

The castle image itself is here, and finally, defined in terms of the Greek myths that Isabella and Franciscus refer to from time to

time. Most of the dialogue is in phallic terms, and includes a bid
for Isabella by Lollio: '. . . if I find you minister once, and set up in
the trade, I put in for my thirds; I shall be mad or fool else.' This
is of course another version of De Flores's point, and Isabella's
reply differs from Beatrice's only in being more clear-sighted:
'The first place is thine, believe it, Lollio, / If I do fall.' In this
world of *actual* madmen, lust is a sordid business deal, but it is also
more frankly recognized for what it is than in the world where
society and 'reason' dominate. The two planes of action combine
in Isabella's important speech after her entry as a madwoman,
frankly tempting her lover:

> *Isabella* Hey, how he treads the air! Shough, shough, t'other way!
> He burns his wings else; here's wax enough below, Icarus,
> more than will be cancelled these eighteen moons.
> He's down, he's down, what a terrible fall he had!
> Stand up, thou son of Cretan Daedalus,
> And let us tread the lower labyrinth:
> I'll bring thee to the clue.   IV, iii, 119–124

The sense beneath the nonsense is evidently telescoping the fall of
Icarus and the business of facing and destroying the Minotaur in
the Daedalus-Theseus-Ariadne myth. The phallic suggestions
clearly start with the evocation of Pasiphae's monster of lust, the
beast born of her union with the bull and then confined by Minos
in the labyrinth; link at this point with the idea of Daedalus, the
fabulous artificer, containing unrestrained lust by the intelligence
and artifice of his labyrinth; and take in also the cunning of
Theseus and Ariadne, with their clue of thread, and the 'fall' of
Icarus. Here in this scene is the final enactment of the character of
Vermandero's castle and an invitation by Isabella to Franciscus to
take more openly the way already – for all she would not admit it –
attempted by Beatrice, and tackle the labyrinth of lust beneath
the 'tame' surface. Characteristically, Middleton has already
allowed himself, in addition to the general parallels and contrasts

of action, one specific remark which links Isabella with Beatrice, Lollio with De Flores:

> De Flores   I could ha' hired
> A journeyman in murder at this rate,
> And mine own conscience might have slept at ease,
> And have had the work brought home.
> Beatrice (*aside*)   I'm in a labyrinth:
> What will content him?   III, iv, 69-73

At this key point in the action the Daedalus myth, with its intricate linking of marvellous artifice and frankly open lust, admirably suits the tone and structure of Middleton's play. It presents pictorially – through the actions of Isabella and her two lovers in the madhouse – what De Flores has already stated in so many words. More important, through the labyrinth image, it unites the utter sordidness of the goings-on in the sub-plot with the more imaginative vision behind and in the play as a whole. The paradox, Middleton is saying, lies in the fact that the public, accepted way of life and the outward appearance of people like Beatrice can remain so apparently secure, when obviously they cannot be taken at their face value in view of the powerful and uncontrollable forces at work underneath.[1]

It is at such points in the play that the comparison with Racine seems to me most compelling. Both *The Changeling* and *Phèdre* depend on a clear, energetic conception of dramatic verse and structure; both are dominated by a key image (the 'castle' or

[1] The sub-plot of *The Changeling* has always presented difficulties. Miss Bradbrook's account (*Themes and Conventions*, pp. 221 ff.) of its relations to the main plot seems to me to dispose of the earlier argument (cf. Hazelton Spencer's in his introduction to the play) that it is merely one of the unrelated lunatic fantasies beloved of the Elizabethans. (However, she has not convinced others – see for instance R. H. Barker, *Thomas Middleton* (N.Y., 1958), pp. 129-30.) In this chapter I have attempted to take the issue further and see the sub-plot as part of the developing castle image. I should add that, though the sub-plot does seem to me substantially good and valuable dramatic writing, some parts of it are feeble and the intended points are barely made. (See in particular the rather repetitive quality of the 'we three' joke and the familiar Elizabethan punning on fools and knaves in the latter half of Act I, scene ii. Later scenes – Act II, scene iii, and Act IV, scene iii – are infinitely more convincing.)

'palace' and its labyrinths) which uses the myth of Theseus and the monster to fuse at once the energy and the destructive power of lust. As in Middleton, the drive of Racine's play comes from those forces of the 'labyrinth' which 'possess' the characters and thus inevitably disrupt normal relations and normal living. Here, for instance, Phèdre, having begun to describe her love for Theseus, ends by identifying her husband with his son and declaring her love for Hippolyte:

> Pourquoi, trop jeune encor, ne pûtes-vous alors
> Entrer dans le vaisseau qui le mit sur nos bords?
> Par vous aurait péri le monstre de la Crète,
> Malgré tous les détours de sa vaste retraite . . .
> C'est moi, prince, c'est moi, dont l'utile secours
> Vous eût du labyrinthe enseigné les détours:
> Que de soins m'eût coutés cette tête charmante!
> Un fil n'eût point assez rassuré votre amante:
> Compagne du péril qu'il vous fallait chercher,
> Moi-même devant vous j'aurais voulu marcher;
> Et Phèdre au labyrinthe avec vous descendue
> Se serait avec vous retrouvée ou perdue.[1]

On the other hand, if Phèdre herself is in the grip of destructive forces, the verse and the play remain clear and firm in texture, seeing both the power *and* the destruction as part of the growing image of the labyrinth.

The end of Middleton's play brings to a halt at last the intricate juggling of different worlds, different values. On a simple plane, Alsemero's perhaps slightly too jolly speech 'What an opacous body had that moon / That last changed on us . . . (Act V, scene iii, 197ff.) formally links all the changelings in the play together. More important, the obvious change in tone in Beatrice's last speech marks the end of her fatal single-mindedness and of the separation of the public and private worlds in Vermandero's castle:

[1] *Théatre Complet de Racine*, Classiques Garnier, p. 563.

O, come not near me, sir, I shall defile you!
I that am of your blood was taken from you
For your better health; look no more upon't,
But cast it to the ground regardlessly,
Let the common sewer take it from distinction:[1]
Beneath the stars, upon yon meteor
    (*Pointing to De Flores*)
Ever hung my fate, 'mongst things corruptible;
I ne'er could pluck it from him; my loathing
Was prophet to the rest, but ne'er believed:
Mine honour fell with him, and now my life.
Alsemero, I'm a stranger to your bed;
Your bed was cozened on the nuptial night,
For which your false bride died.
                  v, iii, 150-162

This is a speech collating complex ideas and relationships (e.g. the relationship of honour to whoredom, of reason and logic to passion and lust) which Middleton has been investigating from the beginning of the play. It is also the moment in the play when Beatrice at last, and with virtually no further prevarication, sees truly. Rightly, therefore, the verse has none of the disturbing hints of rhetorical over-emphasis and illogicality of Act II, scene i:

Methinks I love now with the eyes of judgment,
And see the way to merit, clearly see it . . .

On the contrary, the richer note, implicit in imagery like that of the now (and probably always) unattainable stars, is barely allowed to rise above the tone of flat statement typical of most of the play: 'I that am of your blood was taken from you / For your better

---

[1] Text based on Mermaid edition. Hazelton Spencer's reading of these lines seems to me unsatisfactory:
    Let the common sewer take it from distinction
    Beneath the stars; upon yon meteor . . .
N. W. Bawcutt supports the Mermaid text on these lines (see Revels Plays edition (London, 1958), p. 109). However, Bawcutt changes the second line of Beatrice's speech to read 'I am that of your blood . . .' (Revels edition, p. 108). This certainly makes clear sense, but seems rhythmically inept.

health'. The tone of the speech I think very nicely balances a sense of rightness and sureness in Beatrice's new insight with a realization from Middleton – and from Beatrice herself – that up to this point she had no hope of seeing truly. The mixture of a richer satisfaction in the acceptance, at last, of things as they are, and the utterly impersonal insight – what would otherwise be called the fatalism – of Middleton is very well done. It is I think an improvement on the more operatic Webster, who can nevertheless produce the beautiful fatalism of the Cardinal –

> And now let me be laid by and never thought of

– in this case only slightly over-rich and self-conscious compared with the Middleton verse, which always returns to the flatness of naturalism or of something reaching back towards naturalism:

> . . . my loathing
> Was prophet to the rest, but ne'er believed:
> Mine honour fell with him, and now my life.

As a whole the play makes an impact probably greater than any other of Middleton's. It has the directness of outlook which characterizes *Women Beware Women*; it also seems to me more vital than this play because the peculiar structure allows a statement not of one thing only, viz. the unreality of the apparently real, but also of the frightening energy of the forces at work within the situations Middleton is describing. Beatrice and De Flores in particular, and on a more general plane Vermandero's castle with all it contains and stands for, its beauty and its 'labyrinths', have a passionate intensity unequalled elsewhere in Middleton except perhaps in individual characters. Though the play rarely swerves from the vein of naturalistic writing which makes Middleton such an original figure in the Jacobean drama, it has at the same time an imaginative depth and force comparable to Webster's.

Indeed what we have been observing in *The Changeling* is a

depth of focus unique in Jacobean (and probably any other) drama. The play is not to be placed in the richly evocative line of Shakespearean development; its meaning and significance are the result of a fresh start in Jacobean enquiry and one which depends a good deal on unswervingly naturalistic attitudes in the verse and dialogue. Yet a term like 'naturalism' is after all wrong or inadequate for Middleton's work as a whole and certainly for this play. Here as nowhere else we are presented, not with a flat, naturalistic surface, but with the spectacle of a single complex image – Vermandero's 'castle'– dominating a whole drama. Not only do we look at and admire the progress of the action; at the same time we, as it were, look down through the surface of this dominant image into the complexity of its internal structure. Where in other plays – Tourneur's, some of Marlowe's, Shakespeare's – we watch and participate in the growth of a network of inter-connected images, in *The Changeling* we are presented with something which is much more clearly a single complex image, a product of the whole play which grows in depth like a gradually expanding sphere, the surface of which is firm but also clear enough for us to gaze into the complex centre. The play is therefore unique, though linked with *Women Beware Women* in obvious ways. Together with the rest of Middleton's work it separates itself off from Jacobean drama generally; while at the same time it preserves, within the Middleton *œuvre*, a separate and distinct identity.

A consideration of the major plays of the Jacobean era seems to me to leave Middleton and Tourneur – different though they are – holding the positions of by far the greatest weight and significance. Webster makes his points right enough, and they are points of value. He is not a diluted Shakespeare, or an interesting collector's item in the history of the stage. But both the other major Jacobeans display a quicker intelligence over the whole range of their plays, and the result is that each lays firm hold of a larger area of Jacobean life than Webster can. Webster's best play, for all its insight, exists as a last spasmodic effort in a dying world. It has no firm hold on the experience that gives it birth. Its strength and weakness alike are that it has to attempt a singular achievement: a remarkably individual effort of structure within the play betrays the isolation of Webster's stand. There is no feeling that he has, as Shakespeare, Tourneur, Middleton all have in different ways, firm contact with a world either of richly conceived tradition and natural order, or – as in the case of Middleton – of coarse but substantial middle-class living.

The unmistakable sign of a superior order and stability in both Middleton and Tourneur is the display by each of a consistency of serious and intelligent writing over the whole extent of a given drama. In Middleton, the result of this, or the manifestation of it, is the freshness and sustained clarity of his approach to new and particularized problems. His plays amount to a thoroughly worked out revaluation of Jacobean experience. The problem of order and chaos in tragedy (as evoked, for instance, in the 'castle' image of *The Changeling*) is worked out in fresh terms; points now more and more clearly to new areas of *bourgeois* values in living (cf. the significance in *Women Beware Women* of the transference of mercantile terms and concepts to private life). Middleton of course is far from passively accepting the values and attitudes suggested to him by the society he sees; but his contact with a large and important movement in modern society is one of the things that gives solidity and firmness of structure to his plays.

The body of thought and experience that Tourneur draws on also has an encouraging and sustaining substance, though of course it is vastly different from Middleton's. (This is what makes it nonsense to think of the two as one man, with one aim in drama.) His play looks to a world in which, much more even than in Webster, and certainly more than in Shakespeare, tragedy works itself out in terms of the physical reality of sin. It is a world conceived partly in mediaeval terms, where sin is felt and perceived as a sensuous reality: 'Hast thou beguiled her of salvation, / And rubbed hell o'er with honey?' But also it is a mediaeval world reinvigorated and brought to a pitch of modern relevance by Tourneur's wit, focused on, and by, his dealings with the traditional Revenge ethic. And again, the substance of it all is manifested in the staying-power in Tourneur, the sustained force of his attack as he manipulates the Vendice *persona* throughout the whole, or almost the whole of the action. *The Revenger's Tragedy* is, simply, a more intelligent play than *The Duchess of Malfi*.

A critical map of Jacobean drama and its achievements would therefore reveal Tourneur and Middleton as in charge of larger and richer areas of the Jacobean world than Webster. They write more clearly than he does, and they are sturdier representatives of a sound moral / aesthetic position. Webster's triumph in the later Acts of *The Duchess* is something positive and recognizable; but in other respects he constantly gives himself away. He recognizes that drama, in more particular ways perhaps than poetry, is led to comment on the relation of its achievements to social attitudes and ways of living; but his attempts to do this are fragmentary.[1] Delio, at the end of *The Duchess*, attempts a 'Bear off the bodies' direction roughly parallel with, say, Albany's at the end of *Lear*. The difference is that Delio's speech, or at least that part of it which attempts a positive moral recovery, is utterly surprising in context:

> Let us make noble use
> Of this great ruin; and join all our force
> To establish this young hopeful gentleman
> In's mother's right . . .

---

[1] Cf. perhaps D. H. Lawrence's comments on Hardy and Tolstoy: 'It is the novelists and dramatists who have the hardest task in reconciling their metaphysic, their theory of being and knowing, with their living sense of being . . .' ('Study of Thomas Hardy', *Selected Literary Criticism* (London, 1955), p. 188.)

Nothing in the play has led us to assume that disruption on this social plane of living will be anything but universal and continuing. The only signs of a more stable order in the background are Antonio's opening speech about the moral French court and one or two sane but very short and conventional remarks from Delio and Cariola about the constancy of good friends. Shakespeare, on the other hand, not only has a far greater clarity at the heart of his conception of a tragic world – he is never tempted to the cloying heaviness of Bosola's 'He and his brother are like plum-trees that grow crooked . . .' – but also, and because of this, he deals effortlessly with the simpler problems of establishing order on the plane of social relations. He is untroubled, for instance, in firmly and clearly establishing Kent, Edgar, Albany, in his way the Fool, and (though obviously a chip off the old block) Cordelia as representatives of an order permanently resistant to the powerful chaotic forces of tragedy. In this company, Albany in his minor way has a particular interest. He becomes progressively more responsible as the play goes on and as he sees what is really happening. There is no one like this in Webster. The few poor representatives of morality start off, as they end, very firmly that way inclined; there is no sense in them of a growing moral awareness. Of course it is not essential for Webster, or anyone else, to show us specific characters on whom tragedy has exercised a reformative influence. The ways in which a dramatist can suggest wholeness, order, and sense are not limited to this. The point, rather, is that since Webster has in fact chosen this method of attempting to re-establish order in society, the awkwardness with which he does it betrays his lack of grip in such matters and particularly his lack of grip on, his alienation from, the social scene around him. His drama crumbles at the edges, revealing in this both a blurredness and confusion at the centre, and a lack of firm roots in a prevailing social order.

Substantiality and wholeness in Jacobean drama rest on the

achievements of Tourneur and Middleton. The essence of tragic insight in this period, the establishment of stability-in-chaos, depend upon a fitting together of their separate, complementary insights. Webster sags between these two; his grip on experience is narrower, more indeterminate. However, it can still be said that simple decadence begins elsewhere (and earlier) in Webster than with *The Duchess of Malfi*. It is only *after* considering the singular case of *The Duchess* that we can begin to talk, for the first time in Elizabethan drama, of anything like a simple, uninterrupted line of 'development'. Even then, of course, the career of Middleton in the 1620's interrupts any generalizations about the increasing decadence of Jacobean drama. But the tremendous possibilities for a fresh conception of comedy and tragedy that he outlined are nowhere taken up. The interest of the plays we shall consider in the following chapters of this book will be, increasingly, one of where, and in what manner, a decadent conception of drama took command in the seventeenth century. In the final chapter I shall make some suggestions about the implications of this decline in drama for the course of English literature generally. One of the most interesting problems raised by the collapse of drama is the position which, as a consequence, faced Marvell and later poets.

PART 3
THE DECADENCE

CHAPTER X

DECADENCE AND TRAGI-COMEDY: MARSTON AND WEBSTER

This chapter is concerned with general problems of decadence in Jacobean drama and, more particularly, with the problem of a growing uneasiness in Jacobean attempts to relate the comic and the tragic. Throughout the chapter I shall be using the term 'Jacobean' to refer very roughly to a chronological division (viz., to plays written after 1602), but I shall also want to distinguish some plays which, though written in the Jacobean period (1603–1625), are predominantly Elizabethan in feeling and tone.

The vexed question of decadence in English tragedy has no certain beginnings. The incidence of faithful servants, bluff soldiers, pitiful children, wives not only chaste but militantly so, grows rapidly with the early years of the seventeenth century. Sentimentality, melodrama, unrelated comic 'relief', twisting of plots with a careless indifference to issues raised earlier in the plays – there are clear signs of these things as early as you like to look in Jacobean, or even earlier drama. They take on real significance only when a reader has discovered for himself what Webster, Tourneur, Middleton have to say about a decadent society, and turns then to the minor figures. For many of these, decadence is not merely a threat but a commanding principle. If their touch is light enough, they turn, sometimes successfully, to one or other of the infinite degrees of tragi-comedy; if not, they struggle, more or less in vain, against encroaching instability, and so they appear soft and yielding, melodramatic or sentimental, precisely where Tourneur, Middleton and (at his best) Webster were toughly resistant.

Decadence, more often than not, is simply an avoidance of issues that, in terms of the plays, demand to be faced.

Where such an avoidance of issues shows most significantly in minor seventeenth-century plays, is in that 'blurring of the tragic and comic' Miss Bradbrook pointed to.[1] The Elizabethan impulse had been one which achieved clarity and firmness *without* making rigid distinctions between, for instance, low comedy and intelligent wit, or lyrical writing and comedy, or the tragic and the comic. With the Jacobeans, too often the comic writing either intrudes irrelevantly – fails to interpenetrate the tragic or lyric impulse – or is included only at the cost of loss of focus in the writing. Even Webster's powerful imagination is radically flawed in this way. For instance, Flamineo's satiric comments in *The White Devil* bear only intermittently on the tragic action of the play; and certainly Webster's attempt, in plays like *The Faire Maide* or *A Cure for a Cuckold*, to write 'tragi-comedy' (i.e. to relate the twin elements by treating tragedy *in terms of* comedy) ends most often in a thinly disguised sentimentality. Indeed most of the plays usually thought of as tragi-comedies – particularly Fletcher's – point pretty obviously to a fatal split *between* tragedy and comedy and hence to the emergence of sentimental tragedy in Chapman, Ford, Shirley and, ultimately, the Heroic Drama.

Generalizations of this kind about 'decadence' would probably be endorsed by most critics – up to the point at which they must be applied to particular plays. Miss Bradbrook and Miss Ellis-Fermor, for instance, agree on many of the more general issues, but are quite at odds with respect to particular plays, and even, in the end, on their judgment of what the minor Jacobeans as a whole are worth.[2] More recently, there have been attempts to re-

---

[1] Bradbrook, *Themes and Conventions*, pp. 240 ff. (and cf. pp. 72-73).

[2] Bradbrook, pp. 240 ff. ('The Decadence'); U. Ellis-Fermor, *The Jacobean Drama* (London, 1936), pp. 201 ff. (on Beaumont and Fletcher) and pp. 227 ff. (on Ford). T. S. Eliot's strictures against Fletcher and Ford (*Selected Essays*, pp. 193-204) are of course brilliantly penetrating (though personally I find his valuations of individual plays an-

habilitate the minor Jacobeans in ways which imply that apparently well-recognized critical points about decadence do not, for some reason, apply to writers like Ford and Fletcher. Most of the difficulty stems, I think, from a growing tendency to assume – more readily in Jacobean studies even than elsewhere – that a mere tracing of 'themes' and 'patterns of development' is a sufficient answer to critical worries about individual plays. Thus it is assumed that if Fletcher, for instance, can be shown to write in terms of 'patterns of emotion' we need not enquire too closely into *what* emotions are at stake, or what of value emerges from the 'patterning'. Alternatively, if certain plays can be called 'tragi-comedy', it is therefore suggested that they must be judged by their own standards and not those of Shakespeare and earlier writers. Even Miss Bradbrook tends at times to assume that convention is convention and further enquiry therefore redundant; and certainly her more valuable insights into particular plays and problems are rapidly being submerged by a tendency in recent criticism towards a new version of the insidious and misleading 'doctrine of kinds'.[1] The quality of the writing in individual plays – the degree of its maturity and insight – is clearly the only safe basis for generalizations about the Jacobean (or any other) age. The question of 'tragi-comedy' is particularly important here. There are firm critical distinctions we must make in order to avoid lumping all plays with a 'happy ending' under the one heading.

noyingly ambiguous). Miss Bradbrook's brilliant half-chapter on Beaumont and Fletcher has – or should have had – as many of the answers to the real problems of this kind of play as one has a right to expect in ten pages of criticism. She is at times cryptic to the point of obscurity, but almost all her judgments are extremely valuable and demand to be enlarged or challenged or both. So far, too many of them have been simply ignored. (Among more recent studies of the period, the Pelican Guide No. 2 deals thoroughly and intelligently with some of the questions opened up by Miss Bradbrook.)

[1] Of all intentionalist misdirections in critical thinking, the assumption that a work of art must be judged according to rules of its 'kind' seems to me the most inflexible and misleading. In drama, it is most pervasive in studies of the minor Jacobeans (though once again the Pelican Guide stands out as a welcome exception to general tendencies in criticism – cf. Note 1, Chapter XI).

If we take as a leading case the works of Marston and Webster, there are two plays at least which point to a blend of the tragic and the comic utterly different from conventional 'tragi-comedy'. Both *The Malcontent* and *The Devil's Law Case* are in fact simply late examples of good Elizabethan writing of a kind that was common enough in the Elizabethan age and hence needs no special label like tragi-comedy to describe it. Indeed to call such plays tragi-comedy is dangerous on two counts. First, it wrongly implies that they are distinctively Jacobean in feeling, or are part of a trend culminating in Fletcher. (Fletcher's attempts to link the tragic and the comic are not merely sentimental, but clearly self-conscious in a way quite foreign to the simple Elizabethan assumption that the two *are* linked.) And second, calling plays like *The Malcontent* and *The Devil's Law Case* tragi-comedy tends either to under-value them (on this view they would be *merely* 'tragi-comedy'); or else to overvalue plays like Fletcher's, and some of Webster's own, by incorporating within the *genre* intelligence and energy of a kind it does not in fact have. The Jacobean age could and did produce great drama which saw tragedy in comic terms and in ways distinct from characteristically Elizabethan writing, but this was Middleton's, not Fletcher's, achievement. On the other hand, where Marston and Webster succeed – as they do to a considerable extent in *The Malcontent* and *The Devil's Law Case* – they do so not, as Middleton did, by seeing new directions in which tragedy and comedy could move, but simply by demonstrating that they are still in touch with the proved vigour and intelligence of an earlier age. Certainly this could never be said of Beaumont and Fletcher, or of dramatists like Chapman and Ford who write tragedy at the tremendous cost of *excluding* comedy as far as is humanly possible.

It is for reasons of this kind that Marston's case is interesting. If one compares three of his best-known plays, *The Malcontent* (1604), *Antonio's Revenge* (1599), and *The Dutch Courtezan* (1603-4), the right answers to the question of where decadence has set in are in a sense obvious, but the implications of this and the pin-pointing of what has actually happened rather more difficult. Obviously *Antonio's Revenge* is by far the worst play of the three. It has many of the hallmarks of decadent writing. But pick on one of the most obvious of these, the manoeuvring of plot and action merely to satisfy the lazier audience-appetites, and this seems to apply equally well to the other two plays. In *Antonio's Revenge* the hero, in verse that oddly anticipates the accents and tone of *Hamlet*, plots revenge for a murdered father and interviews his mother to try and prevent her from marrying the murderer. In the course of this Antonio, in Act III, scene iii, comes across the villain's young son, Julio. Much as he likes the innocent boy, Antonio decides to kill him and present the body to the father as a foretaste of what is to come. With typical 'Jacobean' sentimentality, the boy, starved of his own father's affection, practically offers himself as a sacrifice:

> So you will love me, doe even what you will.

Antonio stabs him, and sprinkles his father's hearse with drops of blood as a token of further revenge to come. The verse often lingers affectionately over lines reminiscent, this time, of *Macbeth*, but much more consciously sensuous than anything in the Shakespeare play. With Marston the effect is either dull, or unintentionally comic:

> And now swarte night, to swell thy hower out,
> Behold I spurt warme bloode in thy blacke eyes.
>
> III, iii (p. 104)

The play ends with a Revenge Masque that has none of Tourneur's moral irony in its structure, only the frank and uncorrected delights of dabbling in the victim's blood:

> *Pandulfo* Out with his tong.
> *Antonio* I have't Pandulpho: the vaines panting bleede,
> Trickling fresh goare about my fist. Bind fast; so, so.
>
> V, v (p. 129)

Even the simplest conventional comment on the murder of the innocent Julio is omitted – or forgotten – and all the revengers, including Antonio, are pardoned and escape the consequences of their actions by taking Holy Orders. The tone of the play at the end is one of unqualified approval of all this. The plot itself answers the demands of an audience who want all the horrors of Revenge and none of its more difficult moral implications, and Marston is content to give them this without adding any implicit comment of his own which would correct the oversimplified solution offered by the action.

In the other two plays, the outline of the action at first seems to have much the same implications. In *The Dutch Courtezan* there are hints of tragic complications when the courtezan demands the head of a former lover as a price for her affections, but in the end all is resolved – simply by a warning from the hero to other young men to beware strumpets and court virtuous Love. His apparent death is merely a trick performed to this end, and, incidentally, to test the constancy of his own (extremely virtuous) mistress. In *The Malcontent*, more interestingly, tragedy very nearly overtakes all the main characters, though, once again, they are saved in the end. Ferneze is 'killed', the virtuous Maria besieged in a tower by the usurping tyrant (or rather one of the usurping tyrants), and Malevole and the reformed Pietro (the original usurper) are set by Mendoza to poison each other. Finally, of course, nobody is killed. Even the foolish Ferneze, stabbed by Mendoza as he rushes from the Duchess's bed-chamber, turns out in the end to have been merely wounded. In this play, too, nobody is allowed to die or suffer any particular harm other than a moral shock to the system. From the purely formal point of view, at least, both plays look like the kind of tragi-comedy which indulges in a reversal of the developments the action would seem to expect.

But *The Malcontent* is in fact a healthy play, particularly when compared with *Antonio's Revenge*. The line between decadence and a genuinely 'tragi-comic' vision (if we can for the moment use the term of an essentially Elizabethan play) is not so easy to draw, and certainly it cannot be drawn in formalistic terms, or by treating the 'theme' of a play as an indication of a *genre* to which the writer has committed himself. Both *The Malcontent* and, to a lesser extent, *The Dutch Courtezan*, succeed because for the most part the writing is vigorously substantial and also because, from the beginning, it intelligently anticipates a comedy ending. In *The Malcontent*, in particular, a lot of the dialogue is extremely funny and – more important – it has robustness and point. The thinness of Beaumont and Fletcher could never compete with the Elizabethan wit of Marston at his best:

> *Bilioso* I shall now leave you with my always-best wishes; only let's hold betwixt us a firm correspondence, a mutual friendly-reciprocal kind of steady-unanimous-heartily-leagued –
> *Malevole* Did your Signiorship ne'er see a pigeon-house that was smooth, round and white without. and full of holes and stink within? Ha' ye not, old courtier?
> *Bilioso* O, yes, 'tis the form, the fashion of them all.[1]
>
> I, iv, 89-99

The robust energy of Malevole's 'pigeon-house . . . full of holes and stink within' puts the cloying sensitivity of both Fletcher and Ford in the shade. It also yields – *through* its broad vulgarity – a criticism of court life (the pigeon-house 'smooth, round and white without . . .') which is sharp, relevant comment rather than – as so often in later plays – a loosely directed, largely unrelated comic extravaganza. And most even of the more 'serious' dialogue in this play is tinged by the lightness and point of Malevole's wit. For instance, when Malevole glides from a homily about lascivious Italian courts to another gibing personal attack on Bilioso, there is no very great break in tone. In this speech serious comment and

---

[1] In this chapter I have used Hazelton Spencer's modernized spelling for quotations from *The Malcontent* and *The White Devil*, see *Elizabethan Plays* (London, 1934).

comedy are related by and in the movement from a sophisticated wit rather like Tourneur's, to sheer fun at Bilioso's expense:

> Strong fantasy tricking up strange delights,
> Presenting it dressed pleasingly to sense,
> Sense leading it unto the soul, confirm'd
> With potent example, impudent custom,
> Entic'd by that great bawd, Opportunity –
> Thus being prepar'd, clap to her easy ear
> Youth in good clothes, well-shap'd, rich,
> Fair-spoken, promising, noble, ardent, blood-full,
> Witty, flattering, – Ulysses absent,
> O Ithacan, can chastest Penelope hold out?
>
> *Bilioso* Mass, I'll think on't. Farewell.   III, ii, 45-55

Admittedly the reconciliation at the end includes some over-simple *cliché* writing; but even here there is a clipped, stylized balance about the verse and a light, rhythmic tossing-off of the banalities. The immediate cause of Pietro's repentance, for instance, is another of Malevole's ironic homilies:

> Think this: this earth is the only grave and Golgotha wherein all things that live must rot; 'tis but the draught wherein the heavenly bodies discharge their corruption; the very muck-hill on which the sublunary orbs cast their excrements . . .
>
> IV, v, 120 ff.

Immediately after this Pietro picks up the dialogue in the stilted semi-couplets which clearly Marston recognizes for what they are:

> *Pietro* I here renounce for ever regency!
> O Altofront, I wrong thee to supplant thy right,
> To trip thy heels up with a devilish sleight!
> For which I now from throne am thrown: world-tricks abjure . . .
>
> IV, v, 136 ff.

Few among the lesser Jacobeans can write this kind of verse and have it, in context, accepted with as few qualms as we have about this.

Certainly there would I think be no point in actually labelling this play tragi-comedy. Here Marston's attitudes to the blend of tragedy and comedy are, for all the happy ending, too like those of the Elizabethans generally to make the distinction of a separate label anything more than confusing. There is little in *The Malcontent* which presupposes the need to cultivate a self-conscious approach towards the linking of tragic and comic attitudes.

Turning from Marston to the minor Webster plays (if I can assume for the moment that *The White Devil* is properly considered as such) involves not merely a shift in time of at least eight to ten years; it also increases difficulties of evaluation by presenting us with a far more individual writer. With Webster, even when he is in the grip of a confusion of purpose as radical as that displayed in *The White Devil*, we are seldom in doubt that he is *potentially* a powerful and intelligent dramatist. Marston's works as a whole, though interesting, are hardly a serious issue. Webster's, even when they are bad – in some cases especially then – are.

As with Marston, and indeed most of the minor writers of the seventeenth century, the basic issue is again that of the relations between the tragic and the comic. The chronology – or probable chronology – of Webster's plays is interesting in this regard. *The Duchess of Malfi* (1613–14) is, it seems to me, the only Webster play with claims to greatness, and as such it is (like Middleton's plays) an exception to generalizations about increasing decadence and confusion in seventeenth-century drama. *The Duchess* apart, however, one could reasonably claim that minor plays by (or attributed to) Webster chart an increasingly disastrous separation of 'tragic' and 'comic' elements in drama. Chronologically, Webster's minor plays fall into two groups. First, *The Devil's Law Case* (1610?) and *The White Devil* (1609–12?) may be grouped together, and – for all that they are radically flawed – they display a lively and invigorating talent. *The Devil's Law Case* is I think a good play, and the closest to Marston's sense for characteristically vigorous and intelligent Elizabethan comedy. *The White Devil*, though in the end it fails because Webster could not relate the grimly cynical comments of Flamineo and others to the central tragedy, is clearly the most interesting and powerful Webster play other than *The Duchess of Malfi*. In *The White Devil* Webster is floundering in a chaos of conflicting – and largely unrelated – impressions; but the writing is nevertheless good *enough* to show us that he is floundering because he has attempted more in this play than he did anywhere else except in *The Duchess of Malfi*. The exasperating critical problem which Webster as a whole presents is a sense of power, energy, and intelligence being fragmented most disturbingly just when it is reaching towards deeper, more satisfying experience.

Apart from these two, most of the minor Webster plays are nowadays attributed to the 1620's,[1] and the shift in time coincides with a radical decline in dramatic power and interest. *A Cure for a Cuckold* (1624–5), *The Fair Maid of the Inn* (1625–6), and *Appius and Virginia* (1624–34?) all, in different ways, represent a disastrous and undignified retreat on Webster's part from tragedy informed by comic virtues and attitudes to sentimental over-simplicity. In this second, and last, group of Webster plays there are occasional passages of dialogue which, taken by themselves, are lively and rewarding; but the plays themselves are unbelievably bad. Webster as a whole represents at once the fascination, and the decline of Jacobean drama.

From the early period, then, *The Devil's Law Case* is the Webster play closest to Marston and the Elizabethans. In saying this, however, I do not wish to imply that either Marston or Webster writes

---

[1] The dates for Webster plays in this chapter are taken from G. E. Bentley, *The Jacobean and Caroline Stage*, vol. V, pp. 1239–56. On *The White Devil* Bentley refers to E. K. Chambers, *The Elizabethan Stage*, III, 509–10.

Elizabethan tragedy. They are both, I think, more valuable and interesting writers than either Fletcher, or Ford; and they do have, at their best, a grittiness and solidity which seem to relate them to Elizabethan life more than to later developments. But with both *The Malcontent* and *The Devil's Law Case*, the fusion of the tragic and the comic is achieved only by sacrificing the depth of insight and general significance which tragedy – Elizabethan tragedy at least – has. *The Devil's Law Case* is an amusing and witty play, and as such it stands pretty well on its own feet; but, taken in the context of Webster's writing as a whole, it is also a demonstration of the fact that successful comic writing is usually possible with him only when the pressure of other problems is slackened. With Middleton, Tourneur, and of course Shakespeare, this is not so.

The Devil's Law Case is best seen, then, as a Websterian comedy informed with touches of the bitter cynicism of his tragedies. The action depends largely upon the machiavellian, Flamineo-like story of Romelio, whose incredibly complicated plans to get his bastard (by Angiolella 'the beauteous nun') adopted by his sister, and thus secure her wealth and his own reputation, go consistently awry. When he tries to kill an enemy, Contarino, by stabbing him on his sick-bed, he merely succeeds in effecting his dramatic recovery from illness. Attempting to get his mother's help, he unwittingly tells her he has killed the man she loves. In the end, he faces death bravely – refusing all Christian comforts – but there is no need, for nobody at all has been killed and the question of who marries who is neatly shelved. Romelio need only restore what he has filched, both in goods and honour:

Ariosto Next, you shall marry that Nun.
Romelio Most willingly.

Manoeuvring of this kind (with a strong hint, from the two romantic leads, of the Heroic drama to come later in the century) forms the basis for a Websterian fantasy rather in the Flamineo vein, but here lighter in tone. There are more pen-portraits than ever and endless highly-wrought conceits from Romelio and others – conceits, however, surely grounded in a vigorous Elizabethan conception of wit:

> Come forth then
> My desperate Steeletto, that may be worne
> In a woman's haire, and nere discover'd,
> And either would be taken for a Bodkin,
> Or a curling yron at most; why, 'tis an engine,
> That's onely fit to put in execution
> Barmotho pigs –   III, ii, 94 ff.

The fantasy here is typically Webster (cf. Romelio's Bosola-like jibe '. . . I have heard Strange juggling tricks have been conveyed to a woman in a pudding'), though it contains elements which enable him to continue Romelio's speech to the dagger in verse which is thicker in texture, more like a mixture of the bitterly intelligent wit of *The White Devil* and an earlier, Shakespearean turn of mind:

> . . . a most unmanly weapon
> That steales into a man's life he knowes not how;
> O that great *Caesar*, he that past the shocke
> Of so many armed Pikes, and poyson'd Darts,
> Swords, Slings, and Battleaxes, should at length
> Sitting at ease on a cushion, come to dye
> By such a shoo-makers aule as this, his soule let forth
> At a hole no bigger then the incision
> Made for a wheale!   III, ii, 100–108

The scene as a whole is therefore a fair example of the mixture of tones in that part of the play which centres in the Machiavellian Romelio. It is quite easily flippant enough to fit in with a plot that is far more artificial and conventional than the much more un-usual *Duchess*, or even *The White Devil*. On the other hand, it is thick enough in texture to carry a serious point not entirely divorced from tragedy. The bewilderment and confusion of Webster's tragic universe is present too, though less powerfully, in the conceits of this comic verse, and it culminates in a Webster dirge in Act V when Romelio contemplates death:

> All the Flowers of the Spring
> Meet to perfume our burying:
> These have but their growing prime,
> And man does flourish but his time.
> Survey our progresse from our birth,
> We are set, we grow, we turne to earth . . .
> Vaine the ambition of Kings,
> Who seeke by trophies and dead things,
> To leave a living name behind,
> And weave but nets to catch the wind . . .
>
> v, iv, 131 ff.

At other times, the lighter fantastic comedy which on the whole governs the action (except for the Heroic lovers) is genuinely funny:

> *Crispiano* (a 'civil-lawyer' who in part controls the
> action in a manner analogous to the Duke's in
> *Measure for Measure*):
> Sir, the King of Spaine
> Suspects, that your Romelio here, the Merchant
> Has discover'd some Gold-myne to his owne use,
> In the West Indies, and for that employes me,
> To discover in what part of Christendome
> He vents this Treasure; Besides, he is informed
> What mad tricks has bin plaid of late by Ladies.
> *Ariosto* Most true, and I am glad the King has
> heard on't . . .   III, i, 4-11

Mock solemnity of this kind works well in context and in this particular case is brilliantly followed up by a 'character' of Women from Ariosto. When a play turns from near-tragedy towards artificial comedy, the character-sketch can easily come into its own, especially when preceded by poker-faced changes of tone like these. Ariosto's speech makes the best of the opportunity:

> So heare should I repeat what factions,
> What Bat-fowling for Offices –
> As you must conceive their Game is all i' the night –
> What calling in question one anothers honesties . . .
> Twill doe well shortly, can wee keepe them off
> From being of our Councell of Warre.   III, i, 19 ff.

Though still, of course, nowhere near the easy mixing of the tragic and the comic in Middleton, this play is nevertheless a lively example of a Websterian comedy informed at key points with the bitterly ironic comment of tragedies like *The White Devil* and *The Duchess*.

Most of it, incidentally, is very obviously Webster.[1] Even where the play moves, as it frequently does, into the sphere of contracts, goods, merchandise, the tone retains the Webster fantasy and conceit. Crispiano's defence of the joys of hoarding wealth –

> In taking Clyents fees, and piling them
> In severall goodly rowes before my Deske . . .
>   II, i, 61-62

looks momentarily like Middleton or Rowley, but it is preceded by the figured ironies of:

> Wenching? O fie, the Disease followes it:
> Beside, can the fingring Taffaties, or Lawnes,
> Or a painted hand, or a Brest, be like the pleasure
> In taking Clyents fees . . .   II, i, 58 ff.

Apart from the grotesquerie surrounding it, this is too frankly greed, and recognized as such by the character, i.e., recognized as something to *do* or *be* in the Webster 'Character' vein. With Middleton it would be different. Money, in *Women Beware Women*, is a mode of living, a metaphor that describes and governs all else in life and in the play, and for this reason its effects on characters are partly unconscious (Middleton's point being that

---

[1] It is accepted as entirely Webster's by both G. E. Bentley (V, 1250-1252) and F. L. Lucas (*The Works of John Webster* (London, 1927), II, pp. 217-21.

these people seldom see the relationships between what they say and the springs of action that in fact govern the whole play).

Yet, characteristically Webster though it is, *The Devil's Law Case* is far removed from the two great tragedies. The conceits are more consistently fantastical or melodramatic; the ironies on the whole less bitter. The action as a whole seldom if ever moves away from conventional intrigue or conventional heroics. The position, then, is that though Webster uses his satirical mind in both comedy and tragedy, the end products in each case – even taking this play into account – are not really in the same line of development. Indeed, given the breakdown of the Elizabethan sensibility of which many of Webster's own plays are evidence, probably the only course which could have united tragedy and comedy in their full extent was Middleton's. The other Jacobeans, like Webster, merely transferred some aspects of their tragic writing to a comic, or tragi-comic sphere. Where they succeeded in this, as in *The Devil's Law Case* (or earlier, *The Malcontent*), it was at the cost of temporarily pushing aside the more urgent enquiry of great tragedy.

Where Webster attempts full-scale tragic writing, the dangers that beset the early Jacobean age of drama are most apparent. *The White Devil* is the most powerful Websterian failure of them all. It commands attention because it gives a *sense* of power and energy (albeit fragmented), while at the same time it obviously falls a prey to divisions within the Jacobean sensibility. Tragedy and comedy are here very much at odds, and it is difficult to feel that recent developments in Webster criticism which emphasize the mixing of tragedy with 'comicall satyre' (derived from pamphlets and other sources) really succeed in closing this particular gap. The thesis of Mr Travis Bogard, for instance, is that Webster's tragic vision is unique in being always tempered by a satirical comment at key points, and indeed, all the way through in the case of at least some of the plays. This is, of course, very largely true, at any rate of *The Duchess of Malfi*, and an examination of this kind of mixture of tone and influence in Webster is extremely valuable. But it is not by any means universally true, even with the great Webster plays. Criticism would surely have to admit that, in the case of *The White Devil*, whatever Webster's attempts and intentions may have been, his achievements in the way of a 'satirical counterpoint' are limited to, perhaps, one scene only.[1]

To attack the problem first from a slightly different angle: I think it is once again true to say that Miss Bradbrook's remarks, though brief, go straight to the heart of the critical problems in the play. These problems are many and varied, but they can, for purposes of convenience, be focused on one thing: the innocence or otherwise of Vittoria. As Miss Bradbrook says, compared with the less ambitious (or more securely organized) Tourneur, Webster's intentions towards his villain-heroes or heroines are often difficult to determine. 'There is, as it were, a subordinate side of Vittoria which is innocent. Actually she is guilty, but there is a strong undercurrent of suggestion in the opposite direction. It never comes to the surface plainly, but it is there . . .'[2] This is obviously the crux of the difference between the two great tragedies of Webster. The moral ambiguity was very firmly there in *The Duchess of Malfi*, but in that play Webster seemed to be able to present us with writing, particularly that centred on the Duchess in Act IV, which treated the ambiguity far more firmly and in fact made a triumph out of the very difficulties it raised. The Duchess is tainted by the rashness and violence that surround her (cf. the madmen's comments, and also, as Miss Bradbrook points out, the ominous close to the otherwise appealing 'proposal' to Antonio: 'This is not the figure cut in alabaster / Kneels at my husband's tomb').

---

[1] The phrase 'satirical counterpoint' is taken from Travis Bogard, *The Tragic Satire of John Webster* (California, 1955). See also O. J. Campbell, *Comicall Satyre and Shakespeare's Troilus and Cressida* (Huntington Library, 1938).

[2] Bradbrook, *Themes and Conventions*, p. 187.

On the other hand, compared with Vittoria, the Duchess is much more unambiguously innocent and the play gains immeasurably by this. To put it more accurately, the ambiguity that centres on the Duchess's position is less bewildering, more controlled by the author, than is that centring on Vittoria. With the Duchess, a reader always feels that Webster is viewing the spectacle of innocence inevitably tainted by guilt with controlled and sympathetic irony. The control, particularly in Act IV of the play, is the product of a sustained moral effort of a kind that is lacking in the more relaxed *White Devil*. There, Webster's vision wavers uncertainly from guilt to innocence (or from admiration to horror), unable to focus a possible relation between these, and so the play finds itself condemned to a relatively simple view of both.

It is for this reason that the forces of good in *The White Devil*, mainly Isabella and Giovanni, appear to have a disastrously forthright position attributed to them. They are more continuously and more clearly in evidence than is Delio, the poor representative of sanity in *The Duchess*, but this is nothing to their, or Webster's, credit. They are still vastly outnumbered by those who, in *The White Devil*, stand quite frankly for lust and intemperance, and, more important, the dialogue Webster gives them is by far the least powerful of any in the play. With them he cannot, as he certainly can with Flamineo and Vittoria, make his point convincingly. The nearest he gets to a convincing statement of a powerful moral order is Isabella's reply to Brachiano's 'divorce' speech:

Isabella Forbid it, the sweet union
Of all things blessed! why, the saints in Heaven
Will knit their brows at that.   II, i ,196-8

This has a combination of traditional simplicity and individual freshness of tone that almost, momentarily, turns a reader's attention to Isabella. But in the scene as a whole, as generally throughout the play, the really forceful writing goes to the equally 'conventional' but far from virtuous Brachiano and (else-where) Flamineo:

Brachiano This is the latest ceremony of my love.
Henceforth I'll never lie with thee . . .   II, i, 191 ff.

Cornelia, so clearly intended to provide a vigorous statement of morality in Act I, is less convincing still. Webster gives her a spirited entrance (Act I, scene ii, 313 ff.) and some reasonably forceful dialogue, but somehow, in the face of Vittoria's and Brachiano's passionate lust, she looks like a conventional stage-property, too hastily sketched in to do anything more than con-fuse the moral issues raised by the central love scenes. Much of her dialogue reveals a banality of outlook alarmingly underlined by rhetorical over-emphasis ('If thou dishonour thus thy husband's bed . . .'). In effect, the framework of morality sketched around Cornelia, Isabella, and the sentimental Giovanni seems thin and remote, altogether too feeble to resist the powerful onslaught of Vittoria's and Brachiano's lust and Flamineo's panderism.

In Webster's attitude to the main characters themselves there is the same over-simplification of the issues, the same awkward break in tone. Our first view of Vittoria and Brachiano is one of people quite frankly unrestrained in lust. Not that Webster gloats, as Beaumont and Fletcher and, more importantly, Ford occasion-ally do; his attitude is more like that of Browning towards the Duke in *My Last Duchess*. There is in Webster a sense occasionally of the clinical detachment of the dramatic sketch of villainy. I think Miss Bradbrook is, momentarily, a little naïve in this regard. 'When we first see her [Vittoria] with Brachiano', Miss Bradbrook says, 'the adultery is obviously right from any but a puritanical point of view.' She quotes (without making clear who is speaking):

Give credit, I could wish time would stand still
And never end this interview, this hour,

But all delight itself doth soonest devour.
Let me into your bosom, happy lady,
Pour out, instead of eloquence, my vows . . .
Flamineo See, now they close. Most happy union.

I, ii, 92 ff.

– and her conclusion is: 'There is no argument against the movement and rhythm of such a passage . . .'[1] In the first place this is, of
course, not Vittoria but the rather conventional Brachiano; in the
second, even if anything can be got from the in fact rather placid
and conventional movement and rhythm of this speech, there are
plenty of other indications in this first sight we get of Vittoria with
Brachiano. A reader will hardly need a puritan background to
see them both, as Webster sees them, fatally involved with lust and
adultery. Just before this speech, Flamineo's panderism has inevitably coloured what is to follow and, more important,
Vittoria's eager acceptance knows no check or scruple whatever.
For 40 lines or so Vittoria listens silently (and, as it turns out,
impatiently) to Flamineo's elaborate scheming. There is no sign
that she cares anything for the consequences, and even the drama
that Flamineo is busily working out for her passes her by. Her only
remark is, towards the end of it, the impatient:

How shall's rid him hence?

Besides this there is also the fact that, with the exception of the
feeble Cornelia, everybody in the play, right from the beginning,
seems intent on hastening adultery to its proper conclusion. The
scene is rapidly set by Zanche bringing in carpets and 'the two fair
cushions' for Vittoria and Brachiano to lie on and by the general
approval of almost all concerned. Vittoria herself caps it with the
frankly evil incitement to murder Camillo and Isabella.

However, Miss Bradbrook's general point is of course absolutely
correct. The play as a whole is divided sharply between this side of
Vittoria and a genuine admiration for her; hence in the end we do

[1] *Themes and Conventions*, p.187

not quite know how to take even this opening scene. A complexity of attitudes from the author is of course quite feasible in a drama such as this one. The worrying part of it is that here the two sides are rarely, if ever, intelligently brought together. In the house of convertites scene later in the play there is a suggestion of play-acting from Vittoria which does help a little to break down the otherwise unqualified admiration for the two of them, but in the trial scene even the theatrical bluff from Vittoria is so intelligently and courageously carried out that, as Miss Bradbrook says, nothing but admiration seems possible: 'She hardly seems morally guilty.' This is very difficult to relate to the frank statements of evil and entirely selfish lust in other parts of the play. The only possible way would be to link the intelligent coldness of the writing in the trial scene with the ruthless efficiency with which Webster ushered in lust and adultery at the beginning, and put Webster's own attitude down as, in this play, one of almost completely clinical detachment. Again, the Browning comparison comes to mind. It may just be possible that Webster admires Vittoria much as Browning admires his Duke?– that is to say as a brilliant sketch in evil, too far removed from normal life to be really disturbing? But in this case the play would simply, or largely, be a theatrical *tour de force* in no way comparable to *The Duchess of Malfi*, for instance, and certainly far below Middleton and Tourneur. For though the writing towards the end of the play does change slightly, nothing in the final Acts is powerful enough to disturb a remoteness of this kind. Certainly the sentimentality over Giovanni and Cornelia could do nothing to change it, and even the admirable sketches of Flamineo 'experimenting', as Leech puts it, in new sensations, are rather in the earlier mode than any other: 'There's a plumber laying pipes in my guts, it scalds.' Just here and there, especially with Flamineo, there *are* hints of the more humane attitudes which partly govern the writing in *The Duchess of Malfi*:

> In all the weary minutes of my life,
> Day ne'er broke up till now . . .

And the grim concession to humanity:

> I have a strange thing in me, to the which
> I cannot give a name, without it be
> Compassion.

But in context this cannot carry much weight against the cold efficiency of the rest. If any single view of the play were possible it would have to be one centring on Webster's Browningesque detachment from the events and issues he's describing.

In the last analysis, however, the Browning analogy will hardly hold because Webster is in fact not detached in anything like this way. Most notably, the trial scene presents us with an author inviting admiration, not clinical detachment. The final view of the play must therefore be one of a confusion of moral purpose far more radical than anything even in the apparently more untidy *Duchess*. Here, in *The White Devil*, Webster presents us with admiration and horror fatally unrelated to each other.

To return here to the issue of dissociation of comedy and tragedy with which I started, and in particular to Mr Bogard's view of the play: his contention is that the two attitudes to Vittoria and Brachiano – the horror of Act I and the admiration of Act III – are in fact well brought together by the 'satiric counterpoint' which reaches its highest point in Act IV. For instance he notices, as others have done, that the grand passion of Vittoria and Brachiano is not allowed to go without pretty savage satiric comment from Webster, *via*, of course, Flamineo:

> What a damn'd imposthume is a woman's will:
> Can nothing break it? – [*aside*] Fie, fie, my Lord,
> Women are caught as you take tortoises;
> She must be turn'd on her back. Sister, by this hand
> I am on your side . . .   IV, ii, 148 ff.

The tendency of Mr Bogard's book, however, is to deal not with plays but with sections of plays, and this can be misleading. There is certainly something in this scene that could well be called a 'satiric counterpoint', but this in itself is not sufficient. If the play is to come off, satire must have some more general point than merely to deflate the heroic emotion of one particular scene, and it is difficult in fact to see that it has. It seems, for instance, to leave untouched the worrying break between our varying attitudes to Vittoria in Acts I and III. Even the 'contrasting action' that Mr Bogard notes in Act V, where 'the conspiracy of Francisco and the murder of Marcello undercut the triumph of Brachiano and of Flamineo', is not sharply enough underlined by Webster to make any substantial point, and in any case is not held long enough to solve the more general questions raised by the play. The important contrast is with *The Duchess of Malfi*, where a combination of sympathy and ironic detachment is not merely an isolated fact but the very centre of our view of the key scenes and certainly the core of the dominating Act IV. In *The White Devil*, the scene in the house of convertites does not take charge of the action of the play in anything like the same sense as does Act IV of *The Duchess*. If any single scene does dominate and modify our attitudes towards the whole of *The White Devil* it is, of course, the trial scene, and here the tone is quite different. Rather unaccountably, the satiric counterpoint in this scene is reserved for the pathetically ineffectual Lieger Ambassadors and the Lawyer.

The White Devil is a much more limited and a much less human play, I think, than *The Duchess of Malfi*. Even its moments of grandeur seem cold splendours compared with the warmth of emotion – satirically placed, certainly – that Webster manages to achieve in *The Duchess*. Only at the end, the contemptuous courage of Flamineo and Vittoria does perhaps arouse something more than mere admiration. Webster begins here to touch the theme, convincingly worked out in *The Duchess of Malfi*, of an utterly bewildering chaos:

> My soul, like to a ship in a black storm,
> Is driven I know not whither . . .   v, vi, 248 ff.

Or better still, perhaps, compare Flamineo's last cynicism:

> I have caught
> An everlasting cold; I have lost my voice
> Most irrecoverably . . .   v, vi, 272 ff.

This is obviously brilliant writing, but even so it is cast in the mould of what Mr Bogard himself calls 'choral comment'—it is in fact *too* brilliantly self-contained – and it is therefore not nearly as telling as the more flexible give-and-take of the dialogue in the crucial scenes of *The Duchess*.

Apart from *The Devil's Law Case* and *The White Devil*, there are the several conventionally Jacobean tragi-comedies in which Webster appears to have collaborated with Ford, Massinger, Rowley and others. In each case, either the fact of collaboration or a failure of inspiration has resulted in a diffuseness and deadness of tone that links the group as a whole with Beaumont and Fletcher rather than with anything characteristically Websterian. Here the evidence for a general slackening of pressure in Jacobean dramatic writing becomes more apparent; the tone of the writing is certainly far removed from that of *The Devil's Law Case*, or *The Malcontent*, or *The White Devil*.

The *Faire Maide of the Inne*, for instance, is marked from the beginning with irritatingly suggestive hints of incest (the sister, perhaps? the mother? – Cesario will take on all comers) which turn out to have no real point at all and yet lack even the melodramatic vigour of, for instance, the relationships described in Beaumont and Fletcher's *A King and No King*. Worse, though Cesario turns out to be a villain, and in the end a reformed villain, there is nothing in the tone of the verse to demonstrate these changes. Honesty, villainy, repentance – no matter what spiritua mood he is in he sounds, with a few exceptions, exactly the same

The exceptions are striking, e.g., his complacent patronizing of Bianca in Act IV (far more striking than her own sentimental simplicity):

> *Bianca* I should have dyed sure, and no creature knowne
> The sicknesse that had kill'd me.
> *Cesario* Pretty heart,
> Good soule, alas! alas!
> *Bianca* Now since I know
> There is no difference twixt your birth and mine . . .
> . . . I come willingly
> To tender you the first fruits of my heart,
> And am content t' accept you for my husband,
> Now when you are lowest.
> *Cesario* For a husband?
> Speake sadly, dost thou meane so?   IV, i, 86-98

– and, just before this, his equally self-satisfied soliloquy:

> Pleasures admit no bounds.
> I am pitcht so high,
> To such a growth of full prosperities
> That to conceale my fortunes were an injury
> To gratefulnesse and those more liberall favours
> By whom my glories prosper. He that flowes
> In gracious and swolne tydes of best abundance,
> Yet will be ignorant of his owne fortunes,
> Deserves to live contemn'd, and dye forgotten;
> The harvest of my hopes is now already
> Ripen'd and gather'd . . .   IV, i, 5 ff.

In fact the writing for Cesario in this scene sounds far more like Middleton than Webster![1] But no matter who wrote the scene, the play unfortunately has nothing else in it as good. It rarely looks

---

[1] Lucas notes this 'charming' scene as Ford's, partly on the analogy between 'My fate springs in my owne hand, and Ile use it' and 'I hold fate Clasp'd in my fist . . .' from *'Tis Pity*. Apart from the fact that both examples, especially the second, clearly look back to *Tamburlaine*, this ignores the blind, gloating self-satisfaction of the rest of the *Fair Maid* speech which Ford could only have done in a very uncharacteristic moment. It is indeed much more like the Middleton of Leantio and *Women Beware Women* generally. (See, however, Lucas, IV, 151; and Bentley, V, 1252-3.)

like Webster at his best; it can never compete with Middleton for more than a speech or two here and there.

A Cure for a Cuckold is another instance of Webster's unfortunate liking for weakly conventional tragi-comedy. The clipped speech and short rhythms, plus the general oddness of the writing in the scenes on the Compass affair (the sailor who was proud of being a cuckold so long as he could buy an interest in the child) turn out, not surprisingly, to owe a good deal to Rowley.[1] There is also, in the despised lover Lessingham and his cynical mistress Clare, a vein of psychological naturalism that reminds one of the Middleton-Rowley world. But consistently, these good beginnings turn towards the heroics of Lessingham's search for the one true friend (the man who will second him in a dubious and unnamed quarrel) and the complicated, artificial manoeuvrings which must take place in order to turn quarrels and misunderstandings into friendship. On the whole, Beaumont and Fletcher did this sort of thing with more *éclat*. Webster, in his own attempts to link the worlds of tragedy and comedy, does best in the more individualistic *The Devil's Law Case*, where he does turn his own imaginative and highly fantastic tragic writing to comic ends. In other plays, he and his collaborators lapse into a conventional tone which has all the flatness but none of the insight of Middleton.

From the evidence of plays like *The Faire Maide* and *A Cure for a Cuckold*, it is not really surprising that Webster should have sunk to the level of collaborating in *Appius and Virginia*.[2] Stoic oversimplicity – as the later of Chapman's plays abundantly show – is an easy refuge for the writer tormented by the impressionistic disintegration of the Jacobean world. With *Appius and Virginia* it is not so much that the dialogue is far clumsier and less exciting than Webster at his best; this is certainly so, but on the other hand the play has enough excitement of a who-gets-who kind to keep a

---

[1] Lucas, III, 10-18; and Bentley, V, 1249-50.

[2] Lucas, III, 134-48; Bentley, V, 1245-48.

reader (though probably not an audience?) going to the end. The real trouble is that at all key points the play is intolerably vague, generalized and sentimental. As Mr Lucas, even, who is on the whole well-disposed towards it, is forced to remark, the characters are vaguely drawn. 'Virginius is just a Roman Father, Virginia just a Virgin Martyr, killed almost before she knows her fate . . .'[1] This in itself would not matter, if something else were present in the play to take its place. One could say as much, for instance, of the Morality *Everyman* or, possibly, even of *Oedipus Rex* – if this were all that needed to be said of a play. *Appius and Virginia* fails, not in dealing inefficiently with characters, which would not necessarily matter, but in dealing inefficiently with everything.

The issues turn around the grand villainy of Appius which is set off nicely, but in the end sentimentally, by the meaner-spirited villainy of Clodius and the bluff stoicism of Virginius. Virginia herself is, indeed, so irredeemably 'just a Virgin Martyr . . .' that she hardly counts at all. The plots of the Machiavel hold the interest fairly well right up to Act V, but there is not much substance in this, and all the time Webster is gathering his forces for the sentimental stoicism of the end. Virginius's bluff honesty is only just saved from sinking into sentimentality quite early on by the touch of policy, which looks momentarily as if it might make something of the relationships between the soldier and the extremely politic Machiavel:

> *Virginius (aside)* Thus men must slight their wrongs, or else
>   conceal them,
> When general safety wills us not reveal them.   ii, ii, 249-50

But when you look it in the face, even this is unconscionably weak, and the whole section is coloured by a sense of endearing but almost impossible generosity about the old man. Inevitably, the fruits of this sort of simplicity are gathered in the trial scene, when the interest in Appius's Machiavellian moves is capped by the im-

[1] Lucas, III, 147.

possible stoicism of Virginius's murder of his own daughter. This is far too easy a solution to the potentially interesting questions which have been raised, of worldly power wrongly but intelligently wielded by Appius. Things look up a little when Icilius (Act V, scene i) begins to outline the moral difficulties Virginius apparently never saw, but Virginius replies with platitudes about the oath of Roman knighthood:

> A parcel of it is, as I remember,
> Rather to die with honour, than to live
> In servitude . . .   v, i, 128 ff.

And Icilius in turn replies with a feeble reproof against Virginius's disturbing the peace of the city, and an offer of friendship until they meet the Senate. In the end, the whole sequence turns out to be a device to heighten still further the idealism centred on Virginius, and when Icilius, in Act V, scene ii, renews his attack (having apparently forgotten about it until Virginia's body appears), this provides Virginius with the opportunity to dispense his Roman justice by handing the two ruffians a pair of swords and expecting them to solve the problems of his own behaviour and theirs. Fortunately for the general tenor of idealism that runs through the play, one of them does, and Rome has purged itself of tyrants even in the act of proving that its greatest villain is imbued with the spirit of its greatest general.

> *Icilius* Away with him; the life of the Decemviri
> Expires in them. *Rome* thou at length art free,
> Restored unto thine ancient liberty . . .

The bitter, cynical Jacobean age could never have made anything of material like this. The stiffness and lifelessness of Webster's writing here, and in others of his minor plays, was prophet to the rest.

CHAPTER XI

JACOBEAN COMPROMISE:
BEAUMONT AND FLETCHER'S
TRAGI-COMEDY

'Beaumont and Fletcher' are usually taken to be, for critical purposes, 'boiled down into a single gentleman'. The issue is not who wrote the plays, but what – if anything – is their worth? On this question modern criticism has varied from outright accusations of decadence, to claims that Beaumont and Fletcher can be justified as 'representing their times', and even to statements that they achieve a 'patterning of emotions' which had not been done before and which is therefore worth while in its own right.[1] Without going into the matter in detail at this point, it seems to me that most of the claims that have been made for Beaumont and Fletcher's plays are untenable. If, for instance, they do 'represent their times', then the simple answer is, so much the worse for their 'times'. If – as is true – there is a 'pattern of emotions' observable in their plays, the further question of what this is worth, what 'achievement' the pattern represents, can only be answered in terms which point to a grouping of over-simple concepts, like Love, Friendship, Honour, in a sentimentalized, thinly conceived framework. Admittedly, in most of the plays there are comic

---

[1] Eliot, *Selected Essays*, pp. 193-204 and Bradbrook, *Themes and Conventions*, pp. 240-67, are both severely critical. So is L. G. Salingar in the Pelican Guide No. 2 ('The Decline of Tragedy', pp. 429-35). Others defend Beaumont and Fletcher on the grounds that they developed a new 'kind' of drama (tragi-comedy) based on, amongst other things, a stylized 'patterning of emotions' (cf. U. Ellis-Fermor, *Jacobean Drama*, pp. 201-26; E. M. Waith, *The Pattern of Tragicomedy in Beaumont and Fletcher* (London, 1952); Philip Edwards, 'The Danger not the Death: the art of John Fletcher', *Stratford-upon-Avon Studies I* (London, 1960), pp. 159-77). With this, compare the claim of J. F. Danby that they are valuable because they represent their times, *Poets on Fortunes' Hill* (London, 1952), pp. 177-83.

scenes as well, but the break in tone between these and the lyrical protestations of Honour, Friendship, etc., is so marked that the result is a compromise between tragedy and comedy of a kind which robs both of their impact and value.

On the other hand it is I think clear that the kind of decadence that Beaumont and Fletcher's tragi-comedy represents is not as big an issue as that represented by, for instance, Chapman and Ford. Beaumont and Fletcher have a lightness of touch which is often irresponsible and trifling, but which for the most part also has the negative virtue of not pretending to deal in more than surface impressions. Only the most critically unaware would be seriously compromised by reading a play like *A King and No King*, and failing to see through its flirting with the possibility of incest between Arbaces and Penthea. Moreover the play has, at points, an engaging *naïveté* which, since the deeper implications of the theme are not pressed by Beaumont and Fletcher, can be enjoyed for what it is – a kind of musical-comedy extravaganza on a Jacobean theme. But however we take plays like *A King and No King* and *Philaster*, the main point is to distinguish the lightness of these from the more solemn tones of Chapman and Ford. Decadence becomes a serious issue in proportion to the gravity of its pretensions.

The best way of seeing Beaumont and Fletcher's plays truly is first of all to distinguish from the bulk of their work the one play which looks – and to some extent is – more interesting than a simple Jacobean compromise. *The Maid's Tragedy* (c. 1611), even if it is only by virtue of the dominating quality of one scene, is clearly Beaumont and Fletcher's most interesting effort in the half-light between tragedy and tragi-comedy. By implication, Miss Bradbrook lumps *The Maid's Tragedy* in with the general run of Fletcher plays in which tragedy and comedy are uncritically mingled and where language, plot, and characterization conspire to muddle or sentimentalize the firmer moral grip of earlier writers. These charges are obviously true to a certain extent. The basis of this play, as of the others, is to some extent an 'outrageous stimulation', and after Miss Bradbrook one need waste no further time establishing this. However, one scene at least stands out firmly against this sort of condemnation, and it's at least possible that it makes the play a good deal more interesting than it appears. The question is – as Miss Bradbrook herself has pointed out in other connections[1] – does the firmness and sharpness of this scene exist merely in and for itself, or does it successfully comment on the values and attitudes in the rest of the play?

The scene is, of course, Evadne's barefaced discovery to Amintor, in Act II, scene i, of her liaison with the king. After Aspatia's sentimental 'Go, and be happy in your lady's love . . .' the bridegroom, shrugging off his worries about her, welcomes Evadne. The resulting dialogue tries very hard to move beyond the over-simplified virtues of Fletcher's pre-Heroic tragedy and, before it finally capitulates, incorporates comment that, above all else, recalls Middleton's boldly naturalistic triumph in *Women Beware Women*. In dramatic – or indeed any other – terms, Evadne's first reply to Amintor is startlingly fresh:

> *Amintor* Oh, my Evadne, spare
> That tender body: let it not take cold.
> The vapours of the night shall not fall here:
> To bed, my love: Hymen will punish us
> For being slack performers of his rites.
> Cam'st thou to call me?
> *Evadne* No.
> *Amintor* Come, come, my love,
> And let us lose ourselves to one another . . .
> II, i (p. 26)[2]

After this, Evadne's protestations are deceptively conventional –

---

[1] Bradbrook, *op. cit.*, p. 241.

[2] Page references are to the Mermaid edition throughout.

Amintor I pr'y thee do.
Evadne I will not for the world.
Amintor Why, my dear love?
Evadne Why? I have sworn I will not.

– until Fletcher makes use of this very quality of apparent maidenly
reluctance to make his real point. Based on the discrepancy between the apparent innocence and actual experience of Evadne's
replies, this particular passage, with its echo some fifty lines later,
briefly anticipates the ironic naturalism of Middleton:

Evadne Yes, sworn, Amintor; and will swear again,
If you will wish to hear me.
Amintor To whom have you sworn this?
Evadne If I should name him, the matter were not great.
Amintor Come, this is but the coyness of a bride.
Evadne The coyness of a bride?

Fifty or so lines later, Fletcher makes Evadne drop all pretence in a
passage which does indeed point towards *Women Beware Women*:

Amintor If you have sworn to any of the virgins,
That were your old companions, to preserve
Your maidenhead a night, it may be done
Without this means.
Evadne A maidenhead, Amintor,
At my years?   II, i (p. 28)

It has of course been made plain earlier what Evadne's 'years'
amount to. She is in fact a young woman, and, in terms of the
writing at the beginning of the play, Amintor should have a right
to expect an innocent one also.

There is no doubt about the completely un-artificial directness
of writing of this kind. The real question is, does it comment on
the Heroic and sentimental values of the rest of the play, or is it
merely detachable? When Evadne's resolution is finally made
plain and irrevocable, Fletcher, as so often in this play, anticipates
Heroic attitudes by making Amintor melodramatically forswear
vengeance on hearing the magic name of 'King':

In that sacred word,
'The King', there lies a terror. What frail man
Dares lift his hand against it . . . ? II, i (p. 31)

Obviously this at any rate is badly out of key. Moreover, later in
the play, this same attitude is very easily put aside by Melantius
(and, for that matter, Evadne herself) in favour of another equally
stylized and equally Heroic value: Friendship (e.g. Act III, scene ii).
On the other hand, if we can for the moment isolate Acts II and
III from later developments, here at least the play's two basic
attitudes (conventional romantic sentiment from Aspatia and
Amintor, and hard-headed but in its way quite honest calculation
from Evadne) are so sharply opposed that they must, albeit not
nearly so forcefully as in the greater Jacobeans, comment on each
other. It is important both that the opposing attitudes are jammed
closely together at the beginning of this sequence (Act II, scene i
et seq.), and that the writing for Evadne is powerfully direct.
Aspatia's nostalgia ('When I am laid in earth . . .') and the in-
experienced Amintor's too tender romanticism ('Oh my Evadne,
spare / That tender body . . .') very rapidly have to face up to
Evadne's toughly experienced clear-sightedness:

Amintor Come, this is but the coyness of a bride.
Evadne The coyness of a bride?
Amintor How prettily that frown becomes thee!
Evadne Do you like it so?
Amintor Thou canst not dress thy face in such a look,
But I shall like it.
Evadne What look likes you best?
Amintor Why do you ask?
Evadne That I may show you one less pleasing to you.
Amintor How's that?
Evadne That I may show you one less pleasing to you.
II, i (pp. 26-7)

There are other ironies and changes of tone which I think
escape Bradbrook's charges of being merely woolly and irrelevant.

The comedy scene in Evadne's apartments after the 'bridal' night has a good deal of rather clumsy writing, but most of it is pointed enough, and reasonably 'critical' of a too easy acceptance of the oversimplified values of Heroism, Friendship, and Nobility. Act III opens with the brothers betting on the odds of Evadne's maidenhead and this itself makes a point of a kind well enough. It comments on the pomp and circumstance of the wedding preparations organized by Amintor's private symbol of heroism, the king, much more sharply and efficiently than does, for instance, Aspatia's stylized decline. It is turned more subtly still towards the main part of the tragedy by a fairly simple dramatic irony in exchanges like the one between Amintor and Diphilus:

> *Diphilus* You look as you had lost your eyes tonight:
> I think you have not slept.
> *Amintor* I' faith I have not.   III, i (pp. 37-8)

(Evadne, of course, has not allowed Amintor to 'sleep' with her in any sense of the word.) Fletcher has not an absolute control of the mixed tones this sort of writing demands. Miss Bradbrook objects to:

> I'll be guilty too,
> If these be the effects!   III, i (p. 38)

(from Amintor after seeing Evadne sleeping sweetly after her announcement of the virtual divorce between them). And indeed the lyricism of that whole speech is a little sudden; it's not that it can't be related to the cynicism of the rest of the scene, but rather that one's not sure *how* it's related. Nevertheless, the whole sequence is more intelligently done than, for instance, the more irresponsibly drawn comedy sketches of *A King and No King* or *Bonduca*, and this distinction should be made.

Nothing in the rest of the play quite comes up to the standard of Act II. Evadne's bare-faced 'using' of Amintor (Act III, scene i) to keep the favours of the King is good and comes between the pointed comment of Act II and the feeble reliance on purely conventional writing later on. Here in Act III Evadne re-lives quite convincingly the unscrupulous boldness of her earlier scenes; but in the writing generally in this scene there is an irresponsible wandering of values, sentimental suggestions of a passionate loyalty in a context where this is hardly credible. The following dialogue contains an interesting but far from satisfactory mixture of cynicism and perverted but passionately sincere loyalty. (There is here more than a hint of the Evadne who later on repents and claims Amintor's love for killing the king):

> *Evadne* I swore indeed, that I would never love
> A man of lower place; but, if your fortune
> Should throw you from this height, I bade you trust
> I would forsake you, and would bend to him
> That won your throne: I love with my ambition,
> Not with my eyes. But, if I ever yet
> Touch'd any other, leprosy light here
> Upon my face: which for your royalty
> I would not stain!
> *King* Why, thou dissemblest, and it is
> In me to punish thee.
> *Evadne* Why, 'tis in me,
> Then, not to love you, which will more afflict
> Your body than your punishment can mine.
>
> III, i (p. 43)

For the rest, the play is characterized by the *volte-face* of Evadne under the highly moral correction of her brother Melantius, by the mixture of Heroic or pre-Heroic self-sacrifice –

> Stay awhile –
> The name of friend is more than family,
> Or all the world besides: I was a fool!
>
> III, ii (p. 52)

– and, from Aspatia, affected and masochistic sentiment in her famous 'duel' with Amintor. From Calianax, too, there is comedy very hard to reconcile with the tougher ironies of Acts II and III, and, from him and Melantius, the banquet scene, which is intriguing only in a purely theatrical sense. The question of who will win the battle of wits and effrontery really has little to do with the central problems of the play. Very often the term 'good theatre' is almost deliberately degraded by Fletcher.

As far as Evadne's conversion is concerned, the worry here is not the simple fact of a change in character. In drama as stylized as much of Fletcher's is, this can obviously be perfectly legitimate. It is the change in the level of complexity in the writing – the change in tone from a complex and intelligent Act II to an over-simplified and stylized Acts IV and V – that matters. Even this kind of thing could, theoretically, be justified. I think the opposite movement is, for instance, in the case of Webster's *The Duchess*. With *The Maid's Tragedy*, I would say that the undermining of the sentimental and Heroic values of Act I by the persistent toughness of Act II and parts of Act III makes the beginnings of a very good, though minor, drama. Taking the play up to this stage, Fletcher has briefly established and then powerfully questioned the set of attitudes and values that were to go almost entirely unquestioned in a later generation of tragic writers. Basically, *The Maid's Tragedy* at least poses more serious questions than any other of his plays. Unfortunately, the dramatist's grip slackens noticeably towards the end and he seems content to forget earlier complexities at a stage when they should be remembered. It is not that immensely subtle irony is an absolute necessity. One need only remember Middleton's success in establishing Bianca's real affection for her seducer in *Women Beware Women* to see what might have been done in Fletcher's play. As it is, however, the play stands more as an interesting attempt than a deed accomplished.

Of this, the dramatic, or rather undramatic verse towards the end is an obvious sign. Evadne's speeches to the king just before she murders him are punctuated with stagey remarks that make the whole thing look like a deliberate parody of Shakespearean functional dramatic verse. The already over-emphatic moral speechifying –

> . . . not a blowing rose
> More chastely sweet, till thou, thou, thou, foul canker . . .

– is often made even more ridiculous by Fletcher suddenly remembering that this is dramatic verse, spoken on the stage by one character to another:

> . . . till thou, thou, thou, foul canker,
> (Stir not!) didst poison me.   v, ii (p. 82)

(Come to think of it, how could he stir? – at this point he is tied to his bed!) Constantly the attempts at living dramatic speech look surprised in the face of the banalities which make up the rest:

> Thus, thus, thou foul man,
> Thus I begin my vengeance! (*Stabs him.*)
> v, ii (p. 83)

For all this, *The Maid's Tragedy* is Fletcher's most interesting play and probably his one attempt at drama that reaches beyond the conventionalizing of action and emotion to which he looks forward.

With the rest of Beaumont and Fletcher plays, it is a mistake to take them too seriously. Critics and readers industriously seek in them evidence of the decadence of Jacobean drama, and of course it is there to be found, in plenty. In particular, if we are thinking of earlier comedy and tragi-comedy, the texture of Beaumont and Fletcher's writing is so noticeably thin and artificial that the note of escapism, of an almost deliberate withdrawal from the boisterous toughness of Elizabethan life is unmistakable. The fragile sentimentality of Fletcher's lyric writing is the most alarming example that English literature affords of a retreat from the body and substance of Shakespearean drama. If Fletcher *had* influenced the later Shakespeare – as it is often claimed he did[1] – it could only

---

[1] For an account of the main arguments in the Fletcher-Shakespeare controversy see Harold S. Wilson, '*Philaster* and *Cymbeline*', *Shakespeare's Contemporaries, op. cit.*, pp. 250-62.

have been for the worse. On the other hand there is a sense in which these plays of Fletcher's (i.e. plays other than *The Maid's Tragedy*) have at their best a lightness of touch which places them as reasonably good escapist fun and nothing more. At least one could say that they are not as dangerous to the critically unaware as either Chapman or Ford. There is little point in being shocked at the kind of twisting of plot, for instance, that happens at the end of *A King and No King* if the tone of the play admits its limitations, skilfully avoids dwelling too long on the sensuous details its own values might easily produce, and is obviously prepared to rest content with the very lightest introduction to the problems it raises. True, the audience has been fooled, irresponsibly, into thinking this was a play about incest when, as it turns out in the end, it was only a Gilbertian accident of changelings after all. It *is* decadent, because it runs away from issues raised or hinted at earlier, but it doesn't trifle with them in the powerfully suggestive way that unfortunately characterizes Ford's writing, for instance, at the end of '*Tis Pity*.

Apart from its irresponsible ending, *A King and No King* (1611) has a certain neatness of arrangement which does succeed in making a very minor point. It would not matter a jot if this play were lost to the history of English drama entirely, but, looked at closely, it has at least as intelligent and as fresh an attitude to the Heroic virtues as later, less critical plays of the more generally recognized Heroic period. Arbaces is an engaging and at times very amusing animal. Offered an easy solution to his torments (Act V, scene iv), he at last promises to stop raging at all in sight and have enough patience to hear what Gobrias has to say. He will not even breathe too loud lest it interrupt the narrative, and so he lies down at his father's feet to listen. (Good dog!) This is certainly on the edge of the blurring of tragedy and comedy Miss Bradbrook complains of, but in fact the play as a whole just manages to keep sight of a consistently built scheme of values and so saves some, though not all of the comedy from the charge of irresponsibility. What success the play has is built around the fact that Arbaces, Mardonius, and Bessus are all, in very different ways, essays in or parodies of the Heroic. We are never, as we are in most of the later Heroic plays, allowed to take Arbaces himself seriously for too long. His own rages betray him, and Mardonius's slightly sentimental trust-worthiness and commonsense is just pointed enough to comment effectively on this. Bessus is of course a frankly comic and rather coarse parody of the whole conception. Receiving a challenge to fight a duel, he reads the letter and tots up the possibilities:

> *Bessus* [*reads*] Um, um, um – reputation – um, um, um – call you to account – um, um, um – forced to this – um, um, um – with my sword – um, um, um – like a gentleman – um, um, um – dear to me – um, um, um – satisfaction. – 'Tis very well, sir; I do accept it; but he must await an answer this thirteen weeks.
> *Gentleman* Why, sir, he would be glad to wipe off his stain as soon as he could.
> *Bessus* Sir, upon my credit, I am already engaged to two hundred and twelve; all which must have their stains wiped off, if that be the word, before him.
> *Gentleman* Sir, if you be truly engaged but to one, he shall stay a competent time.
> *Bessus* Upon my faith, sir, to two hundred and twelve. . . . All the kindness I can show him, is to set him resolvedly in my roll the two hundred and thirteenth man, which is something; for I tell you, I think there will be more after him than before him . . .
>
> III, ii (p. 53)

In this setting, the engaging animal quality of Arbaces is just sufficiently stressed to be established as part of a crude but welcome slant to the whole business. There are certainly in this play very dangerously suggestive hints of the sensuous delights of incest (e.g. the frankly uncorrected delights of Penthea's kiss, Act IV, scene iv), but they are rapidly passed over in favour of a comic investigation of Heroism and Stoicism. In many ways this, though irretrievably minor, is an engagingly human play.

Philaster (*c.* 1610) represents another very common strain of Fletcher tragi-comic writing. Here again, the play is just light enough in tone to make it, where time permits, worth a very quick reading through. It is not as good as *A King and No King*; it is not nearly as dangerous as, for instance, Ford's *'Tis Pity*. It relies far too much on a mixture of Heroics and a very gentle nostalgia (cf. Bellario's patient sufferings and the devotion of her life to Arethusa). It errs, as Fletcher's plays commonly do, in the direction of unrelated comedy, but the tone of most of the play is light enough to make this no great sin, and at least some of the comedy is mildly funny:

> *Pharamond* You will not see me murder'd, wicked villains?
> *1 Citizen* Yes, indeed, will we, sir; we have not seen one for a great while. v, iv (pp. 180-1)

The comedy is not critical of Pharamond's stiffly inadequate dialogue; it merely makes it laughable. But in context, this cannot be a really serious matter, except perhaps in the sense that it points the way English drama is going.

The best the play has to offer is a frankly decorative lyricism which is slight enough to do no great harm, and which has interest of a kind in that, again, it is symptomatic of what is happening to English drama – and English sensibility – after Shakespeare. Lacking the fresh insight of a Middleton, a dramatist would, presumably, have seen little in post-Elizabethan society to give body and substance to his work. One clear sign of this is Fletcher's pleasantly escapist lyricism which culminates in Bellario's last speech in Act V:

> But yet all this
> Was but a maiden longing, to be lost
> As soon as found; till, sitting in my window,
> Printing my thoughts in lawn, I saw a god,
> I thought, (but it was you,) enter our gates.
> . . . I did hear you talk,

Far above singing. After you were gone,
I grew acquainted with my heart, and search'd
What stirr'd it so; alas, I found it love!

v, v (pp. 189-90)

It is important not to build this up, as Miss Ellis-Fermor, for instance, tends to do, into a contemplation of 'the perfumed beauty of certain isolated, pathetic figures . . .', or (in the plays as a whole) 'a beauty which, however it be rooted in falsity, bears again and again a singular and lovely flower'.[1] A critic dare not, surely, dismiss what is admitted to be a fundamental falsity and sentimentality of conception as easily as this, or merely in favour of suggesting there is some real value in detached bits of poetry and action which seem 'beautiful' (or worse, 'perfumed'!). Plays like *Philaster* must be admitted to be little more than an escape from more pressing worries. If this is not in some way admitted in the cadenza-like passages themselves, then the writing is indeed dangerous, instead of merely pleasant.

But few nowadays would read these plays as Miss Fermor at times tends to do. The real danger with them is in the obvious signs of a drastically inflexible approach to drama which will and does grow on writers as the century advances. Even Fletcher's best play, *The Maid's Tragedy*, has passages which clearly forecast the hardening of drama into a set of over-simple, preconceived attitudes towards love, friendship, royalty, honour, etc.:

> *King* Draw not thy sword; thou know'st I cannot fear
> A subject's hand; but thou shalt feel the weight
> Of this, if thou dost rage.
> *Amintor*   The weight of that!
> If you have any worth, for Heaven's sake, think
> I fear not swords; for, as you are mere man,
> I dare as easily kill you for this deed,
> As you dare think to do it. But there is
> Divinity about you that strikes dead

[1] Ellis-Fermor, *op. cit.*, p. 212.

My rising passions; as you are my King,
I fall before you, and present my sword
To cut mine own flesh, if it be your will . . .
III, i (p. 45)

And in *Philaster*, more obviously still, there is a growing sense of
the writer moving words around like counters. In the more
'serious' parts of the play, terms like 'love', 'value', 'worth',
'virtue', 'honour' are used like talismans to charm a sleepy
audience. This sort of thing, though perhaps not vitally serious in
Fletcher's own case, since most of his plays attempt little, undoubtedly looks forward to the gigantic bluff of Heroic tragedy
and the disappearance of any true sense of the 'dramatic' from the
English stage. It is increasingly a pity, and increasingly significant,
that Fletcher could make only one very small attempt in his plays
to incorporate the sort of attitudes so brilliantly established by
Middleton.

CHAPTER XII

DECADENCE: THE HOLLOWNESS OF CHAPMAN AND FORD

The seriousness and solemnity of tone in Chapman and Ford is much more worrying than anything in the lightly irresponsible Beaumont and Fletcher. Indeed, the dangers of taking minor Jacobean drama at face value are well illustrated by the case of writers who – like Chapman and Ford – appear to be making a serious point when in fact they are only making a sentimental one. There are serious criticisms that can be levelled against Webster, Tourneur, and even Middleton, but each of these makes his point in the teeth of such criticisms. With Chapman, Ford, and to some extent Fletcher, controls have so broken down that the drama is struggling to make any point at all. These writers, then, must firmly be placed (even Miss Bradbrook, finally, hesitates here) well below the three great Jacobeans, and this fact, and the reasons for it, are a good part of the interest that remains in their plays. With Chapman, it is mainly a matter of his being, for all his apparent intelligence, wrong-headed about the moral issues he thought, or rather would like to have thought, dominated the Jacobean scene. At various times he is a propagandist alike for Marlovian and Stoic virtues, and it seems that he must have felt the hopelessness of these causes so keenly that it drove his writing often into stiffness, sentimentality, and moral confusion. At any rate, whatever the causes, these characteristics are there in his plays, and they prevent him from making a central point as effectively as, say, Webster, for all his apparent confusion, does.

But Chapman, like Ford, mesmerizes critics. 'Decadent' writing becomes a serious issue when its pretentions cannot readily be recognized for the bluff they are. Beaumont and Fletcher have a lightness of touch which, however thin and superficial the point it is making, at least advertises its own inadequacy. With them, the lightweight sentimentality is only rarely mistaken by critics for serious philosophy. Chapman, on the other hand, makes claims both to complexity and depth of meaning, and all too often he is taken at face value.

Basically, Chapman's plays are simple – for the most part over-simple – in outlook. His best play, *Bussy D'Ambois* (1604), recognizes this and makes at least something out of a Marlovian exuberance which nevertheless must surely, in Jacobean England, have been a lost cause.[1] *Bussy* is a play which on the whole staves off the complex verbal jugglings of the *Byron* plays; and, though dangerously inflated in places, it does not give in to the brashness of later plays like *Caesar and Pompey*, where themes are rhetorically underlined often to the point of absurdity. In *Bussy D'Ambois* Chapman is content with a simple enthusiasm – satirically placed – for his hero. Bussy's opening soliloquy warns of the dangers of greatness and, rather stiffly and unconvincingly, claims a conventional Virtue as the only guide in high places. But what he and Chapman eventually come to mean by this is that greatness of spirit, even if tinged with rashness, is the only thing that will place a man on a higher moral level than the rest. 'Sin is a coward, madam, and insults / But on our weakness . . .', Bussy advises Tamyra. The dilemma of all the early Chapman heroes and heroines is that there is a 'natural' order in society and in the universe; but, on the other hand, nature herself urges Man to overstep the bounds. The 'natural' order exists to be challenged; and will destroy the man of daring who challenges it. Obviously a dichotomy like this – between, for instance, outrageous daring

[1] For a critical account which presents Chapman as philosophically and emotionally the heir of Marlowe, see Edwin Muir, ' " Royal Man ": Notes on the Tragedies of George Chapman', Bluestone and Rabkin, *Shakespeare's Contemporaries*, pp. 230-8. Mr Muir's thesis, however, seems to me unacceptable in that it fails to make the all-important distinctions between the quality of the writing in *Bussy D'Ambois* and later Chapman plays.

and restraint – is a drastically over-simplified attitude compared
with, notably, Shakespeare's intelligent and subtle approach to
problems of man and the universe. Indeed it is obvious that
Chapman looks back enviously, particularly in his earlier
tragedies, to an apprenticeship with the Marlovian school of
rhetoric and to a world where morality simply meant action and
aspiration. But, in this one play, Chapman achieves a directness of
impact which is impressive – at least up to a point – because,
while not pretending to any great complexity, it cuts deeper than
any simple, nostalgic yearning for the *Tamburlaine* world. It
recognizes, clearly and firmly, at once the attraction of Bussy's
reckless daring, and the inevitability of his defeat:

> Then these divines are but for form, not fact:
> Man is of two sweet courtly friends compact,
> A mistress and a servant: let my death
> Define life nothing but a courtier's breath.
>
> v, iv, 82-85

After this, there is the more defiant oration as the hero dies:

> O, my heart is broken!
> Fate nor these murtherers, Monsieur nor the Guise,
> Have any glory in my death, but this,
> This killing spectacle, this prodigy:
> My sun is turn'd to blood, in whose red beams
> Pindus and Ossa (hid in drifts of snow,
> Laid on my heart and liver) from their veins
> Melt like two hungry torrents, eating rocks,
> Into the ocean of all human life,
> And make it bitter, only with my blood . . .
>
> v, iv, 131 ff.

Here the sun-blood simile clearly predicts the rhetorical over-
emphasis and confusion of later plays. (It is worth noting that
Marlowe himself in similar vein would have been much more
straightforwardly rhetorical, less inclined to the confusion of the
Pindus and Ossa figure and less inclined to the masochistic sug-

gestions of the conclusion: 'And make it bitter, only with my blood.') But the opening lines ('Fate nor these murtherers . . .') are Chapman in his better, and more simply direct, vein. And this directness of personal response is something which Chapman manages convincingly in one play only, *Bussy D'Ambois.*

In view of the large claims made for Chapman's later work in books like Mr Ennis Rees's *The Tragedies of George Chapman: Renaissance Ethics in Action*,[1] it is important to stress that Chapman's attitude towards Bussy – for all the simplicity of the play generally – is mixed. *Bussy* is not, as Mr Rees thinks, a play which rejects the hero's claims entirely in order to look forward to the stoic ideals of later heroes like Clermont D'Ambois. Admittedly, Bussy is not to be equated simply with Chapman. Other characters than Bussy (for instance, Henry III), other images, modify the total impression and we are clearly meant to see through Bussy's boastfulness to some extent. Nature has driven him beyond the mean and consequently his outbursts are placed, often, as wild and uncontrolled:

> *Bussy* (to *Monsieur*) That your political head is the curs'd fount
> Of all the violence, rapine, cruelty,
> Tyranny, and atheism flowing through the realm:
> That y' ave a tongue so scandalous, 't will cut
> The purest crystal; and a breath that will
> Kill to that wall a spider: you will jest
> With God, and your soul to the Devil tender;
> For lust kiss horror, and with death engender:
> That your foul body is a Lernean fen
> Of all the maladies breeding in all men:
> That you are utterly without a soul . . .
> *Monsieur* Why, now I see thou lov'st me.
> Come to the banquet.   III, ii, 479-499

[1] E. Rees, *The Tragedies of George Chapman: Renaissance Ethics in Action* (Cambridge, Mass., 1954), and cf. U. Ellis-Fermor, *op. cit.*, esp. pp. 67-76.

The later Chapman plays are dated as follows (E. K. Chambers, *op. cit.*, vol. III, pp. 251-60): *Charles, Duke of Byron* 1608; *The Revenge of Bussy D'Ambois c.* 1610; *Caesar and Pompey c.* 1613?; *Chabot Admiral of France c.* 1613?. (*Chabot* is considered by G. E. Bentley to be later, *c.* 1621-2: *The Jacobean and Caroline Stage*, vol. V, pp. 1088-91.)

But, on the other hand, there is no doubt about the admiring way Chapman plays up the brave rise of Bussy at court, unsupported by any wealth except that represented by his own courage (cf. the unqualified approval behind and in the speech of Nuntius on the fight, Act II, scene i, 35ff.). Bussy is far more than merely an empty foil to the wiser Henry, and Chapman himself can be felt – despite a certain stiffness in the metaphor – very much behind Monsieur's sudden burst of enthusiasm:

> . . . here will be one
> Young, learned, valiant, virtuous, and full mann'd;
> One on whom Nature spent so rich a hand
> That with an ominous eye she wept to see
> So much consum'd her virtuous treasury.
> Yet as the winds sing through a hollow tree
> And (since it lets them pass through) let it stand;
> But a tree solid (since it gives no way
> To their wild rage) they rend up by the root:
> So this whole man
> (That will not wind with every crooked way,
> Trod by the servile world) shall reel and fall
> Before the frantic puffs of blind-born chance,
> That pipes through empty men and makes them dance . . .
> v, ii, 32 ff.

This early play is Chapman's best, and, drastically limited and flawed though it is, it cannot be seen merely as clearing the ground for a presentation of nobler, wiser heroes later on.

And in fact the attempt in the later plays at something deeper, or more complex, than the naïve enthusiasm of *Bussy D'Ambois* is increasingly disastrous. Chapman clearly wanted to get beyond the simple, Marlovian outline of his early work, but the resulting 'complexity' and 'seriousness' is of the surface only. The *Byron* plays follow logically from *Bussy D'Ambois*, and here the dilemma of the Natural Man is repeated; but the gap between the statements of its two sides – a daring idealism on the one hand, and on the

other the impossibility of upsetting the order of Nature for long –
is far greater than it was in *Bussy* and so the plays are, morally,
more confused. A reader is puzzled as to just how to take the
awkward division of attention between the foolish but largely
sympathetic figure of Byron and the wiser but less convincing
Henry. The very transitions in the writing between the two
themes are too crude and too stiff to present any problem really
accurately. Finally, with the later plays, Chapman's attention
begins to swing away from his earlier sympathies more and more
towards the Clermonts and Chabots and Catos. But by this time,
for all the attempt at a wise and deep stoicism, the writing is so
flat and dull that nothing is achieved: the culminating moral intention is dissipated either in sheer dullness or in academic
philosophizing. Roughly, this still seems to me the only way to
take the Chapman *œuvre* – i.e. with the simple *Bussy D'Ambois* at
the head of a pretty unimpressive list – and theses which make him
out a powerful moralist or philosopher are disastrously wide of the
mark.

What has misled many critics into thinking the later plays are
good and convincing is the apparently complex language. Most
obviously in this connection, there is the extended simile that
Chapman leans so heavily on in the *Byron* plays, *The Revenge of
Bussy D'Ambois*, *Chabot*, and others. Frequently, the stiffness of
these similes is emphasized by longish classical allusions that do not
lend themselves readily in English blank verse to anything more
than academic subtlety:

> What place is this, what air, what region,
> In which a man may hear the harmony
> Of all things moving? Hymen marries here
> Their ends and uses, and makes me his temple.
> *Byron's Conspiracy:* I, ii, 22-25

But classical allusions are a comparatively minor worry. The main
trouble is the simile itself:

Clermont 'Twas but your fancy, then, a waking dream:
For as in sleep, which binds both th' outward senses,
And the sense common too, th' imagining power
(Stirred up by forms hid in the memory's store,
Or by the vapours of o'erflowing humours
In bodies full and foul, and mix'd with spirits)
Feigns many strange, miraculous images,
In which act it so painfully applies
Itself to those forms that the common sense
It actuates with his motion, and thereby
Those fictions true seem, and have real act:
So, in the strength of our conceits awake,
The cause alike doth [oft] like fictions make.
                    The Revenge of Bussy D'Ambois: v, i, 41-53

Now what can this possibly mean? On close inspection, the literal
meaning is clear enough (though what this sort of verse must be
like in the theatre one can only speculate!). It is, however, adver-
tising itself as poetry complicated in at least a verbal sense. A
reader (or audience) must keep in mind the attempted distinction
between the 'outward senses' and the 'sense common', disentangle
the subordinate clauses with their vague subjects and possessive
pronouns, and cope at the same time with Chapman's confusing
habit of grouping ideas in brackets. But the fact that there is
nothing *basically* complex here – and hence that the verbal
juggling is merely empty – is best seen in terms of Chapman's
rhythm. The all-too familiar idea of the imaginary power – complete with the 'forms' of 'the memory's store' and the humours –
acting to make the unreal 'real' is set in the inflexible 'For as . . . so
. . .' simile; and the whole passage moves with the plodding gait
of the simple, literal mind:

> In which act it so painfully applies
> Itself to those forms that the common sense
> It actuates with his motion . . .

Most of Clermont's speeches are stiff and literal-minded in this

way, and the academic ring of the 'philosophizing' makes nonsense
of the pretended complexities:

> *Clermont* Good and bad hold never
> Anything common; you can never find
> Things' outward care, but you neglect your mind.
> God hath the whole world perfect made and free,
> His parts to th' use of th' All; men then that [be]
> Parts of that All, must, as the general sway
> Of that importeth, willingly obey
> In everything without their power to change . . .
>> *The Revenge of Bussy D'Ambois:* III, iv, 55 ff.

A couple of pages of this produce only the remark from Renel:

> What should I say? As good consort with you
> As with an angel; I could hear you ever.

The mind that could think in this language, and this rhythm, is not
essentially different from the mind which – at times even in the
later plays – admits to a simple, Marlovian exuberance:

> . . . kings had never borne
> Such boundless empire over other men,
> Had all maintain'd the spirit and state of D'Ambois;
> Nor had the full impartial hand of Nature
> That all things gave in her original,
> Without these definite terms of Mine and Thine,
> Been turn'd unjustly to the hand of Fortune,
> Had all preserv'd her in her prime, like D'Ambois.
>> *Bussy D'Ambois:* III, ii, pp. 95–102

Energetic, patterned verse of this kind is a mode very dear to
Chapman's heart, and the simplicity of it throws light on the
falseness of those sections of his later plays which pretend to a
deeper complexity. Chapman should indeed have stuck to the
Bussy theme and frame of mind – though this of course must have
been in fact impossible in view of the demanding complexity of
the Jacobean (or indeed any other) age.

The last plays, according to Mr Rees, reveal the growing strength of Chapman's 'Christian Humanism', the combination of strength, humility, and maturity towards which he had been working all his life. By this account, looking at Chapman's tragedy as a whole, Bussy and Byron are satirical figures, condemned very strongly by Chapman: 'Clermont, Cato, and Chabot stand as the dramatic embodiments of the ideal towards which man should strive.'[1] One's first reaction to a sentence of this kind is that the inclusion in it of the name of Chabot gives away more of the writer's thesis than he can possibly afford. Chabot 'embodies' nothing at all – or at any rate nothing more than a vague, sentimentally conceived ideal of conduct. And so indeed with the whole range of Chapman's later plays. The academic ring we noted in Clermont's speeches from *The Revenge of Bussy D'Ambois* becomes, if anything, duller and more pretentiously boring as Chapman strives harder for his idealized, Humanist-stoic philosophy. *The Tragedy of Caesar and Pompey*, for instance, gives us pages of Cato and Athenodorus 'arguing' so stiffly, and in such slow, literal-minded verse, that the whole effect is like an unintentional parody of Socratic dialogue:

> *Cato* Are not the lives of all men bound to justice?
> *Athenodorus* They are.
> *Cato*   And therefore not to serve injustice:
> Justice itself ought ever to be free,
> And therefore every just man being a part
> Of that free justice, should be free as it.
> *Athenodorus* Then wherefore is there law for death?
> *Cato*   That all
> That know not what law is, nor freely can
> Perform the fitting justice of a man
> In kingdoms' common good, may be enforc'd.
> But is not every just man to himself
> The perfect'st law?
> *Athenodorus* Suppose!

[1] Rees, *op. cit.*, pp. 31 *et seq.*

The Hollowness of Chapman and Ford

Cato   Then to himself
Is every just man's life subordinate.
Again, sir, is not our free soul infus'd
To every body in her absolute end
To rule that body . . . ?   IV, v, 62–76

It would be hard to conceive a nobler or more utterly lifeless dialogue than this one, where Cato is proving that it is right for him to commit suicide!

Perhaps, after all, Chapman is merely a well-intentioned bore and not a writer one would think of as thoroughly hollow and decadent. But then he *is* taken seriously by many – even by those who have qualifications to make – and virtually only one writer I have been able to discover seems prepared, or able, to see through the empty rhetoric.[1] When pretentiousness of the kind evident in plays like *Caesar and Pompey*, for instance, can pass itself off successfully as important drama, the emptiness of the 'profound' philosophizing is indeed alarming rather than simply boring. In the case of Chapman the attempt at a wise philosophy of life – an attempt which at first sight may seem the reverse of decadence or giving in – seems if anything more dangerous than the frank enjoyment of sin that Fletcher and Ford go in for.

---

[1] See J. W. Wieler, *George Chapman, the Effect of Stoicism upon his Tragedies* (N.Y., 1949). Mr Wieler's thesis is, roughly, that Chapman's growing interest in Stoicism involves a marked decline in dramatic power, especially in the last plays.

There is also a very interesting and lively article on Chapman by Peter Ure ('Chapman's Tragedies', *Stratford-upon-Avon Studies I*, pp. 227–47). Mr Ure writes very impressively indeed on the question of Chapman's interest in his rebellious heroes and the relation this bears to his interest in a stable 'moral authority'. He also – like Wieler – points the decline in dramatic power from *Bussy D'Ambois* onwards. However, the disturbing quality in Mr Ure's article is his assumption that writers who can be shown to be doing something different from Shakespeare must therefore be doing something valuable: 'It is this "emptying" of the drama, as Yeats called it, of human character and its replacement by heroic energies which helps to differentiate the plays of such workers in the heroic mode as Fletcher and his successor Dryden from those of Shakespeare . . . . Chapman, although faintly and far-off, anticipates both the magnification of life with which Dryden amazes us, and the neo-classical critics' advocacy of Philosophy as a guide . . .' (p. 246). In reply to this one might surely ask: in what sense does Dryden's – or Chapman's – 'magnification of life, amaze us? and in what sense do any of these writers embody 'Philosophy' as a guide?

For numbers of recent critics and readers, Ford has quietly but firmly established his claims over the last big area of Jacobean dramatic sentiment and passion. As with Chapman, few seem prepared to realize the dangers of the kind of claim he certainly does make. The worries that Miss Fermor and others have, for instance, about his writing seem scarcely to touch what they regard as his peculiar virtues – the quietism of emotional stress in *The Broken Heart*, incidental beauties of phrase throughout the dramas, a lyricism of emotion far less violent than Webster's, etc., etc. For a long time, in fact, the general feeling has been that one must censure Ford for his obvious faults of style, structure and the like, place him a good deal below Webster and Tourneur, but at the same time give him credit for doing something earlier writers scarcely envisaged.[1]

Ford certainly has a cunning turn of phrase. He is, for instance, better than most at the old Jacobean game of imitating and using other writers. Webster himself would have been reasonably well pleased at this from *The Broken Heart*, stiff and rhetorical though it is:

> *Orgilus* .. So falls the standard
> Of my prerogative in being a creature!
> A mist hangs o'er mine eyes, the sun's bright splendour
> Is clouded in an everlasting shadow;
> Welcome, thou ice, that sitt'st about my heart:
> No heat can ever thaw thee. (*Dies*) v, ii (p. 250)[2]

But far too often, cunning of this kind is instrumental in underlining a moral confusion which, for all its technical beauty of phrase, should put a reader on his guard immediately. What are

---

[1] Of the recent books on the subject that I have read, only the Pelican *Age of Shakespeare* sees Ford truly (see pp. 438-40). The following may be taken as representative of the group of critics who see Ford as (at least in some plays) an important and valuable writer: U. Ellis-Fermor, *Jacobean Drama*; H. J. Oliver, *The Problem of John Ford* (Melbourne, 1955); Robert Ornstein, *The Moral Vision of Jacobean Tragedy*. (To some extent Miss Bradbrook appears to adopt a similar, or related, position. See *Themes and Conventions*, pp. 250 ff.)

[2] Page references for Ford quotations are taken from the Mermaid edition.

we to make, for instance, of Ford's attitude to Giovanni's raptures over his sadistic murder of his sister in Act V of *'Tis Pity*?

> The glory of my deed
> Darkened the mid-day sun, made noon as night...
> I digged for food
> In a much richer mine than gold or stone
> Of any value balanced.   v, vi (p. 159)

Of this particular speech, more later. For the present, the issue is the more difficult and dangerous because frequently in these plays we have to notice Ford deliberately declining to modify the tone of his verse as the action demands. It's difficult to tell when he's sincere and when, on the other hand, he's ringing emotional changes, painting a passion, only to deny its relevance a few lines further on. The reconciliation scene between Soranzo and Annabella in Act IV, scene iii, of *'Tis Pity* is impossible to judge accurately, except by reconstructing, as it were after the event, Ford's probable motives and intentions. Apparently, Soranzo is, within the dialogue's limited terms, sincere:

> Forgive me, Annabella. Though thy youth
> Hath tempted thee above thy strength to folly,
> Yet will not I forget what I should be,
> And what I am – a husband; in that name
> Is hid divinity: if I do find
> That thou wilt yet be true, here I remit
> All former faults, and take thee to my bosom.
> IV, iii (p. 144)

There is nothing here which could give a foothold for the dramatic irony which is in fact supposed to be taking place. When, later on, Ford *states* that Soranzo didn't mean a word of what he was saying to Annabella, we quite frankly don't believe him. Certainly the verse looks weak enough here, but it is very doubtful if it is intentionally so. The speech is softly sentimental, rather than deliberately Machiavellian on Soranzo's part. Coming to these lines for the first time, a reader's conclusion would have to be that a real (and hence very significant) change of heart was intended. Ford's later denial of this is annoyingly hollow because, even when looking back in the light of Soranzo's later, sadistic conduct towards Annabella, it is impossible to see anything ironical or even politic in these lines. A quick contrast with one of Ford's own much more convincing examples of a character's changes of heart forming dramatically feasible 'emotional patterns' at the expense of naturalism should make the point: Vasques, Soranzo's faithful retainer, is given alternating spurts of honesty and Machiavellism which are etched in consistently enough throughout the play, and lightheartedly enough, to be perfectly acceptable. Soranzo's case, unfortunately, is rather more typical and certainly more important. With him, at any rate in this scene of 'reconciliation' with Annabella, Ford clearly wants, quite irrelevantly as far as the action of the play is concerned, a scene of apparently genuine and touching marital reconciliation. What matter if later on it turns out that one of the parties didn't mean a word of what he was saying?

Always the danger is that Ford is obviously in deadly earnest in these plays. Compared with Beaumont and Fletcher, he is serious even in his apparently irresponsible patterning of whatever emotions and passions come to hand. In Beaumont and Fletcher there is, for the most part, what we would today probably call a Coward-ish lightness of tone and intention which plainly warns a reader not to take the issues and conclusions too solemnly – and this can be so even where the overall intention is in a sense a 'serious' one. Ford cannot be taken in this way. His designs on the reader, whether they come off or not, are intended to carry as much tragic weight and import as Tourneur's or Webster's.

Ford, then, is the real villain of the piece in Jacobean tragedy. He is untrustworthy. This judgment applies notably to the emotional quietism for which he is perhaps most famous. In the eyes of his supporters, his originality and value lie at least partly in his delicate suggestion of deep emotions which never achieve literal expression because they are bravely and virtuously kept beneath the visible surface of a character's expression and dialogue:

> They are the silent griefs which cut the heart-strings:
> Let me die smiling.   *The Broken Heart* v, iii (p. 253)

As a comment on the quite obviously audible griefs of Lear and the Duchess of Malfi, for instance, this in itself might have had a considerable point to make. (At least Ford could not have known that it would be made much more significantly in, of all ages, the nineteenth century, by Chekhov!) In fact, however, the significance of the quotation is so modified by its context as to be lost in sentimentality and confusion of moral purpose. Before looking at this more closely, we must glance quickly at the still more vicious case of *Love's Sacrifice*.

Love's Sacrifice (1632?)[1] is the play in which the heroine Bianca, in night-attire, visits her lover's bedside, only to tell him that nothing but words and kisses can pass between them. We are asked to believe in the efficacy of this kind of virtue and in Fernando's easy capitulation to it, and in the end we must also subscribe to Ford's eulogies of Bianca's unspotted virtue. 'Love's Sacrifice' appears to be, amongst other things, the payment Bianca must make for having sworn fidelity to a mere husband. Even the Duke finally recognizes this, and castigates himself for ever having had an unworthy doubt of his wife's 'honour':

> Whither now
> Shall I run from the day, where never man,
> Nor eye, nor eye of Heaven may see a dog
> So hateful as I am? Bianca chaste!   v, ii (p. 333)

It is all too easy; the conventionalizing of motives and character glances too contemptuously at the real difficulties of the situation.

---

[1] The dates for Ford's plays are taken from G. E. Bentley, *The Jacobean and Caroline Stage*, vol. III, pp. 433-64. Strictly speaking Ford is, of course, a Caroline playwright. Salingar, however, comments that '... he can be regarded, in stage history, as a belated Jacobean (*The Age of Shakespeare*, p. 439).

The pretended morality of the play gives itself away most obviously, again, in the scenes of self-sacrifice and muted passion from hero and heroine towards the end. In Act V, scene i, Bianca regales the Duke her husband with apparently reckless praise of her lover:

> I'll tell ye, if you needs would be resolved;
> I held Fernando much the properer man.
>
> v, i (p. 327)

She must be taken as at least partly sincere in this, but the trouble is it looks as if it should be wholly sincere. As such it might well make its point – i.e. suggest a serious questioning of the validity of conventional moral law as against the force of spontaneous natural feeling. In fact, however, Ford leaves us in doubt as to what relation all this bears to Bianca's earlier puritanical restraint and, not content with this, confuses the issue further still when, *with practically no change in the tone of the dialogue*, he makes her protest that she, not Fernando, was the guilty party from start to finish in the affair. If she is still chaste, it is not her fault. Apparently, then, her boldly amoral praise of her lover was not quite what it seemed to be, but in fact was really concealing some other, less obvious emotion in order to delude the Duke into thinking she alone was at fault and so sparing Fernando. Or was it? In any case, heroic self-sacrifice of this kind is almost always suspect; particularly when it tempts an author to confuse issues of tone, significance and morality in this way.

The Broken Heart (*c.* 1627–31?) on which Ford's reputation as a stoic dramatist mainly rests, is innocent in comparison with the humbug of 'virtue' represented in *Love's Sacrifice*. By and large, it is a simpler play, resting its case on a combination of stoicism and sentimentality which is familiar enough in literature. Nevertheless it has, dangerously, pretensions to tragic status and these have imposed on critics who should have been far less gullible than Lamb, whose ingenuous comparison between Calantha and the Spartan boy started off the train of deference to Ford in modern times:

> I do not know where to find in any play a catastrophe so grand, so solemn, and so surprising as this of *The Broken Heart*. This is indeed, according to Milton, to 'describe high passions and high actions'. The fortitude of the Spartan boy who let a beast gnaw out his bowels till he died without expressing a groan, is a faint bodily image of this dilaceration of the spirit and exenteration of the inmost mind, which Calantha with a holy violence against her nature keeps closely covered, till the last duties of a wife and a queen are fulfilled . . .

Whatever we may think about the myth of the Spartan boy, the comparison with Calantha is absurd. Calantha's 'Spartan' resolve is set in a tide of sentimentality and melodrama which sweeps over and dominates it in a way characteristic of Ford's most weakly undramatic writing. The play, especially in Act V, is properly labelled 'undramatic' because its verse and dialogue are opportunist rather than critically directed towards a dramatic point. The masque begins the final statement of Calantha's 'masculine' reserve, but it is in its way as melodramatic and false as Giovanni's dagger in Act V of *'Tis Pity*. It draws attention to itself as an exhibitionist display of feeling. The 'tragic' news comes in suddenly, with no dramatic warning, and this sets the tone for Calantha's display of 'courage':

Armostes The king your father's dead.
Calantha To the other change.   v, ii (p. 245)

As the scene goes on, it becomes clear that Ford, instead of building up the stoic or would-be stoic values that should underly this, is lovingly and carefully decorating their outward effects. Our attention is on the splendidness of the mask which conceals feeling, not on the significance of the feeling's being concealed. Calantha's action appears as affectation rather than the 'masculinity' of spirit ascribed to her by Bassanes.

Moreover, the rest of the play's action colours Calantha's fine moments. Ithocles is more like a character from *Sandford and Merton* than the creation of a mature human being. He is a genuine Man of Sentiment in the true eighteenth-century meaning of the term, and his sister is tarred with the same brush. Her too incredible chastity and honour yield the play yet another scene (Act III, scene v) of stoic suppression of emotion, but she dies sentimentally. Dying of grief would never have occurred to the Spartan of Lamb's analogy! Most of the characters (Calantha, Penthea, even Ithocles) are kept from happiness by accidents which in context appear merely pathetic, and in consequence a general air of sadness and sentimentality pervades the action, colouring especially the would-be stoic scenes from Calantha, Penthea, Ithocles. Incidentally, this is relieved at at least one stage of the action by genuinely amusing comedy. Act I, scene iii, shows Orgilus in Tecnicus's garden pretending to be a scholar, and his dialogue with Euphranea and Prophilus is good. Only, one is reminded of Miss Bradbrook's point: the comedy has little if anything to do with the central tragedy of broken hearts. It is merely irrelevant 'comic relief'.

'*Tis Pity* (1629?–33) is the most interesting of all Ford's plays. Apart from the 'reconciliation' scene already mentioned, there clearly isn't a great deal of muted passion of the *Broken Heart* kind. In '*Tis Pity* Ford makes in a sense the most honest statement in all Jacobean drama of the glories of incest. 'Honest' is possibly the wrong word – certainly a strange word – for this. Until perhaps right at the end, Ford never finally commits himself to any firm position in regard to Giovanni's attitudes and desires. There is from the first a Marlovian recklessness in Giovanni's speech which is obviously meant as a correcting comment from the author; but at the same time it is a sign of the play's decadence and laxity that this sort of comment is never as forcefully put as is Giovanni's quite genuine case for the joys of incest. The two attitudes are never in balance or control. The feebleness of the Friar's conduct and dialogue scarcely helps to right the balance of the play, and of course in the end Giovanni's speeches – in any case compromised by the melodrama of the dagger scene – give themselves over finally to an uncontrolled hymning of the delights and glory of incest and of the 'martyrdom' of Annabella:

> Go thou, white in thy soul, to fill a throne
> Of innocence and sanctity in Heaven.
> Pray, pray, my sister . . . !
>   If ever after-times should hear
> Of our fast-knit affections, though perhaps
> The laws of conscience and of civil use
> May justly blame us, yet when they but know
> Our loves, that love will wipe away that rigour
> Which would in other incests be abhorred.
>   v, v (p. 157)

And:

>   The glory of my deed
> Darkened the mid-day sun, made noon as night . . .
>   v, vi (p. 159)

The obviously dangerous recklessness of Giovanni's atheistic talk to Annabella just before this hardly touches or even comments on the lyrical exuberance of his attitude here. Ford's own values, in fact, have at the end swung right behind Giovanni's. He is enjoying it all immensely and has forgotten even a pretence of critical comment. He even gives Giovanni a hero's death – he is slain only by the overwhelming odds presented by the banditti. The play closes with a set of fairly conventional moral remarks from the Cardinal (of all people!) and of course (also from the Cardinal) the amusing but odd speech:

> We shall have time
> To talk at large of all: but never yet
> Incest and murder have so strangely met.

Of one so young, so rich in nature's store,
Who could not say, *'Tis Pity she's a Whore?*
v, vi (p. 163)

'Tis Pity is obviously Ford's best play. It is more open in its
designs on an audience than either *The Broken Heart* or *Love's
Sacrifice*. It is infinitely more vigorous and courageous than
Perkin Warbeck. It makes a reasonable attempt to state boldly and
vigorously Giovanni's claims. The attempt, however, is in good
measure doomed from the start. Plays must inevitably refer to a
moral framework, and though they don't of course have to adopt
uncritically the moral standards they find in respectable society,
there is no sense in deliberately and wantonly controverting these.
A playwright who is even tempted to do this will inevitably feel
the pull of 'normal' values, and unless he is good enough to
balance these seriously and acutely against attractions of the
Giovanni-Annabella kind, the moral framework and form of the
play will be, as here, unbalanced. The critical intelligence which
should be brought continuously to bear on Giovanni and Annabella is never alert enough to cope with the vigorous challenge
which they certainly do make. They get away with far too much
of the author's unqualified approval.

A comparison with incest plays and themes in Fletcher and
Middleton makes a good number of the points one would wish to
make in establishing Ford's position. *A King and No King* pulls a
bigger bluff than anything in Ford. The issues between Arbaces
and his 'sister' are side-stepped shamelessly at the end of this play.
But it is consistently lighter in tone than *'Tis Pity* and so, though it
is easier to dismiss it, perhaps contemptuously, it is never as big a
threat to serious standards in the drama. By the same token, however, it is far too lightweight to touch Ford's real point or serve as
a touch-stone of any kind by which to judge or place his work.
Women Beware Women, on the other hand, does expose the moral
dangers in Ford's outlook. Middleton of course relegates incest to

a sub-plot and this in itself is significant, but on the surface, similarities are certainly there. Putana, for instance, could have stepped straight out of a Middleton play, and the ethical questions of why love should be forbidden between sister and brother or uncle and niece are there in both plays. The difference obviously is in Middleton's exposure of the whole world of buying and selling love which surrounds Isabella in *Women Beware Women*. Isabella is in a sense innocent of course (at least of incest), though her obtuseness in the matter of her mother's supposed adultery and her own is significant. But the real point that Middleton insists on is the link between Isabella's situation and the rest of the play. She is, in the first place, obviously paralleled by Bianca and she is also quite obviously placed as the subject of the buying and selling in matrimony which governs the play. This, not the simple glory of adultery, or the simple condemnation of it, is the significance of her characterization:

> *Fabricio* See what you mean to like; nay, and I charge you,
> Like what you see: do you hear me? there's no dallying;
> The gentleman's almost twenty, and 'tis time
> He were getting lawful heirs, and you a-breeding on 'em.
>
> I, ii (p. 271)

Remembering this and the toughness of texture and attitude in *Women Beware Women* as a whole, Ford's development of a familiar Jacobean theme can be readily unmasked. Even his best play has pitfalls that, surprisingly, few even of the Jacobeans could match. For just as the personal relations given us in his plays (like Giovanni's love for Annabella in *'Tis Pity*, or Bianca's sacrificial outburst to her husband in *Love's Sacrifice*) are for the most part treated in isolation, valued by Ford for themselves alone rather than for their relations with wider and deeper problems; so the more generalized 'moods' and 'emotional patterns' which govern the plays are isolated phenomena, insubstantial and unhealthy because they are there for their own sake. Ford's plays are irresponsibly written in the sense that the governing emotional patterns – like the hymns of praise for incest in *'Tis Pity* – are never brought up in a social or intellectual context which could test, probe, and modify them. The cloying texture of much of the verse comes from the fact that such patterns in Ford are almost always allowed to exist uncriticized and unfocused; they lack the substance which comes from a playwright looking – as Middleton virtually alone of the later writers did – towards values created in and by the business of living and common experience. Plays which are about comparatively isolated phenomena (like incestuous relations between brother and sister) must, if they are to avoid sentimentality and insubstantiality, also be based at least in part on the *relations between* themes like incest on the one hand, and the 'normal', the toughly intractable nature of everyday living on the other. Truly dramatic writing is virtually the reverse of Ford's because, while it is in no sense restricted to the ordinary or the everyday, it never isolates phenomena from the nourishing context of common social or personal relations.

CHAPTER XIII

CONCLUSION

DRAMA AND POETRY
IN THE SEVENTEENTH CENTURY

I think it is clear that the course of Elizabethan-Jacobean tragedy demonstrates at once a growing tendency towards idealistic thinking and attitudes (either of the quietly sentimental or the Heroic kind) and the fact that such a tendency must always be fatal to drama. Great drama sets its face unequivocally against the assumption that there is any ideal state (in ethics, belief, love, reality) divorced from, or superior to, actual life 'the real state of sublunary nature'. More firmly than any other artist, probably, a dramatist knows – or should know – that life is not merely something to be 'endured' or 'defied', but on the contrary the nourishing force which moulds and gives substance to a work of art. The trouble with Chapman, Ford and the Heroic writers is precisely their failure to recognize the real business of drama – that is, to see the difficulty, toughness and vulgarity of life as a source of spiritual and intellectual food. With late seventeenth-century dramatists in particular the insubstantiality, the lack of fibre in typical passages of their verse, betrays a desire to look beyond experience without becoming involved in it more than is humanly possible.

Thus there is a clear connection between the stoic resignation of Chapman's hero-philosophers (cf. especially Clermont and Cato) and the emotional quietism of many of Ford's best-known characters:

Calantha   O, my lords,
I but deceived your eyes with antic gesture,
When one news straight came huddling on another
Of death! and death! and death! still I danced forward;
But it struck home, and here, and in an instant.
Be such mere women, who with shrieks and outcries
Can vow a present end to all their sorrows,
Yet live to court new pleasures, and outlive them:
They are the silent griefs which cut the heart-strings;
Let me die smiling.   *The Broken Heart*, v, iii (pp. 252-3)

From here it must have been an easy step to Heroic defiance:

To Honour bound! and yet a Slave to Love!
I am distracted by their rival Powers,
And both will be obeyed ...
No man condemn me, who has felt
A woman's Power, or try'd the Force of Love:
All tempers yield, and soften in those fires:
Our Honours, Interests resolving down,
Run in the gentle Current of our Joys:
But not to sink, and drown our Memory:
We mount agen to Action, like the Sun,
That rises from the Bosom of the Sea,
To run his glorious Race of Light anew;
And carry on the World. Love, Love will be
My first Ambition, and my Fame the next.
                              Oroonoko, v, iv, 1-19

On the surface, Southerne's verse looks different in quality and design from Ford's, but in fact Ford's quietism ('They are the silent griefs which cut the heart-strings . . .') is very like the other side of the coin from Southerne's inflated rhetoric. Both assume that the ordinary business of living is intolerable, and hence look towards a sentimentally conceived ideal where all impurities shall be purged by lyric grace or burning passion. To many of the later seventeenth-century dramatists, exaggerated quietism or exaggerated defiance are simple alternatives, and the choice of one or the other doesn't matter very much so long as the exigencies of truly dramatic thought and feeling can be avoided.

It was this movement away from the broad, popular energy of the Elizabethan dramatic experience which signed the death-warrant of tragedy on the English stage for two hundred years or more. More than any other form of literature, drama – and *a fortiori* tragedy – is always threatened when the poet's range is narrowed, and when, by force of social or other circumstances, he is cut off from deeply popular energy of the kind evident in, for instance, Shakespeare's *Henry IV, Lear, Antony and Cleopatra*. Shakespeare used to be thought of as the supreme artist who could write on many levels at once and translate sophisticated ideas and themes into language the rude mechanicals could easily grasp. If anything, the reverse is true. Shakespeare is not a theatrical genius popularizing an Elizabethan metaphysic (or 'world-picture'), but a great writer whose individuality and intelligence are nourished by popular movements of which he is himself a part. To take a broader view: the decline of tragedy in the seventeenth century is not merely a matter of writers losing the technical facility of appealing to audiences like those of the Globe Theatre, or even of writers succumbing, as Beaumont and Fletcher certainly did, to the blandishments of a corrupt court and audience. Questions of the theatre (its practice, techniques, audiences, etc.) are never more than surface manifestations of much deeper trends in social, personal and intellectual living. And in fact the decline of tragedy in the seventeenth century is clearly part of, or one manifestation of, a general withdrawal from the popular energy of Elizabethan times towards a more sophisticated, self-conscious art. Thus it is clear that the whole way of English living and thinking is changing during the seventeenth century towards the self-consciousness of Cavalier and Restoration society, and that artists are tending more and more to reflect - and in some cases even to capitalize success-fully on - these changes of outlook and emphasis.

But whatever one's judgment on social and intellectual movements in the seventeenth century – clearly in some ways they were a necessary and valuable development – it is clear that they tended to make the writing of tragedy virtually impossible. Tragedy – English tragedy at least – flourishes in societies where the playwright is in touch not merely with an intellectual *élite*, or with any one class in society, but with, amongst other things, broadly (and often vulgarly) comic elements such as those represented by the Falstaffian world in Shakespeare, or the bourgeois world of 'factorship' in Middleton, or the prostitution and 'maintenance' in Tourneur. Moreover, just as tragedy withers with any great degree of social or intellectual refinement, so the social relationships which maintain it best involve disruptive forces and a kind of brutality, rather than simply a 'well-ordered' and stable society. The concept of an 'organic' society is a valuable one in literary criticism, but used valuably I think it must include as part of its meaning the possibility of a society where levels of experience and living impinge on each other violently – even disruptively – rather than smoothly and efficiently. The important thing is that levels of experience, and classes in society, should indeed interact, rather than remaining simply detached. The deeper and wider the interaction, the more fruitful are the possibilities for an art-form like tragedy; though clearly the interaction will also liberate an energy which produces tensions as much as simple satisfactions. Poetic drama never looks to, or depends on, a statically conceived picture of a Golden Age. More important for our purposes here, tragedy never flourishes when the intellectual climate is, as it was by Marvell's time for instance, predominantly self-conscious and cultivated. It is the function of tragedy – and I think of drama generally – to develop a more vulgarly robust set of attitudes than Marvell or his age dared to contemplate. The achievement of a Marvell may in some ways be called 'dramatic'; but in a more central and real sense it represents and relies on forces that were inimical to drama.[1]

It would seem then that the concept of a unified sensibility in the great Elizabethan and Jacobean poets up to Marvell must be modified slightly by a consideration of the relations between drama and poetry. Clearly poetry and drama in the seventeenth century *are* related, and often in ways which demonstrate Eliot's points about that oneness of thought and feeling which the seventeenth century at its best achieved. Yet there are movements in late sixteenth and seventeenth century poetry which, even though they can rightly be described as dramatic in some senses, nevertheless oppose – at times successfully and valuably – much of what the drama itself had stood for. As early as Marlowe himself, for instance, there is at points a clear and remarkable break in tone, attitude and orientation between poetry and drama, and this is a break significant of later developments in the two fields and in literature generally. Thus *Hero and Leander* impinges on the drama, but only in the very broad sense that its tragedy is an exploration of a dominant Elizabethan theme – the ways in which people partake of, and are related to, powerful natural forces and impulses. Hero and Leander are in fact destroyed – that is, the clear assumption is they would have been if the poem had been finished by Marlowe – by the fruition of the impulse to love and fertility essential to their very being.[2] Leander's special pleading to Hero is related to the common appeals of sonneteer lovers to their ladies:

---

[1] I think that most of the generalizations about tragedy and drama in this paragraph apply to other literatures as well as English. Admittedly, the French classical theatre presents difficulties. Both Racine (in tragedy) and Molière (in comedy) seem to disprove the claim that drama 'withers with any degree of social or intellectual refinement'. However, I think it is probably true that both Molière and Racine, for all their inclinations towards socially acceptable modes and ideas, were in fact in touch with a much wider range of society than is apparent on surface impressions.

[2] See S. L. Goldberg, 'The Orchard of the Hesperides', *The Melbourne Critical Review*, No. 1, 1958, pp. 42-51.

> Like untuned golden strings all women are,
> Which long time lie untouched, will harshly jar.
> Vessels of brass, oft handled, brightly shine;
> What difference betwixt the richest mine
> And basest mold, but use . . .

> Ah, simple Hero, learn thyself to cherish!
> Lone women, like to empty houses, perish.

And Hero's beauty is such that it deceives nature itself, tempting the bees to drink honey from her veil:

> Her veil was artificial flowers and leaves,
> Whose workmanship both man and beast deceives;
> Many would praise the sweet smell as she passed,
> When 'twas the odor which her breath forth cast;
> And there for honey bees have sought in vain,
> And, beat from thence, have lighted there again.

Once beauty and freshness of this kind reach fulfilment, they naturally perish. There is no possibility of permanent fulfilment for Hero and Leander – as in fact is clear from warning notes struck early in the poem (cf. the incongruity of the innocent Hero meekly sacrificing turtles' blood at the shrine of Venus: 'There might you see the gods in sundry shapes, / Committing heady riots, incest, rapes . . .').

Very broadly, attitudes of this kind could be said to relate to the kind of interest we saw Shakespeare taking in man's participation in natural processes and forces which turn out in the end to be both fruitful and destructive. On the other hand, the sophisticated lightness of tone the poem has in Marlowe's (though not Chapman's) section points consistently to an emphasis and orientation very different from Marlowe's own plays and different also from Shakespeare's, Tourneur's, Middleton's. All these playwrights – even Marlowe himself in parts of *Faustus* – could write witty and intelligent comedy, but the fabric of the verse in *Hero and Leander* establishes a quite unexpected Marlovian triumph based on a wit

and sophistication astonishing from the writer of *Tamburlaine,
Faustus,* etc. There is nothing in Marlowe's plays outside *Edward II,*
and little even in Elizabethan drama generally, which could give
more than occasional hints as to the identity, background, and
personality of the writer who saw the triumph and defeat of love
in this way:

> Love is not full of pity, as men say,
> But deaf and cruel where he means to prey.
> Even as a bird, which in our hands we wring,
> Forth plunges and oft flutters with her wing,
> She trembling strove; this strife of hers, like that
> Which made the world, another world begat
> Of unknown joy. Treason was in her thought,
> And cunningly to yield herself she sought.
> Seeming not won, yet won she was at length;
> In such wars women use but half their strength.
> Leander now, like Theban Hercules,
> Entered the orchard of th' Hesperides,
> Whose fruit none rightly can describe but he
> That pulls or shakes it from the golden tree.

Marlowe's triumph in *Hero and Leander* is certainly a real one; but
the poem achieves subtlety and life at the cost of excluding, or
keeping at bay, many elements on which Elizabethan drama depended for its very life: the triumphant, greasy vulgarity of
Falstaff, the imagery of flies blowing Cleopatra's body 'into
abhorring', the uncompromising accusation in Lear's 'Howl,
howl, howl, howl! O! you are men of stones . . .' In *Hero and
Leander* there is an obvious and necessary narrowing of focus. It is a
'dramatic' poem in the sense that it 'enacts' and demonstrates the
validity of its own view of life (and this, incidentally, is one which
it would be difficult to see any play envisaging); but its outlook
and basis are fundamentally divergent from those of the Elizabethan playwright.

In itself this is of course natural enough. But after *Hero and*

Leander the strain of sophisticated poetry grows, and crystallizes in the verse of Jonson and Marvell. Neither of these adopts Marlowe's position, but both have in common with the Marlowe of *Hero and Leander* a degree of elegance, and a sophistication of feeling and intelligence, which would be fatal to the drama. Some of Jonson's poems, like 'Sealed of the Tribe of Ben', adopt the driving energy of his own plays, but the lyrics have for the most part a robustness which is perhaps related to, but in the end quite divergent from, that of *Volpone*. *Penshurst*, admittedly, does evoke a world of nature and natural living which has some of the freshness of Shakespeare and the Elizabethans generally:

> And if the high-swollen Medway fail thy dish,
> Thou has thy ponds that pay thee tribute fish,
> Fat aged carps that run into thy net,
> And pikes, now weary their own kind to eat,
> As loath the second draught or cast to stay,
> Officiously at first themselves betray;
> Bright eels that emulate them, and leap on land . . .

But even in this passage – and more clearly still in the rest of the poem – the emphasis is on man's ability to *extract* order, civilisation, and a degree of sensible, unpretentious living from the natural world. As with Marlowe, the themes are related in a very broad sense to those of Elizabethan drama, but the whole cast of mind is more consciously cultivated, less prepared to seek drive and energy from the worlds of Falstaff, Vendice, Antony and Cleopatra, the changelings of Middleton, etc.

But the related strengths and limitations of Marvell[1] are the most revealing case when we are thinking of a developing seventeenth-century poetry *vis-à-vis* the drama. Marvell is, of course, well after the great age of Elizabethan drama and he takes the elegance of *Hero and Leander* and Jonson to extremes; though in the end it is

[1] See S. L. Goldberg, 'Andrew Marvell', *The Melbourne Critical Review*, No. 3, 1960, pp. 41–56. I have included some detailed comment on *Appleton House* in this chapter largely because Mr Goldberg's article is not generally available.

possible he does far more with it than anybody before him. In poems like *Appleton House* he is concerned – probably below the level of full consciousness – with what has now, in the seventeenth century, become the necessary interpenetration of a high degree of sophistication with what one is tempted to call the remnants of Shakespearean natural energy and vitality. The relativism in the 'grasshopper' stanzas is a case in point. These stanzas follow immediately from the 'Cinque Ports' in which Fairfax is seen ambiguously as having abandoned the ambitious world for nature (Appleton House); but once he has done this it is obvious that nature offers no simple retreat from the cares and responsibilities of civilization:

> But he preferr'd to the *Cinque Ports*
> These five imaginary Forts:
> And, in those half-dry Trenches, spann'd
> Pow'r which the Ocean might command.

Immediately after this, man is pictured in the meadows of Appleton House, 'diving' into the 'unfathomable grass' and, later, mowing it (i.e. completing the fulfilment towards which the grass has been growing); but while all this is happening men are also seen, first half-satirically (as grasshoppers), and then as actually dwarfed by the real grasshoppers which, in the context of the growing meadows, easily dominate men by climbing the tall grass:

> And now to the Abbyss I pass
> Of that unfathomable Grass,
> Where Men like Grashoppers appear,
> But Grashoppers are Gyants there:
> They, in their squeking Laugh, contemn
> Us as we walk more low then them:
> And, from the Precipices tall
> Of the green Spir's, to us do call.

Finally the whole section turns round on itself once again and pictures men as confidently – even indiscriminately – dominating the meadow which after all is there for them to use:

> The tawny Mowers enter next;
> Who seem like *Israelites* to be,
> Walking on foot through a green Sea.
> To them the Grassy Deeps divide,
> And crowd a Lane to either Side.
>
> With whistling Sithe, and Elbow strong,
> These Massacre the Grass along;
> While one, unknowing, carves the Rail,
> Whose yet unfeather'd Quils her fail.
> The Edge all bloody from its Breast
> He draws, and does his stroke detest ...

The point I wish to make is that here undoubtedly is a great poet capitalizing on the very sophistication and the civilizing process which defeated late seventeenth-century drama. Marvell's elegant, intelligent wit enables him to produce valuable poetry of a kind barely conceived earlier, even by Jonson and Marlowe. Both *Appleton House* and *The Garden* have an elegance of line and form which is in danger of attenuation but which also enables Marvell to achieve a sinewy line of thought, or thinking, of a kind rarely attempted by, say, Donne (the metaphysical poet most clearly and obviously related to the dramatists). Clearly Marvell would never dare to plunge head-first into experience as Donne – for all the careful organization of his poems – often does. Marvell could not by any stretch of the imagination have writen 'For God's sake hold your tongue and let me love ...' or 'Kind pity chokes my spleen ...' But he could organize his shorter, less disturbing line into poetry which is certainly not escapist and which holds a developing thought more continuously and more firmly in mind than Donne's more violent verse can readily do. With Donne, even when he is at his most violent, there is a feeling that the thought is to some extent limited by having been given a pre-existent shape.

(The stanza-form and to some extent the whole structure and shape of the Songs are in fact surprisingly neat for verse which is often violently disruptive in texture.) Marvell's poetry – particularly the second half of *Appleton House* – gives much more strongly the impression of genuinely leading on from one position to the next, or – if this seems too neat to fit the poem – of allowing a fresh direction of thinking to emerge *from the poetry* as it has developed and been written up to a given point within the poem.

Clearly it will never be possible to draw up a neat, schematic picture of seventeenth-century literary developments and achievements or of the course they took in later years. For instance, when we place some of the emphases developed by Marlowe, Jonson, Marvell *vis-à-vis* those emerging from Elizabethan tragedy, even the brilliant formulations of Leavis and Eliot of the 'unified sensibility' of the best poets of the age need modification or development. And later periods in English literature present further difficulties. Clearly social and intellectual movements in the seventeenth century were tending to develop a kind of self-consciousness which poetry has never since abandoned except in the hands of writers as individual as Blake. (Though the fact that Blake's really great poems are short and few in number is suggestive of the price he had to pay for being outside the stream which led Romantics like Wordsworth, Keats and Coleridge to make the subject of poetry very largely the poet himself.) And certainly the step from Romanticism to a symbolist self-consciousness in Western poetry generally must have been a short and easy one to take. On the other hand, not merely was this growth towards artistic self-consciousness inevitable (there are clear signs of it even in the last plays of Shakespeare); equally clearly, in defeating the drama, it produced poetry which, like Marvell's and the best of Pope, is freshly individual, framed to deal valuably with new situations and new movements.

On the other hand, poems which are completely out of touch

with the energy and roughness of vulgar speech and vulgar living will, like much of Pope's smoothly efficient *Essay on Man*, prove insubstantial and flaccid. And moreover, from the late seventeenth century onwards, there is in English literature a thinning down, an attenuation of the substance and form of poems as well as plays consequent upon the victory of civilization over what classical critics and writers like Dryden call the 'barbarity' of the Elizabethan age. This indeed is the real clue to the value of Elizabethan drama now. It presents attitudes and values which are not merely historically important, but which are in fact insights doubly valuable since they are not available in any but Elizabethan terms. After the mid-seventeenth century, nobody could have written or even conceived an Elizabethan tragedy. Poems like the best of Marvell, Pope and later on the Romantics are far too good to ignore; but they are clearly looking in very different directions from those developed by the Elizabethan drama they helped to defeat.

Indeed if it were not for the growth and dominance of new forms, particularly the modern novel, the outlook for literature as a formative influence on English life and sensibility in modern times would be bleak. The insights developed by poetry from Marvell onwards are varied and immensely valuable; but *taken alone* they would be insignificant because too narrow in range, too unadventurous in scope and outlook, to take the place of the drama. With the collapse of drama, any literature will tend to lack body and substance. But with the achievement of George Eliot, Lawrence, Conrad and others, English literature recovered a breadth, depth and substance lost when sophistication and civilization combined to dismiss tragedy from the English stage. Had Middleton's broad hints as to fresh directions the drama might take been anywhere developed and explored, the course of English literary history might well have been altered. In fact they weren't, and it looks as if the reasons for his lead being ignored were very much those which tended to encourage the empty rhetoric of Heroic, eighteenth-century, and Romantic 'tragedy'. Poetry does respond – though intermittently – to the strain of artistic self-consciousness which culminated in modern Symbolist verse; drama never has and probably never will.[1] To recover its earlier scope and depth, English literature, and English life, had first to work out its salvation independently from the stage. Or perhaps it would be truer to put it this way: after the eclipse of tragedy in the seventeenth century, a fresh impetus was needed, and one which could disentangle itself from the history of the stage and yet develop broader – and coarser – attitudes than modern poetry at least is capable of doing.

The first major step in this direction was taken when George Eliot showed that modern society, in the shape that is to say of Middlemarch society, was not something that artists and poets need run away from, but on the contrary, and for all the biting criticisms she herself made of it, the source of the energy, the activity, and the moral choices by virtue of which we now live.[2]

---

[1] Apparent exceptions to this rule, such as plays by Maeterlinck and Yeats, seem to me far too insubstantial to count for much. They lack both the grittiness and the energy of good drama (or, if it comes to that, of good literature).

[2] For a development of this point of view, see my article '*Middlemarch* and Modern Society', *The Melbourne Critical Review*, No. 6, 1963, pp. 44-45.

INDEX

Figures in bold type denote a major entry

Index

Index